Culture and Consciousness

PERSPECTIVES IN THE SOCIAL SCIENCES

Culture and Consciousness

PERSPECTIVES IN THE SOCIAL SCIENCES

Edited with Introductions by

GLORIA B. LEVITAS

GEORGE BRAZILLER
NEW YORK

For Mike

Acknowledgments

American Anthropological Association—for "On the Concept of Function in Social Science," by A. R. Radcliffe-Brown, from *American Anthropologist,* Vol. 37, pp. 394–402, July–Sept., 1953; reproduced by permission of the American Anthropological Association. "Anthropological Implications of Sickle-Cell Gene Distribution in West Africa," by Frank B. Livingstone, from American Anthropologist, Vol. 60, 1958; reproduced by permission of the American Anthropological Association.

Basic Books, Inc.—for selections from Vol. II of the *Collected Papers of Sigmund Freud,* edited by Ernest Jones, M.D., Basic Books, Inc., Publishers, New York, 1959; from *Structural Anthropology,* by Claude Lévi-Strauss, © 1963 by Basic Books, Inc., Publishers, New York; and from *Phenomenological Psychology* by Erwin Straus, © 1966 by Basic Books, Inc.

Beacon Press—for "Philosophical Anthropology and World Law," by F. S. C. Northrop, from *Forms and Techniques of Altruistic and Spiritual Growth,* edited by Pitirim A. Sorokin; reprinted by permission of the Beacon Press, © 1954 by the Beacon Press.

Blaisdell Publishing Company—for selection from *Social Causation* by R. M. MacIver (Waltham, Mass.: Blaisdell Publishing Company, a Division of Ginn and Company, 1942) ; reprinted by permission of the publisher.

Thomas Y. Crowell Company and Methuen & Company, Ltd.—for selection from *King Solomon's Ring* by Konrad Z. Lorenz; copyright © 1952 by Thomas Y. Crowell Company, New York.

Farrar, Straus & Giroux, Inc.—for selection from *The Science of Culture,* by Leslie A. White, by permission of Farrar, Strauss & Giroux, Inc.; copyright © 1949 by Leslie A. White.

Sigmund Freud Copyrights, Ltd., Mr. James Strachey and the Hogarth

by Harold C. Conklin, from *Southwestern Journal of Anthropology*, Vol. 11, Winter, 1955.

The University of Chicago Press—for selection from *The Nature of Culture* by Alfred Louis Kroeber; by permission of The University of Chicago Press; copyright 1952 by The University of Chicago. "Social Order and Anomie" by Émile Durkheim as it appeared in the *University Observer*, Chicago, 1947. The University of Illinois Press—for selection from *Theory of Cultural Change*, by Julian H. Steward.

Like an iceberg, an anthology can include within its pages only a small fraction of the information that is available. This small fraction, moreover, is supported by a structure of knowledge which is itself highly imperfect. Much must be ignored, omitted, slid over—sometimes out of conscious choice, sometimes from ignorance. It has been my intention to offer a few selections that hopefully shed some light upon the problems, theories, and methods of the social sciences. To the extent that I have succeeded in giving the reader a glimpse into some of the arguments that have emerged as part of the growing pains of the social sciences, I owe a debt of gratitude to many people.

First, I wish to thank George Brantl—the best editor and teacher I have ever known. His ability to ask the right questions, to suggest appropriate ideas without imposing his own views, and to maintain his patience and good humor is, in good part, responsible for whatever balance and order appears in this book.

I would also like to thank Irving Levitas for his many invaluable suggestions, his willingness to hear me out and to argue with me, and for the use of his extensive library.

To Dr. Robert Popkin, his wife, Elizabeth, and to Mrs. Helen Seeherman, I owe still another debt—in part, intellectual, for their patience in listening and discussing sections of this book and its problems with me. Their many kindnesses to my family provided me with the time and freedom to do the extensive research of which this anthology is merely the end product.

Last, I would like to thank my family—my parents, my mother-in-law, my husband, and children for their gifts of love and the time that this endeavor took from them.

Contents

Contents

Introduction

W HEN, IN 1830, AUGUSTE COMTE proclaimed the creation of the social sciences and gave the name "sociology" to his basic science of human behavior, he optimistically looked forward to the day when application of scientific knowledge to social problems would cure the social ills that plagued mankind.

Quite obviously, history has not proceeded according to the plans laid out for it by Comte—or by his numerous successors. Our own world has fallen heir to many of the problems that plagued Comte's, and we have managed to invent a few more of our own. The triumphs of the natural sciences paradoxically have increased social difficulties. Even more ironic, the progress of the social sciences themselves, which continually introduce new factors into the environment, has accelerated the pace of change and thereby made the social future less predictable.

There can be little doubt that the social sciences have lagged far behind the natural sciences in technological ability. Yet it is foolish to claim, as do so many critics, that the social sciences are, therefore, not sciences at all, and that they have added little to human knowledge since their establishment by proclamation over a century ago. Their critics insist on measuring the social sciences against standards of achievement that science itself has proven to be illusory. Today we recognize that complete predictability does not exist—even in physics —at certain levels of behavior. Moreover, science has taught us that nature may not be completely knowable; that the separation between

1

subject and object is not always possible, and that, therefore, the expectation that science can predict and shape the future is an illusion.

Despite these findings, some social scientists and a good portion of the public refuse to recognize that the limitation of our ability to perceive some phenomena without interfering with them obtains not only in the social sphere, but has been one of the great stumbling blocks to scientific research conducted on purely objective models. What is more, the search for certainty and absolute conclusions tends to obscure the cumulative nature of scientific theories and the relative impermanence of scientific explanations during those eras in which knowledge is growing at exponential rates. Attacking the social sciences for their inability to surpass limitations inherent in all phenomena is futile and wasteful. In saying this, I do not wish to imply that the social sciences have achieved their potential. In fact, the development of the social sciences has been very uneven, partly because they could not use the traditional methods of physics—experiment in a controlled environment—and partly because the social sciences have had to wrestle all along with problems of value and interference. To complicate the picture further, the social sciences deal with far more complex material than do the natural sciences, and conceived as they were in the image of the natural sciences, they were saddled with a view of the world as a static, objective mechanism; a view incompatible with the nature of social phenomena, which is unstable and embedded in human subjectivity.

If, as a result, there appears to be a great deal of dross among the few golden nuggets mined by social scientists during the short century-and-a-quarter of their existence, it is, nevertheless, capricious to deny the progress that social sciences have made toward deepening and broadening our understanding of the relationships among the multiple factors that mold social behavior. The public has, however, persisted in adhering to the illusion that social sciences ought to predict and shape the future—and it is this illusion that obscures the solid achievements of the field and generates confusion over its aims.

Public ambivalence toward the social sciences may also be attributable to growing difficulty in understanding the language of sociology and anthropology; a difficulty that sometimes leads to a suspicion that the conclusions of months of research, couched in obscure terminology, merely explicate the obvious. Because of our familiarity with the essential facts of social life, we tend to react to new sociological discoveries with a sense of *déjà vu*. Our intuitive understanding of much social behavior breeds a contempt in us that is directed against those who attempt to bring these rules to consciousness.

On yet another level, public ambivalence reflects an intelligent awareness that, in the long run, too much control may be as dangerous for mankind as too little control. This ambivalence does little to clarify the position of the social sciences or to promote a more mature attitude toward both their values and limitations.

The value of the social sciences lies in their ability to inform us about the workings of social processes. Such knowledge may give us a transient ability to manipulate our social behavior—providing, of course, that we can agree on the ends toward which we are working. Agreement on goals, however, can only occur as a result of the growing self-awareness that is itself a primary aim of scientific endeavor. Our ability to choose among alternatives is also enhanced by knowledge. But it seems presumptuous of us to believe that our choices will be made for eternity, and it is only vanity that leads us to think that in making choices we guarantee man's future development. No one expects biologists to predict the direction or form of future evolution of animal species; yet some are disappointed because social science is unable to predict the future evolution of society!

Prediction for the purpose of control, however attractive it may appear as a technological tool, is not only impossible in a temporal world of ever-changing forms, it is also not the only standard by which science may be judged. Science is not a category but a process by which we obtain information. It is characterized by its attitudes and procedures, its cumulative nature and its ability to provide models that explain events that have occurred in the past. Moreover, like art, science affords aesthetic pleasure in the discovery and elucidation of the structures or systems that underlie complex social behavior. Sociology and anthropology are sciences that systematically, through the use of a varied kit of scientific methods—some objective, some adapted specifically to their human subjects—try to discover the latent structures that support social and cultural processes.

Anthropologists were at one time principally interested in understanding human evolution. They hoped to develop a retrodictive or explanatory science that would disclose the processes by which cultures had developed from simple kinship organizations to complex territorial powers. They wished to understand how a group of people connected by bonds of marriage could evolve into nations connected by bonds of law and government. They wanted to know how hunting and gathering people had discovered and developed techniques of agriculture and animal domestication; how they developed simple tools and complicated chemical processes; how they "invented" or discovered language and writing, art and architecture, religion and ritual, cooking and chemistry. Though sociologists, too, professed an interest in history and origins, they were generally more concerned with explaining current processes: they looked for the implicit rules that appear to determine the interaction of human groups. Sociologists have tried to explain the nature of the social bond; to reveal the factors that cause competition and cooperation; they have tried to outline and describe the role played by social stratification in framing behavior. Sociologists have outlined the functions of politics, art, religion, economics, and they have also drawn our attention to the social functions of acts that appear to be either useless or damaging to the delicate social fabric. Their insight has led us to suspect that disruptive though they appear, warfare, crime, disease, suicide, drugs, and economic depressions may on some occasions serve to cement social bonds rather than destroy them. Together, sociology and anthropology have built up a corpus of information that defines and describes in great detail the process by which human organizations are held together by an invisible web of rules, laws, or sanctions. Until the development of the social sciences, many of these rules were sensed intuitively because they were embedded in the individual mind as part of the processes involved in personality development. "Sciencing," in the words of Leslie White, is the process of bringing to consciousness rules, laws, structures, and functions that are often obscured or only dimly perceived by rational thought.

The manner in which the social sciences use the knowledge they have painstakingly wrested from their studies depends ultimately upon what they conceive their goals to be. In this sense the social sciences are no different from the natural sciences, which have had to confront the recognition that their discoveries, too, could be used for good or bad ends, and that, in fact, a scientist's good intentions could not preclude the development of unforeseen, evil consequences. The discovery of atomic power, though the most graphic example of the woes to be found in the scientific Pandora's box, is hardly the sole example. Less dramatic, but perhaps equally threatening, is the technological progress that has resulted in widespread water and air pollution; the production of virulent strains of disease as a by-product of antibiotics; and overpopulation as the result of improved standards of hygiene and medicine. Every advance made by science has exacted a price from humanity, and the most pressing problem faced by man today is that of minimizing the price he is forced to pay for scientific progress.

It was Comte's belief that one of sociology's principal roles would be the prediction of future scientific discoveries, and he supposed that this ability would lead to the development of methods of control in advance. To a degree, of course, sociology can predict scientific discoveries—but the effects of these discoveries on human life is not so easily ascertained. Each new discovery, by altering the situation and changing the environment, places severe limitations on our powers of prediction. In addition, we must consider the environmental effects of the attitudes and discoveries of the social sciences, for these are today a significant factor in framing opinion and thereby affecting man's future.

The exponential development of the social sciences has added more data than can be absorbed—even with a liberal use of computers and mathematics. The result has been specialization. The tendency toward specialization itself adds to the confusion as each new specialty attempts to delimit its field of interest, jealously guards its prerogatives, and tends to look with disdain on the efforts of its colleagues. Nowhere are the bewildering results of specialization more obvious than in the social science textbook. Confronted by a text, the curious reader is rewarded for his interest by a series of definitions of categories such as "family," "kinship," "role," "race," "culture," "stratification," "art," "science," "personality," "education," and so on. The texts do little to integrate the material, and they discuss methodological problems separately; as a result it is possible to read through a textbook without ever getting a clear idea of what sociologists actually do, or why they organize their data this way. Synthesis is left to the reader. If he lacks a historical or philosophical background, he can do little more than wade through this ocean of fact.

Anthropologists, who use textbooks infrequently and who are less involved in the problems of their own cultures, present a somewhat more cohesive picture. The public assumes that an anthropologist is simply a peculiar human being who collects exotic data about primitive peoples. The anthropologist is a romantic figure—close kin to the novelist—who offers more entertainment and fewer threats of manipulation than does the sociologist. The public believes it knows what anthropology is and does, although many students of the subject have themselves become less clear about the matter. In fact, the differences between anthropology and sociology—particularly between social and cultural anthropology and sociology—are largely historical. The two fields remain distinct today largely in terms of their differing historical tradition and in some divergent methodological techniques. Today anthropology, too, is specialized. It consists of dozens of new subfields: cultural ecology, medical anthropology, psycholinguistics, ethnomusicology, culture-personality—to name only a few. Each pursues its questions somewhat independently of the rest and utilizes eclectic methodologies developed in anthropology or borrowed from the other social sciences.

Today's social sciences are attempting to solve numerous new problems that have emerged as a result of growing technology and acceleration of change, but they are also interested in restating some of the old questions in terms of their increased knowledge. As a result, the questions asked today are often very different from those asked in the nineteenth century. Since science is not a purely objective process but one that constructs what it discloses, it is often more difficult to see what the problems are than to solve them. The framing of questions presents a great deal of difficulty in scientific work. Interest in particular problems can evolve naturally from developments within the social sciences themselves, but it may also be generated by social events and by changing attitudes and values in the natural sciences.

Anthropologists are still searching for clues to man's cultural evolution, and they are also interested in studying societies as functioning systems *qua* systems. As they have uncovered more information, they have had to revise many of the assumptions upon which their early research was based. For example, when anthropologists assumed that all people evolved through stages from savagery to civilization, they searched for data by which they could classify societies and place them at their proper "level." When growing knowledge suggested that there were too many exceptions to the rule of unilinear evolutionary progress, the anthropologists were forced to revise their picture of evolution in order to accommodate the exceptions.

Both anthropology and sociology, however, have been greatly influenced by the natural sciences—and shifts in their assumptions rest largely on discoveries in the natural sciences. When the social sciences assumed that the world was a giant mechanism, they were reflecting the view of the physicists. Assuming that the social world worked like a machine, they looked for simple, linear, cause-and-effect sequences. They believed that events at one level could be explained by events that occurred at another, lower level. What is more, they did not fully realize the complexity of interactions that go into the formulation of a single event. Thus the early social scientists tended to seek the "cause" of social behavior in a biological factor, or an environmental factor, or psychological, or economic factors. One of the earliest anthropological thinkers, Gustav Klemm (1802–1867) explained differences in human behavior as the result of innate differences in human mentality. Klemm identified two races: a "passive" and an "active" race. The active race comprised the upper strata of European society, the passive consisted of virtually everyone else. Klemm also suggested that geography played a significant role in human development: "Men who inhabit the forest areas," he wrote, "grow up with limited horizons, while coast dwellers reflect upon the constant changes due to the sea—changes which foster their powers of concentration."

To be sure, few social scientists ever viewed society in such simplistic mechanical terms, but many anthropologists adopted a biological view of culture which was itself highly mechanical. Greatly influenced by Charles Darwin, anthropologists wished to discover how man had been transformed from an apelike creature into Homo sapiens. Their emphasis was upon man as a biological organism undergoing physical evolution. Because the most significant difference between men and apes appeared to be the former's development of language and culture, the sciences of linguistics and archeology were added to physical anthropology. At the same time, growing European contact with primitive societies stimulated an interest in ethnography (the descriptive study of primitive cultures) and this, too, became a part of anthropology.

The most influential early contributors to anthropological development—men like J. J. Bachofen, J. F. M'Lennan, and H. J. Sumner Maine—were contemporaries of Charles Darwin and they conceptualized cultural evolution as essentially analogous to natural evolution. Lewis Henry Morgan (1818–1881), whose major contribution is considered to be his analysis of kinship systems, was primarily an evolutionist who set out to furnish an evolutionary discription of progress in terms of institutions, which he correlated with economic and intellectual achievements.

Even Edward B. Tylor (1832–1917), who exhibited much more acute critical faculties, was inclined toward asserting the priority of mechanical evolution over other factors. Tylor, considered the father of anthropology, defined the term "culture," gave anthropology its subject matter, recognized the effect of contact and idea-diffusion on evolutionary processes, and was very much aware of the inadequacies of the metaphysical concept of cause and effect for which he attempted to substitute the mathematical concept of "function." Nevertheless, Tylor, too, affirmed his belief that "the institutions of men are as distinctly stratified as the earth upon which he lives. They succeed each other in series substantially uniform over the globe . . . shaped by similar human nature. . . ."

By and large, the evolutionists equated societies with "species," saw development in terms of the "survival of the fittest," believed that cultural innovation was equivalent to "mutation" and that social or cultural development was autogenic; that is, that it developed automatically in a single, predetermined direction. These early thinkers assumed that all cultures progressed through similar stages of development, and these stages were generally described in terms of their economic base and in relation to some ethnocentric, value-oriented concept of civilization as the equivalent of nineteenth-century Europe. The evolutionists complacently assumed that the development of civilization would continue in the future. They regarded the primitive peoples as "survivals" of an early epoch and suggested that they, too, would evolve naturally to achieve civilized status. Some anthropologists felt that they would evolve more quickly if civilized westerners interfered; most were content to observe them without interference.

As archeologists, linguists, and ethnographers brought in more data, anthropology was forced to recognize, as Tylor had suggested, that cultures were not evolving isolates but had, in fact, been in constant and frequent contact with each other. Interest shifted from questions directed at ascertaining evolutionary stages and levels to questions about culture contact. Recognition that cultures borrowed or absorbed "traits" of other cultures obstructed attempts to place cultures into rigid, linear sequences. Anthropologists accordingly became more interested in studying the differences between cultures than in explaining the similarities. They asked why cultures borrowed certain traits and not others, and they attempted to find out why evolution proceeded at different rates. They badly needed data and they needed a methodology by which they could compare traits or complexes of traits in one culture with their equivalents in another.

Although anthropologists had early recognized that geography did not provide an adequate explanation of human cultural difference, they were not unaware of the influence of climatic factors on development. Alfred Kroeber (1876-1960) organized his data in terms of "culture areas." He did not assume that environment determined cultural forms, but he did perceive a correlation between environment and culture. Knowledge of what that connection is, and how environment interacts with culture, eludes us even today; most anthropologists concede that environment plays a limiting role. Others, particularly among the ecologists, argue for a more inclusive definition of environment and suggest that environment is creative—and, if conceived holistically—determinative of cultural forms.

Meanwhile, development of psychology during the nineteenth century gave support to one of anthropology's basic tenets: the psychological unity of man. Freud's key to the structure of the mind gave social scientists a tool by which they could analyze social behavior in terms of individual psychology. A voluntaristic tradition in American philosophy, which emphasized free will and the power of the individual to affect society, also influenced social thought. Freud saw psychology very much in simple evolutionary terms: Culture, for him, was repression and its function was to maintain social bonds at the expense of individual freedom of expression. Although the Freudian tradition was in many respects diametrically opposed to the liberal tradition, which exalted free will and the individual, both traditions focused attention upon the individual. In equating culture with repression, moreover, Freud attempted to explain the origins and functions of cultural institutions in terms of models taken from individual psychology. Noting the resemblance between the highly patterned behavior of neurotics and the "rituals" of religion, Freud suggested that religion had its source in human anxiety and that its function, like that of neurotic ritual, was both to allay anxiety and to prevent human beings from coping with their problems scientifically. Freud's influence on social thought can hardly be underestimated. Though the simple psychological reductionisms of many Freudian theories have been rejected, his outline of the mechanisms of the mind has proven to be a powerful tool for social science in its studies of enculturation.

In terms of its effect on social institutions, the most influential concept of the nineteenth century was that of Karl Marx. Marx was an evolutionist who saw the world in terms of a struggle among species. Unlike most evolutionists, who were quite willing to wait for evolutionary changes to occur naturally, Marx believed that man could, and should, hasten the process along. Reacting against the social Darwinists who had used the notion of survival of the fittest to justify the status quo, Marx attacked both the laissez-faire economic theories and the puritan ethic of the nineteenth century. His call to revolution in the name of Utopia was very much in the Comtean spirit, though like Comte he was admittedly vague about the nature of his Utopia. Marx attributed all human behavior to the influence of institutions, which reflected economic motives. Like Freud's ideas, Marx's concepts are very much alive today—but simple reductionisms, explanations of social behavior solely in terms of economic motives, are largely out of fashion.

Evolutionary theories dominated nineteenth-century thought. But there were some who, while influenced by evolution, were more interested in societies as ongoing processes. Oriented to the present rather than the past, interested in current rather than historical problems, these men attempted to shift the focus of attention in the social sciences to a study of social groups as they functioned at the time. Partly in reaction to the historicism and biologism of their predecessors, and partly as a result of developments within the social sciences, which had, in collecting data, suggested that the study of differences was more fruitful than the attempt to perceive similarities of social behavior, some of these social scientists tried to cut themselves completely away from evolutionary ideals and from biological and physical analogies. Émile Durkheim's (1858–1917) explicit purpose was to expose and define a level of behavior that was purely and distinctively social. ". . . Disregarding the individual as such, his motives and his ideas, we shall seek directly the states of the various social environments . . . in terms of which the variations of suicide occur," said Durkheim. Durkheim implied that society was an emergent—*sui generis*—a phenomenon that had its own laws of development, and these laws were neither reducible to, nor explicable except, in terms of society itself. At about the same time, William Graham Sumner (1840–1910), one of the prominent American sociologists of the late nineteenth century, had explored the unvarying nature of folkways and suggested in a similar vein that while the group benefits by individual experience, the "folkways" were not creations of purpose or initiative. Sumner believed that the individual had little or no effect upon society and that, therefore, the science of sociology should proceed without reference to the individual or his desires.

Before Durkheim, though Comte had coined the name "sociology" for his science, there was neither a coherent body of data nor a method of approach that could be called "sociological." The social philosophers, whose ideas formed the bedrock upon which sociology rests, had all speculated on the origins of society and upon the manner in which it functioned. The great social thinkers—John Stuart Mill, John Locke, Thomas Hobbes, Nicolò Machiavelli—had tried to explain social behavior by introspection. Though most of them were astute observers and were widely read, they had no technique for amassing or comparing data and in fact, tended to conceptualize the world in terms of their idiosyncratic relationships to it. Though this is no place for personality studies, we cannot ignore either the peculiar social milieux in which these men worked and lived, or their reactions to these milieux. It is hardly an accident that Machiavelli, surrounded by the intrigue of the Florentine court, should have seen society in terms of intrigue and power; nor is it a coincidence that Locke, raised in the liberal traditions of England, saw the origins of the state in terms of the social contract.

Given the excesses of philosophy and the psychologism of social thinkers, given also the attempts to counteract the influence of religious thought and replace it with scientific techniques, Durkheim's suggestion that sociology discard philosophy and introspection and replace these with the collection of data and statistics was understandable. However, his insistence that sociology excise metaphysics, ignore the individual mind, and concentrate upon statistical regularities led in its turn to scientistic excesses.

Durkheim's examination of suicide was undertaken to prove that even an act as personal as self-destruction had a social base and thus could be predicted from statistical data. In turning his attention solely to macrophenomena, he assumed that the subject of sociology was society divorced from the men who made it. Like the physicist who can predict the movement of molecules without being able to predict the act of any particular molecule, Durkheim's statistical method attempted to restrict scientific investigation in sociology to a particular level of behavior.

Sumner's research into folkways, Durkheim's statistical forays, and Georg Simmel's attempt to analyze society in terms of the interaction of social forms, irrespective of content, all reflected reactions in the social sciences against evolutionism, reductionism, psychologism, philosophy, and religion. In anthropology, at about the same time, Alfred Kroeber proclaimed his belief that culture was "superorganic." The term "superorganic" had actually been invented by the great evolutionist Herbert Spencer and was originally based on his analogy of society with a biological organism. In embracing the "superorganic" theory, Kroeber was reacting against biological ideas which had, to him, suggested a priority for racist explanations of culture. But there can be little doubt that Kroeber, too, had been influenced by the Durkheimian view and by anthropological antecedents that included Franz Boas. Franz Boas (1858–1942) was perhaps the most influential of all anthropologists—at least in America—and it was he who set the stage for acceptance of the notion of the superorganic. Durkheim had succeeded in defining the subject of sociology and suggesting a method for its study; Boas achieved the same ends in anthropology. Boas himself was interested in statistics. But the method he favored for the study of society was that used by field naturalists. Inability to perform experiments in controlled environments had appeared to be one of the most severe limitations faced by social scientists in their attempts to develop a methodology. In its place, Boas set anthropologists gathering data in the field. The anthropologist was to act as a "participant" observer. He was trained to observe carefully, and he was also trained in linguistics. Franz Boas wished to make certain that the meaning attached to observed acts was, in fact, the meaning attached by the people—not some erroneous explanation invented by an ethnocentric anthropologist. In using subjective techniques, Boas aimed at a higher objectivity and he stressed cultural relativism over universals. The

Boasian view forced the anthropologist to view culture from two vantage points, and clearly recognized that in studying man, objectivity—free of cultural bias—could be gained only by including subjective methods of observation.

Boas was very much interested in the American Indians and very involved in the ethnographic present. He was consequently less interested in problems of history than in cultures as functioning systems. Under his guidance, American anthropology concerned itself more and more with problems of "functionalism." Interest in historical reconstruction waned as interest in the structures and functions of social acts grew. The excessive claims made by evolutionary theorists had been eroded by the recovery of data that contradicted the concepts of unilinear evolution. Difficulties in obtaining information about the past, moreover, led many anthropologists to believe that they could never really discover answers to questions of origin and that, therefore, they would do better to look for answers to questions of function. Boas did not believe that cultures could be graded evolutionarily, nor did he see them as "inferior" or "superior."

During the early years of the twentieth century, anthropology appeared to be moving confidently away from its theoretical base in evolutionary and biological ideas toward concern with structures and functions. It was moving from system-building philosophical generalizations to a concern with data; away from ethnocentric concepts of cultural universals, to concepts of cultural relativism. Sociology, too, had begun to take shape as a distinct discipline—primarily in the United States. In Europe, by and large, it still remained tied to philosophy. Comte had attempted to give sociology a working base, but like his contemporaries, he was largely an evolutionary philosopher and had not concerned himself with defining methodology. Comte had differed from Spencer, largely in his assumption that manipulation of the social order was a necessary corollary of social improvement. Spencer, on the other hand, believed that progress would occur without interferences. Evolution's lesson for Spencer and for Sumner was the necessity of noninterference. Ranged against this view were Lester Ward (1841–1913) and Lewis Henry Morgan, who were equally convinced that manipulative action on the part of sociologists would speed social evolution.

Though Émile Durkheim had, to some extent, changed the direction of sociological thought by shifting interest from these philo-

sophical arguments toward methodology, he had not abandoned
the idea that sociology should have social value. His concentration
upon a few specific research topics and his emphasis upon the use
of quantitative techniques—as if in ironic proof of his contention
that individual volition had little to do with sociological development—soon came to dominate both sociological theory and methodology. Durkheim felt about sociology somewhat as Boas did about
anthropology; that the science could proceed no further without concrete data. But while Boas emphasized field work and concentration
upon the people's interpretations of themselves, Durkheim's approach
suggested that a sociology divorced from people was the most valid.
Though Durkheim could hardly have intended it, sociology there-
after shifted its interest from problem solving to data collection. The
advent of World War I raised these tendencies to a peak. Until the
war, the social sciences had managed to maintain a semblance of
their belief in progress and evolution. But the disillusionment that
set in with the war conclusively undermined theories of progress.
Bitter and disillusioned, the social sciences wholeheartedly embraced
functionalism, turned away from theorizing, and retreated behind a
concept of science as value-free and concerned with amassing knowledge. Sociologists—and to a lesser extent, anthropologists—insisted
that their major concern was not problem solving but data collection.

Commentators upon the sociological scene are fond of pointing
to the period between the two world wars as a time of "betrayal" of
nineteenth-century science. In fact these years cannot be understood
simply as reactions against excesses of evolutionary theory, but as
an extension—sometimes *ad absurdum*—of scientistic tendencies that
had been obscured by the philosophical battles of the nineteenth
century. The enthusiastic proponents of the social sciences who had
once expounded a philosophy of action seemed to have, in accordance
with demands of scientific method geared to production of predictive
models, moved away from questions of value, problems of metaphysics and application, toward a view of the social world as an object
outside of and divorced from man. Their efforts produced some truly
astonishing rationalizations whose contradictions could not be exposed
as long as philosophical or metaphysical ideas were to be excised
from scientific concerns.

The social disciplines called themselves "mental sciences" but
attempted to treat their abstractions as if they were material things.

They argued that all the so-called material objects that science studied were really only inferential abstractions made by the human mind. Therefore, the inferential abstraction known as society or culture was exactly the same as a material object. Proceeding from this intellectual sleight-of-hand, they then contradicted themselves further by refusing to consider the effect upon the social world of mental inferences—on the ground that the mind had no material existence and therefore was not a fit subject for scientific study! Nor was this their only logical contradiction. Sociologists strove to be objective and value-free: that is, they refused to allow preconceptions about society to contaminate their data. They did not realize that every question they asked—as well as the method by which they proposed to answer it—reflected and supported their particular intellectual orientation. They claimed to be value-free, but failed to realize that every scientific experiment expresses a commitment to specific scientific values. Their inability to understand that science actually constructs what it discloses led them away from an attempt to understand the nature of ideology and of subjective systems of thought to an emphasis on the study of mechanical processes.

Initially, both sociologists and anthropologists set out to use the methods of physics and biology to develop their sciences of human behavior. At the same time, some of them also insisted that social behavior was a "level of behavior" distinct from the physical behavior of animals, the mechanical behavior of inorganic objects, and the psychological behavior of individual men. Just as a biologist should not attempt to account for the behavior of a frog in terms of matter-in-motion—a method of explanation known as "reductionism" because it assumes that phenomena at one level can be understood by reducing or transforming them to phenomena at a lower level— so the social theorists refused to account for social behavior as the effect of geographical, racial, biological, or psychological factors. Only social or cultural factors were to be admitted into evidence to explain social events. But the attempt to escape the traps of premature reductionism by creating a level of social determinism simply substituted another mechanical determinant for the geographical, psychological, or biological determinisms of the past. In asserting that the actions of men were subject to law and causally determined and that the laws were to be understood in phenomena separate from the men who made them, the social and cultural sciences maintained the dual view of Descartes, which separated man as an observer from the world that he observed. By so doing, the social sciences threatened to transform men into mere objects since, as we have seen, the ideas of the social sciences have themselves come to play an important role in altering the direction of human evolution. To add to the confusion, the social sciences attempted to slip the knot of determinism upon which their science was based by claiming that man was uniquely able to make his environment. Knowledge of the workings of social machinery would enable men to control it. This temporal echo of the Calvinist doctrine of grace, which assumed that grace was predetermined and that men could gauge whether or not they possessed it by success in life, gave freedom with one hand and took it away with the other.

Once the social sciences, and particularly sociology, had embarked into this sea of contradictions, they nearly sank under the weight of their methodological problems. They had to consider society or culture a "thing"—an object divorced from the men who made it. They could produce actuarial tables with a high degree of predictive success, but the phenomena they predicted were often only peripheral to men's major problems, and many of the problems that urgently needed attention were ignored in the interest of data collection. Furthermore, many of the questions asked by sociologists were products of unconscious assumptions about human nature. In denying the relationship between human motives and social phenomena, the sociologists refused to subject these to study. As Alex Inkeles so astutely pointed out in his discussion of the relationship between personality and social structure, "The student of a social structure seeks to explain the action consequences of a particular set of institutional arrangements. In order to do this, he must correctly estimate the meaning of these arrangements or their effect on the human personality."

Lacking metaphysics, moreover, the social sciences could not locate the source of many of their problems: the dualistic model of the universe, which in separating objective from subjective facts, refuses to recognize the role played by human thought in framing science. The social sciences have labored prodigiously to maintain this inept dualistic model (whose basis has largely been destroyed by the new physics). The direction and development of the social sciences can be understood largely as an attempt to transform the social realm with all its complexities, creativity, and open-endedness into a mechanical, determined object that will stand still to be dissected and analyzed.

Though the point of view which divorces the acts of men from the men themselves had tremendous effects upon the social sciences, it did not go unchallenged. For Charles Horton Cooley (1864–1929) sociology's principal value lay in the role it could play in developing human self-awareness, in promoting the extension of sympathy, and in fostering cooperation by developing a scientific basis for morality. Cooley wished to emphasize the meaning of human social life and he concentrated on the ethical implications of sociology as well as upon the effect of human ideas upon each other. His emphasis, like that of George Mead (1863–1931), provided the base for a dynamic study of society as an ongoing process. His goal was to suggest a synthesis between society and the individual, which he perceived simply as different aspects of the same thing. Instead of conceiving the individual as regulated by society, which exists outside him, Mead, Cooley, and their followers suggest that the kinds of experiences available to the individual account for the regularities in his behavior. His self—a product of interaction between social demands and individual needs—is conceived as regulating his conduct.

Linguists, concerned with man's acquisition and use of symbols, also tended to stress the individual's role. Foremost among these was Edward Sapir (1884–1939), who rejected the idea that the individual was nothing more than a passive recipient of culture. Sapir criticized the "superorganic" for its static nature and he also rejected the dualistic model upon which it was based. He believed that the genesis and development of cultural patterns could be discovered in studies of enculturation, but he was not convinced that cultural patterns could be disconnected from the organization of ideas and feelings which constituted the individual.

Out of Germany as well, which had maintained criticism of positive science and of the mechanical, dualistic view of the world, a new picture of the universe had emerged—in physics and philosophy first, and later in German social science. Although the German philosophical tradition had accommodated itself to the scientific revolution by framing its propositions so that they supported science, the maintenance of a philosophical tradition welded to science paved the way for criticism of the assumptions upon which science itself was based.

Max Weber (1864–1920) emphasized a theory of social action and advocated an approach to sociological material known as *"verstehen"* or understanding. Insisting that observed facts, no matter how expert the procedures for obtaining them, are of little significance unless evaluated, he maintained that the observer had to attempt to understand what the behavior of individuals or groups means to them. Weber's emphasis upon the role of value and meaning in the social sciences added another influential voice to those already raised in alarm at the implications of "objective" studies of human behavior.

For Karl Mannheim (1893–1947) the solution to the problem lay elsewhere. Mannheim believed that the social sciences badly needed a perspective from which they might view and assess their own activities. A social science unaware of its effects and committed to values and procedures that were largely unconscious could, by conceptualizing men as objects, actually remake the world into the mechanism it had embraced as its model. Mannheim's sociology of knowledge represented a firm step in the direction of self-consciousness. His "sociology of science" provided a method by which the social sciences could recognize and assess the influence of value systems and of the ideologies that underlay their methods, models, and procedures.

The worship of objectivity, the insistence that the objective model of the natural sciences was the only model suitable for the social sciences, had led to incessant sociological arguments over methodology. Peculiarly enough, these arguments reflected a very unscientific method of thought that resembled the attitudes of primitive magicians rather than those of scientists. When a magician sets out to make rain, he conducts a ceremony which is designed, through imitation or sympathetic magic, to "create" rain. If his ceremony succeeds, the magician is convinced, of course, that it has caused rain. If his ceremony fails, however, the magician does not usually attribute the failure to the inadequacies of his model of what causes rain. Instead, he is convinced that something is wrong with his method. Perhaps he did not observe the proper taboos, or he made some error in the ritual chant, or he mishandled his ritual paraphernalia. Instead of trying to correct his model, he assumes that it is his method that is incorrect. To Robert M. MacIver, sociology's overconcern with method suggested such magical thinking. Moreover, the sociologists' attempt to excise metaphysics led them to evaluate even their own methodology in

purely operational terms. MacIver's attempts to deal with the underlying philosophical problems of sociology suggest that social science
exhibits a special type of causal process that demands attention to
values.

Criticisms from within the social sciences have been paralleled and
often exceeded by criticism from outside the field. Although often
astute, outside criticisms are frequently too naïve to come to grips
with the complex problems of the social sciences. In asking "Are the
Social Sciences Really Inferior?" Fritz Machlup expertly sums up both
lay and professional doubts. His outline of the essential difference
between the social and natural sciences suggests that dissension in the
social sciences reflects not inferiority but, perhaps, a higher order of
complexity.

Today's social sciences reflect a view of the world as complex and
at least partly unpredictable. Taken as a whole, they indicate that
science is not a monistic method of approaching problems but is, in
fact, an attitude toward phenomena that can make use of whatever
methods prove adequate in yielding models that explain these phenomena. Today's sciences do not assume that events can be understood
in terms of simple cause-and-effect mechanisms. The concept of linear
sequences no longer obtains: it has been replaced by a concept of
the world as a simultaneous act. Thus, what appears to be cause may
also be effect, furthermore any cause may have numerous effects—and
the decision to see one aspect of a total environment as "cause" and
another as "effect" is dependent upon human subjectivity. The world
that physics has revealed to us is a strange one because it defies our
understanding of it in rational or pictorial terms. We cannot conceive—without mathematical symbols—of the peculiar relationship
between matter and velocity. Events take place in a field, or total
environment, and it is this total environment that appears to determine events, not any sequence of cause and effect; antimatter exists,
the splitting of the atom releases tons of energy; phenomena hundreds
of times smaller than the atoms have been discovered and these do
not seem to abide by the laws that govern larger phenomena. The
complacency with which nineteenth-century physics assumed it had
achieved most of the answers to questions about the natural world
was based upon ignorance. The naïve assumption that the world was
a dichotomy in which we, the observers, stood outside to discover the
"truth" about what was observed, has been shattered. Pure objectivity

never is and never was. Man not only influences everything he observes, he is responsible for creating his own behavior. His position
vis-à-vis the natural and social worlds is a product of his own creative
imagination.

Paradoxically, while physics has been forced to confront the problems of value and meaning, subject and object, which once disturbed
only the social scientists, some social scientists have embraced the
belief that only the objective stance is capable of yielding knowledge.
Among the most thoughtful proponents of this view is George Lundberg. He would admit into evidence only sensory data or acts that
can be perceived through the senses. His "operational" view has numerous supporters among the ecologists, whose examination of cultures suggests to them that ideas and values do not, in fact, help to
shape human culture but are actually culturally elaborated structures
that function to increase survival possibilities. For the ecologists,
values are determined by need, and though they may appear to shape
culture and society, in fact they are irrelevant. The ecologists regard
man as a biological organism, and they see social forms as contribut-
ing to human survival. While they recognize that unilinear explanations of human behavior are not adequate, the ecologists tend to
equate culture with technological proficiency in manipulation of the
environment. Mind, and its products, are taken into account only
where they can be operationally validated or made into material
objects. The ecological approach has uncovered some fascinating data,
which suggest that such cultural items as witchcraft are neither
capricious nor nonfunctional, but in fact may tend to maintain a
society's adaptation to its particular niche. Its most significant influence, however, may result from its attempt to shift the interest of the
social sciences from the analysis of static objects to the study of the
dynamics of adaptation.

Games theory, as represented here by Omar K. Moore and Alan
R. Anderson, visualizes society in evolutionary terms as if it were a
player making strategic choices to maximize his survival. The environment is pictured as the opponent, and prediction of human behavior
is made by applying games mathematics to the choices made by society
as it attempts to maximize its survival. Application of games theory
has tended to corroborate the ecological point of view: namely, that
cultural forms and structures that appear to be completely irrational
elaborations, in fact, have survival value. Although men may be fully

aware of the rationality of their acts, more often they act in what appears to be an irrational manner but thereby effect their own survival. Games theory can deal with only a few variables and since social events usually involve many variables, games theory is a tool with restricted but undeniable value.

The introduction of mathematics, physics, geography, and statistics into the social sciences has created a revolution in thinking. Not less important has been the effect of new discoveries in biology. Konrad Lorenz's popularization of the science of ethology has brought to the attention of a wide public what appears to be a revolution in anthropological attitudes. While no anthropologist would ever concur in the notion that the behavior of monkeys is the same as the behavior of men, most are willing to concede that the analysis of animal behavior—the ritual performances of birds, the social structures of monkeys, the behavioral reactions of rats to stress—may provide hypotheses about human behavior that are well worth serious investigation. A renewed interest in the connections that exist between biology and culture has led, in both anthropology and sociology, to a willingness to relinquish some basic myths about the uniqueness of man and of culture. Willingness to see human behavior as a continuum from animal behavior has reopened a great many questions that were once ignored by the social sciences as reductionist. Discoveries in biology and medicine, for example, have yielded a great deal of new information that suggests explanations for some of the racial variations that have long puzzled men. Many anthropologists have turned to the study of disease and nutrition in an attempt to assess the roles played by these in inhibiting or encouraging cultural evolution, or in affecting social behavior. One of the seminal papers in this field is that by Frank B. Livingstone which discusses the distribution of the sickle cell gene in Africa. By tracing the distribution and incidence of the sickle cell gene in human populations, anthropologists have been able to corroborate linguistic evidence of cultural connections. Moreover, since the sickle cell gene is an adaptive mechanism that in its heterozygous form enhances immunity to malaria, study of those groups who carry the gene has yielded much interesting information about cultural practices and their effects upon disease. Most recently, an anthropological approach to medicine suggested that a particular neurological disease, kuru, once believed to have a genetic base, was in fact transmitted by cultural practices.

Ritual cannibalism rather than genetic defect appears to be the mode of transmission of this disease. Although kuru affects only a small number of New Guinea natives, the implications of the discovery that this disease may be carried by a slow virus has already begun to affect thinking about similar diseases such as muscular dystrophy and multiple sclerosis.

Provocative as are these attempts to link cultural processes with biological needs, much work must be done before we can accept such ideas as proven. But they have brought much new excitement—as well as argument—into the social sciences.

While the ecologists and biologists have concentrated their attention upon environment and organisms, other researchers have maintained and reenforced the traditional connections between the social and the psychological sciences. Replacement of the simple notions of the relationship between culture and personality that informed early work in the field have stressed, as does Talcott Parsons, the dynamic processual relationship between personality development and social structure. In anthropology, early formulation of models that saw personality as culture writ small have been replaced by more complex models, which have replaced the notion that culture and personality are identical, and stress instead the complementary natures of the numerous personalities that make up even the simplest cultural systems.

The initial concern with emotional aspects of behavior has been enriched as well by a growing interest in intellectual, or cognitive, aspects of the mind. Once again, the linguists have played an important role in suggesting directions for the development of cognition studies. Harold Conklin's "Hanunóo Color Categories" suggests that revelation of the differences in cultural conceptualization of basic visual phenomena (arrived at through participant observer techniques) provides interesting clues to some possible causes of cultural growth. Such studies may help explain differences in evolutionary development of different peoples.

Melford Spiro's analysis of religious systems is, in some ways, a more traditional approach to problems of psychology and culture—it reflects the continual attempts made by anthropologists to refine the conceptual tools of psychology for their own use.

On a somewhat more pragmatic level—but one whose conceptions cannot be separated from the central problems of the social sciences—

are the numerous recent attempts to apply the knowledge of the social sciences to help solve human problems. The social action theory first proposed by men like Robert Merton and Talcott Parsons, as well as the attention paid to applied anthropology, has eased problems of cultural change in some cases, while it has supplied situations for experiment that are otherwise extraordinarily rare. Such thoughtful studies as William Gamson's on the manner in which group dynamics rather than rational procedures may determine the outcome of action programs are not only enlightening, they have immediate social value.

Of all the recent developments in the social sciences, however, the one that promises most is the reappearance in the social sciences of philosophical speculation. Although such speculation was characteristic of anthropology and sociology in their beginnings, disappointment with the rationally based system-building of the evolutionists, and with the somewhat naïve phychologism of the social philosophers, led to almost complete rejection of speculation in favor of narrow, empirical approaches. Reemergence in physics of questions of value and meaning, subject and object, interference and separation, has paved the way for a reassessment of the value of philosophical speculation in the social sciences. A willingness to recognize these problems; in fact, the sense that it is necessary to support the scientific structure with a philosophical base, today informs the work of even the most dedicated operationalists.

Emergence of philosophical questions into the social sciences is a sign that the rift between body and mind, man and nature, subject and object, is mendable. Each thoughtful critique of dualism has its own perspective. For Claude Lévi-Strauss, renewed attention to history is the first step toward understanding. For F. S. C. Northrop, the discovery of the source of the symbol in the neurons of the brain suggests that the ultimate goal of science—explanation of all phenomena in terms of a single law—is not beyond the realm of possibility. Fear that such reductionism reduces man to "nothing more" than an animal, or, in the final analysis, to a material object, is in fact nothing more than a residue of categorical thinking. For Erwin Straus, definition by category, which suggests differences in levels of behavior and abrupt breaks in quality between man and animal or man and nature, must be replaced by definition in terms of processes. All phenomena—mental, physical, and cultural—are embedded in each other, incomprehensible without each other. Man has his origins in the world of matter, and he is only recently removed by his consciousness from the world of animals. What we wish to understand is the process by which he has moved along the continuum from unthinking matter to self-consciousness. What we wish to learn is how this evolution has been effected, and how the emergence of consciousness fits into and alters the evolutionary scheme.

By concluding on this philosophical note, I do not wish to suggest that all anthropologists and sociologists approve of this renewed interest in philosophical speculation, nor do I wish to suggest that there is any agreement as to the role of consciousness or the place of meaning in the social sciences. Far from it. The old arguments over method still exist, though they are not, perhaps, as shrill as they once were. Man is conceptualized as "nothing more" than matter in motion; as an animal; as a victim of cultural forces; as a being whose mind and body are inexplicable except as a whole; and, on the other extreme, as a purely mental phenomenon—a consciousness free to create itself. Each point of view has its value, as long as the assumptions upon which it is based are clearly stated. The view that most adequately fits today's model of the physical world is, however, the one that sees man and mind, man and culture, man and environment as interacting processes.

It is unfortunate, however, that the public should regard the arguments and the heated debates of the social scientists as symptoms of disorganization, or proof of the nonscientific status of the social sciences. As any good social scientist will tell you, arguments and conflicts are not necessarily divisive; they are often methods by which social cohesion is maintained.

Our social sciences are growing at an exponential rate; they are bewilderingly diverse, difficult, and far richer than they were in the past. Their transformation, from disciplines that sought mechanical answers to cause-and-effect questions to ones that seek more accurate and ever-changing models to explain social and cultural behavior, has not been without pain. But these are only growing pains, not, as many people believe, a symptom of serious disease. In fact, the divergent tendencies of the social sciences, their growing specialization, their willingness to maintain continual argument and debate, as well as their attempts to synthesize, are unmistakable symptoms of development.

We are no longer constrained to view society or culture as something divorced from the men who made it. We are free to study society as a process rather than a material object. Our constant awareness that science and understanding, heredity and environment, biology, psychology, and culture are not categories but processes of interaction, indicates that the dualistic separation of mind and body is not a necessary corollary of scientific method. In facing the possibility that the world may indeed be a very different place from what we now imagine, we may have to surrender our childish search for absolutes—and to recognize the world for the creative and constantly evolving process that it is.

PART I ○○○

Society and Culture:

Theories and Methods

Auguste Comte

Positive Philosophy

In suggesting a science of society, Comte was a child of his time, heir to optimism engendered by man's successful discovery and application of the natural sciences. The notion that the world ran by mechanical laws; that these laws were knowable; and that discovery of these laws would enable men to predict and therefore control their social behavior, informed the founding of social sciences, whose goal was the achievement of Utopia. The fact that the Utopian optimism of Comte has been proven to be an illusion should not blind us to the importance of Comte in suggesting the possibilities of a science of society. Although he conceived this science mechanically as offering "positive" truth, his suggestion that scientific methods be applied to the study of social problems was the impetus that served to shift the emphasis in the social sciences from purely rational speculation that required no proof to scientific method that utilized perceptual and later mathematical techniques for validation.

I HAVE SHOWN THAT THE physical laws which are the basis of the theory of motion and equilibrium, and therefore all their consequences, are as applicable to the mechanical phenomena of living bodies as to any others (allowing for the difficulties arising from a complication of details); and we have seen, in a more special manner, that the study of animal mechanics, in the province of biology, must begin with such an application, and would be wholly unintelligible without it; but we have now to go much further, showing that the application must extend even to the social form of existence. As to the first of these laws, Kepler's law of inertia, improperly so called—seen in its true light as the law of mechanical persistence—is merely a particular case of the tendency of all natural phenomena to persevere in their state, unless disturbed; a tendency specially established with regard to the most simple and general phenomena. I have traced back the biological case of Habit to this principle, modified only by the characteristic intermittence of the corresponding phenomena. In social life, less rapid and more durable than individual life, we see an analogous exemplification in the obstinate tendency of every political system to perpetuate itself. In physics, again, we have noticed, in acoustics, phenomena which prove that, in the smallest molecular changes, there is a disposition to the reproduction of acts which were before supposed proper to living beings, and which evidently come under the law of mechanical persistance. It is impossible to deny here the subordination of all natural effects to some universal laws, modified according to the conditions of each case. It is the same with the second law of motion—Galileo's law of the reconciliation of any common motion with various particular motions—which is extensible to all phenomena, inorganic and organic—all active and passive mutual relations being radically independent of any action which is precisely common to the parts concerned. In biology, we find this true in the cases of sensibility and contractility: for, our impressions being purely comparative, our appreciation of partial differences is not interfered with by any general and uniform influence. In sociology, we find it again; any disturbance in the interior of any political system being due to the unequal progressive action on the different parts which, if participating in the movement in any equal degree, would be unaffected by a much more rapid progression. We discern an analogous case in the physico-chemical province, in thermometrical effects referrable to mutual inequality, and we shall no doubt encounter many more when the science is further developed. As to the third law of motion—Newton's law of the equivalence of action and reaction—its universality is more striking than in the other two cases; and it is the only case of the three in which the principle has hitherto been perceived and proposed. If we adapt our observation to the spirit of the corresponding phenomena, there is no doubt that the equivalence of action and reaction may be as readily observed with regard to physical, chemical, biological, and social effects as in the case of mechanical effects. Besides the mutual quality inherent in all actions, it is certain that the general estimate of mechanical reaction, in the combination of masses and velocities, everywhere meets with an analogous appreciation. If Berthollet has shown the chemical influence of mass, before misconceived, an equivalent discussion would manifest no less clearly its biological or political influence. The close and prevalent interconnection which distinguishes vital, and yet more social phenomena, and in which all aspects are mutually dependent, is eminently fit to familiarize us with the universality of this third law of motion. Each of the three laws on which rational Mechanics is founded is, in fact, only a mechanical manifestation of a general law, applicable to all possible phenomena. In order to illustrate this most important aproximation, it must be extended, further, to the famous general principle by which D'Alembert completely connected questions of motions with questions of equilibrium. Whether it is regarded, as I propose, as a happy generalization of the third law of motion, or is still regarded as a distinct idea, it is in conformity with a universal conception by which the dynamical is always connected with the statical appreciation—the laws of harmony being always maintained in the midst of the laws of succession. Sociology here again affords us the most decisive exemplification (though often only implicit) of this general relation; because the two aspects are more marked and more interconnected than in any other case. If we could thoroughly know the laws of existence, I have no doubt that we should find them all, as in mechanics, to be mere questions of action. But, though we must proceed in an inverse manner, we proceed upon the same conception of the necessary convergence between the statical and dynamical conclusions. It is only that the universal principle is employed in a new mode, in conformity with the nature of the phenomena; of which sociological speculation has often presented important examples. The laws of rational mechanics are then only the earliest philosophical manifestation of certain general laws, necessarily applicable to the natural economy of any kind of phenomena whatever. Though they must first be recognized in regard to the simplest and most general case of all, it does not follow that they are due to the mathematical spirit, which at present is the chief obstacle in the way of their being understood. The conception results from the first scientific reaction of the positive spirit proper to organic studies, and sociological speculation particularly, on fundamental ideas which have hitherto seemed proper to inorganic researches. Its philosophical value lies in its establishing an identity between the primary laws of the two extreme orders of natural phenomena: and the delineation I have now offered is intended to point out here, in the only case compatible with the extreme imperfection of science, the first type of the new character of universality which must belong to the chief positive ideas under the natural ascendency of the true philosophical spirit. We have no equivalent case at our command: and in more complex subjects, these general laws can only go a part of the way in directing our speculations; though they will always afford valuable scientific guidance and suggestion, because they must always govern more special laws, relating to other abstract modes of existence and activity. Whether, as we may hope, these more special laws may in time obtain universality among their respective phenomena or not, we are now authorized in conceiving the whole system of our knowledge as susceptible, in certain respects, of a true scientific unity, independently of the logical unity, though in complete agreement with it.

Vilfredo Pareto

On the Equilibrium of the Social System

The idea that a science of society could use the methods and models of physics had begun with Comte. Vilfredo Pareto (1848–1923) attempted to apply these mechanical concepts to produce what he called "social physics."

Pareto firmly upheld the concepts of empiricism and believed that sociology must begin by studying concrete cases. General principles would come later. Unlike Comte, whose Utopian vision enlisted science as an aid to man, Pareto's social physics aimed solely at discovery of the "truth" whether or not this truth was socially beneficent or not.

In the selection that follows, Pareto suggests that the conflict between individual and social tendencies can be understood in terms of the physical theory of equilibrium.

2063. An exhaustive study of social forms would have to consider at least the chief elements that determine them, disregarding those elements only which seem to be of secondary or incidental influence. But such a study is not at present possible, any more than an exhaustive study of plant or animal forms is possible, and we are therefore obliged to confine ourselves to a study covering a part only of the subject. Fortunately for our project, not a few of the elements have an influence upon human proclivities and sentiments, so that by taking account of residues we indirectly take account of them as well.

2064. The influence of the first group of elements (soil, climate, and so on) is undoubtedly very important. A comparison of the civilizations of peoples of the tropics and peoples of temperate zones would be enough to show that; and many books have been written on the subject, but so far with no great results. We shall make no direct examination of such influences here, but account for them indirectly by taking as data of fact the residues, proclivities, and interests of human beings who are subject to them.

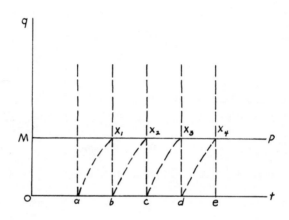

FIGURE I

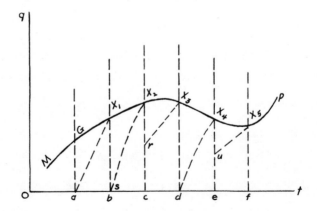

FIGURE II

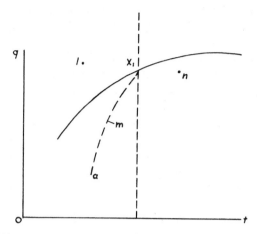

FIGURE III

2065. To go farther still in our avoidance of difficulties, we shall confine our investigations to the peoples of Europe and of the Asian and African sections of the Mediterranean basin. That will free us of the many serious—and unsolved—questions that are connected with race. We must necessarily take account of the influences upon a given people of other peoples, for the various peoples of the regions indicated have at no time in history been entirely isolated. But military, political, intellectual, economic, and other kinds of power through which those influences have been exerted depend upon elements such as sentiments, state of knowledge, and interests; and the influences therefore, may be inferred, in part at least, from those elements.

2066. But however many, however few, the elements that we choose to consider, we assume at any rate that they constitute a system, which we will call the "social system"; and the nature and properties of that system we propose to investigate. The system changes both in form and in character in course of time. When, therefore, we speak of "the social system" we mean that system taken both at a specified moment and in the successive transformations which it undergoes within a specified period of time. So when one speaks of the solar system, one means that system taken both at a specified moment and in the successive moments which go to make up a greater or lesser period of time.

2067. *The state of equilibrium.* If we intend to reason at all strictly, our first obligation is to fix upon the state in which we are choosing to consider the social system, which is constantly changing in form. The real state, be it static or dynamic, of the system is determined by its conditions. Let us imagine that some modification in its form is induced artificially (virtual movements). At once a reaction will take place, tending to restore the changing form to its original state as modified by normal change. If that were not the case, the form, with its normal changes, would not be determined but would be a mere matter of chance.

2068.   We can take advantage of that peculiarity in the social system to define the state that we choose to consider and which for the moment we will indicate by the letter X. We can then say that the state X is such a state that if it is artificially subjected to some modification different from the modification it undergoes normally, a reaction at once takes place tending to restore it to its real, its normal state. That gives us an exact definition of the state of X.

2069.   The state X is ever in process of change, and we are not able, nor do we care, to consider it that way in all its minute detail. If we desire to figure on the fertility of a piece of land, we do not set out to watch how the grain grows in the sown field every minute, every hour, every day, or even every month. We take the annual crop and let it go at that. If we want to figure on the element of patriotism, we cannot follow each soldier in every move he makes from the day when he is called to arms to the day when he falls on a battle-field. For our purposes it is enough to note the gross fact that so many men have died for their country. Or again, the hand of a watch moves and stops, stops and moves, yet in measuring time we disregard that circumstance and figure as though the movement of the hand were continuous. Let us therefore consider successive states X_1, X_2, X_3 . . . reached at certain intervals of time that we fix on for the purpose of getting at the states which we choose to consider and which are such that each one of the elements that we elect to consider has completed its action. To see the situation more clearly, we might look at a few examples. Pure economics affords a very simple one. Let us take a person who in a given unit of time—every day, we will say—barters bread for wine. He begins with no wine, and stops bartering when he has a certain quantity of wine. In Figure 1, the axis of time is Ot, and ab, bc, cd, de . . . are spaces representing equal units of time. The axis of the quantities of wine is Oq.

At the beginning of the first unit of time, the individual has no wine —his position is at *a*; at the end he has the quantity bX_1 of wine— his position is at X_1. Exactly the same transaction is repeated every day, and at the end of every day, or of every unit of time, the individual's position is at X_1, X_2, X_3. . . . All those points fall within a line, *MP*, parallel to *Ot*, and the distance between the two lines is equal to the quantity of wine that the individual acquires through exchange each day. The line *MP* is called the line of equilibrium and, in general, is the line determined by the equations of pure economics. It does not have to be a line parallel to the axis *Ot*, for there is no reason why exactly the same transaction should be repeated every day. It may, for example, be the line *MP* in Figure 2: *ab, bc, cd* . . . are still equal units of time, but at the beginnings of the various periods the individual's position is at *a, s, r, d, u* . . . and at the ends at $X_1, X_2,$ X_3, X_4, X_5. . . . The line MX_1, X_2, X_3, X_4, X_5 . . . is still called the line of equilibrium. When it is said that pure economics gives the theory of the economic equilibrium, it means that pure economics shows how the final positions, X_1, X_2, X_3 . . . are reached from the points *a, s, r, d, u* . . . and nothing more. Now let us consider the more general case. In Figure 2, *ab, bc, cd* . . . are no longer equal to one another, but represent different periods of time, which we choose in order to examine a phenomenon at the end of each of them, the length of the period being determined by the time required for an element to complete the particular action that we have chosen to consider. The points *a, s, r, d, u* represent the state of the individual at the beginning of the action; X_1, X_2, X_3 . . . the state of the individual when it is completed. The line MX_1, X_2 . . . *P* is the line of the state *X* (§ 2076).

2070. That definition is identical, barring the mere difference in form, with the one given in § 2068. In fact, if we start in the first place with the definition just given of the state X_1, we see that the action of each element having been completed, society cannot of itself assume any form other than the form X_1, and that if it were made artificially to vary from that form, it should tend to resume it; for otherwise, its form would not be entirely determined, as was assumed, by the elements considered. In other words, if society has reached a point X_1 (Figure 3), following such a path aX_1, that at X_1 the action of the elements which we choose to consider is complete; and if society is artificially made to vary from X_1, the variation can be brought about only: (1) by forcing society to points such as l, n . . . which are located outside the line aX_1; or (2), by forcing it to a point m on the line aX_1. In the first case, society should tend to return to X_1; otherwise its state would not be completely determined, as was assumed, by the elements considered. In the second case, the hypothesis would be in contradiction with our assumption that the action of the elements is complete; for it is complete only at X_1, and is incomplete at m; at the latter point the elements considered are still in action and they carry society from m to X_1.

Using the definition we gave in § 2068 as the point of departure, we see, conversely, that if after society has been artificially made to vary from the point X_1, it tends to return to X_1, the phenomenon indicates one of two things: either, as in the first case above, that society has been brought to the points l, n . . . which are different from the points determined by the elements considered, or that society has been brought to a point m, at which the action of the elements considered is incomplete. If instead of reaching the points X_1, X_2, X_3 . . . successively the system were to traverse the line X_1, X_2, X_3 in a continuous movement, there would be nothing to change in the definitions just given. One would need merely to say that if the system were made artificially to deviate from the line X_1, X_2 . . . it would tend at once to return to it; and that if the effect of the elements is to impel the system along that line, their action would not be complete unless the system were located on that line, and on no other.

2071. So we get the precise and rigorous definition that we said . . . we were intending to give of the state we are about to consider. To become more familiar with it let us now look at some analogies, much as one looks at a sphere to get some conception of the shape of the Earth.

For a concrete example, the state X is analogous to the state of a river, and the states X_1, and X_2 . . . to the states of the same river taken day by day. The river is not motionless; it is flowing, and the slightest modification we try to effect in its form and in the manner of its flow is the cause of a reaction that tends to reproduce the original state.

2072. For an abstract case, the state X that we are considering is analogous to the state of dynamic equilibrium in a physical system, the states X_1, X_2 . . . to successive positions of equilibrium in that system. The state X, one might also add, is analogous to the state of equilibrium in a living organism.

2073. We might look for analogies in a field closer to our own. The states X_1, X_2, X_3 . . . are like the states that pure economics considers in an economic system; and the analogy is so close that the states of the economic system may be regarded as particular cases of the general states of the sociological system.

2074. There is another analogy that we cannot disregard if we would go somewhat deeply into this matter. The state X is analogous to the state called a *statistic* equilibrium in the kinetic theory of gases. To make that clearer, suppose we consider a particular case, the consumption, for instance, of cigars of a given quality within a given territory. The states X_1, X_2, X_3 . . . represent hypothetically, the annual consumptions of such cigars. Let us begin by assuming that they are all more or less equal. Then we would say that the consumption of cigars is constant. By that we do not mean that every individual smokes the same number of cigars each year. We know very well that such numbers vary widely. But the variations more or less offset one another, so that the resultant is zero or, to be more exact, approximately zero. To be sure, it may happen that so many of these variations will be in the same direction that the resultant will no longer be approximately zero, but such a probability is so slight that we need not consider it; and that is what we mean when we say that the consumption is constant. If, instead, the probability is not so slight, fluctuations around the constant total of consumption will be observable, such fluctuations following the law of probabilities. But suppose X_1, X_2, X_3 . . . represent increasing consumptions. We can then repeat, with the proper modifications, everything we have just said. We are in no sense assuming that the individual consumptions are on the increase. We know they are extremely variable. We are speaking of a *statistic* equilibrium, where variations offset one another in such a way that the resultant is an increasing total consumption. And such increasing total consumption may have a probability so great as to eliminate fluctuations depending on probabilities; or a probability not so great, and then fluctuations will occur. So, in preparing ourselves by studying particular cases of that sort we find it easy to grasp the general significance of X_1, X_2, X_3 . . . for consumptions varying in any manner whatsoever.

2075. Extend to an entire social system what we have seen to hold for a system of consumers of one brand of cigars, and the result will be a clear conception of the analogy we have in view for the states $X_1, X_2, X_3 \ldots$

2076. We could continue to designate the social states that we elect to consider . . . with the letters X and $X_1, X_2 \ldots$, but that manner of designating soon begins to weary and one would prefer to have them given names. We could choose a name at random, but it is perhaps better to borrow it from something more or less like the thing we intend to designate by it. So, stopping at the mechanical analogy, we will call the states X and $X_1, X_2 \ldots$ *states of equilibrium.* But the meaning of the term as we use it has to be sought strictly within the definitions that we gave in §§ 2068–69, due attention being paid to the argument in § 2074.

2077. We have now simplified our problem by deciding to consider certain successive states instead of the numberless imperceptible mutations that lead to them. We now have to go on along that path and try to reduce the problem of mutual correlation and the number of elements that we are to consider to greater simplicity.

2078. In our study we stop at certain elements, just as the chemist stops at chemical elements; but that in no sense means that the elements at which we stop are not reducible to a smaller number, or even, at a hazard, to one; just as the chemist does not claim that the number of chemical elements is not still further reducible or indeed that some day they may not be recognized as different manifestations of one single element.

Herbert Spencer

Social Growth

Although Herbert Spencer is frequently linked with Auguste Comte as cofounder of the social sciences, the two men were, in many respects, diametrically opposed in their thinking. Both shared the belief that a science of society was possible, but while Comte hoped to use his social science to create Utopia, Spencer's understanding of evolution lent itself to justification of political laissez-faire. Spencer's ability to utilize evolutionary theory in analyzing social behavior formed a base from which more sophisticated views of the nature of society later emerged. Spencer believed that the structural complexity of all things in nature increased while the behavior of their parts became more specialized and coordinated. Society, he believed, was analogous to the organism, and must be understood as a unit comprising complementary —rather than equivalent—parts. Spencer's analogy provided a valuable tool by which societies could be classified, and his evolutionary scheme with its stress upon the adaptive qualities of human society is implicit in most ecological thinking today.

SOCIETIES, LIKE LIVING BODIES, begin as germs—originate from masses which are extremely minute in comparison with the masses some of them eventually reach. That out of small wandering hordes have arisen the largest societies, is a conclusion not to be contested. The implements of pre-historic peoples, ruder even than existing savages use, imply absence of those arts by which alone great aggregations of men are made possible. Religious ceremonies that survived among ancient historic races, pointed back to a time when the progenitors of

41

these races had flint knives, and got fire by rubbing together pieces of wood; and must have lived in such small clusters as are alone possible before the rise of agriculture.

Between this trait of organic evolution and the answering trait of super-organic evolution, there is a further parallelism: the growths in aggregates of different classes are extremely various in their amounts.

Glancing over the entire assemblage of animal types, we see that the members of one large class, the *Protozoa,* rarely increase beyond that microscopic size with which every higher animal begins. Among the multitudinous kinds of *Coelenterata,* the masses range from that of the small Hydra to that of the large Medusa. The annulose and molluscous types, respectively show us immense contrasts between their superior and inferior members. And the vertebrate animals, much larger on the average than the rest, display among themselves enormous differences.

Kindred unlikenesses of size strike us when we contemplate the entire assemblage of human societies. Scattered over many regions there are minute hordes—still extant samples of the primordial type of society. We have Wood-Veddâhs living sometimes in pairs, and only now and then assembling; we have Bushmen wandering about in families, and forming larger groups but occasionally; we have Fuegians clustered by the dozen or the score. Tribes of Australians, of Tasmanians, of Andamanese, are variable within the limits of perhaps twenty to fifty. And similarly, if the region is inhospitable, as with the Esquimaux, or if the arts of life are undeveloped, as with the Digger-Indians, or if adjacent higher races are obstacles to growth, as with Indian Hill-tribes like the Juangs, this limitation to primitive size continues. Where a fruitful soil affords much food, and where a more settled life, leading to agriculture, again increases the supply of food, we meet with larger social aggregates: instance those in the Polynesian Islands and in many parts of Africa. Here a hundred or two, here several thousands, here many thousands, are held together more or less completely as one mass. And then in the highest societies, instead of partially aggregated thousands, we have completely aggregated millions.

The growths of individual and social organisms are allied in another respect. In each case size augments by two processes, which go on sometimes separately, sometimes together. There is increase by simple multiplication of units, causing enlargement of the group; there is increase by union of groups, and again by union of groups of groups. The first parallelism is too simple to need illustration; but the facts which show us the second must be set forth.

Organic integration . . . must be here summarized to make the comparison intelligible. The compounding and re-compounding, as shown us throughout the vegetal kingdom, may be taken first, as most easily followed. Plants of the lowest orders are minute cells, some kinds of which in their myriads colour stagnant waters, and others compose the green films on damp surfaces. By clusterings of such cells are formed small threads, discs, globes, etc.; as well as amorphous masses and laminated masses. One of these last (called a thallus when scarcely at all differentiated, as in a sea-weed, and called a frond in cryptogams that have some structure), is an extensive but simple group of the protophytes first named. Temporarily united in certain low cryptogams, fronds become permanently united in higher cryptogams: then forming a series of foliar surfaces joined by a creeping stem. Out of this comes the phaenogamic axis—a shoot with its foliar organs or leaves. That is to say, there is now a permanent cluster of clusters. And then, as these axes develop lateral axes, and these again branch, the compounding advances to higher stages. In the animal-kingdom the like happens; though in a less regular and more disguised manner. The smallest animal, like the smallest plant, is essentially a minute group of living molecules. There are many forms and stages showing us the clustering of such smallest animals. Sometimes, as in the compound *Vorticellae* and in the Sponges, their individualities are scarcely at all masked; but as evolution of the composite aggregate advances, the individualities of the component aggregates become less distinct. In some *Coelenterata,* though they retain considerable independence, which they show by moving about like *Amoebae* when separated, they have their individualities mainly merged in that of the aggregate formed of them: instance the common Hydra. Tertiary aggregates similarly result from the massing of secondary ones. Sundry modes and phases of the process are observable among coelenterate types. There is the branched hydroid, in which the individual polypes preserve their identities, and the polypidom merely holds them together; and there are forms, such as *Velella,* in which the polypes have been so modified and fused, that their individualities were long unrecognized. Again, among the *Molluscoida* we have feebly-united tertiary aggregates in the *Salpidae;* while we have, in the *Botryllidoe,* masses in which the tertiary aggregate, greatly consolidated, obscures the individualities of the secondary aggregates. So, too, is it with certain annuloid types; and . . . with the *Annulosa* generally.

Social growth proceeds by an analogous compounding and re-compounding. The primitive social group, like the primitive group of living molecules with which organic evolution begins, never attains any considerable size by simple increase. Where, as among Fuegians, the supplies of wild food yielded by an inclement habitat will not enable more than a score or so to live in the same place—where, as among Andamanese, limited to a strip of shore backed by impenetrable bush, forty is about the number of individuals who can find prey without going too far from their temporary abode—where, as among Bushmen, wandering over barren tracts, small hordes are alone possible, and even families "are sometimes obliged to separate, since the same spot will not afford sufficient sustenance for all;" we have extreme instances of the limitation of simple groups, and the formation of migrating groups when the limit is passed. Even in tolerably productive habitats, fission of the groups is eventually necessitated in a kindred manner. Spreading as its number increases, a primitive tribe presently reaches a diffusion at which its parts become incoherent; and it then gradually separates into tribes that become distinct as fast as their continually-diverging dialects pass into different languages. Often nothing further happens than repetition of this. Conflicts of tribes, dwindlings or extinctions of some, growths and spontaneous divisions of others, continue. The formation of a larger society results only by the joining of such smaller societies; which occurs without obliterating the divisions previously caused by separations. This process may be seen now going on among uncivilized races, as it once went on among the ancestors of the civilized races. Instead of absolute independence of small hordes, such as the lowest savages show us, more advanced savages show us slight cohesions among larger hordes. In North America each of the three great tribes of Comanches consists of various bands, having such feeble combination only, as results from the personal character of the great chief. So of the Dakotahs there are, according to Burton, seven principal bands, each including minor bands, numbering altogether, according to Catlin, forty-two. And in like manner the five Iroquois nations had severally eight tribes. Closer unions of these slightly-coherent original groups arise under favourable conditions; but they only now and then become permanent. A common form of the process is that described by Mason as occurring among the Karens. "Each village, with its scant domain, is an independent state, and every chief a prince; but now and then a little Napoleon arises, who subdues a kingdom to himself, and builds up an empire. The dynasties, however, last only with the controlling mind." The like happens in Africa. Livingstone says—"Formerly all the Maganja were united under the government of their great Chief, Undi; . . . but after Undi's death it fell to pieces. . . . This has been the inevitable fate of every African Empire from time immemorial." Only occasionally does there result a compound social aggregate that endures for a considerable period, as Dahomey or as Ashantee, which is "an assemblage of states owing a kind of feudal obedience to the sovereign." The histories of Madagascar and of sundry Polynesian islands also display these transitory compound groups, out of which at length come in some cases permanent ones. During the earliest times of the extinct civilized races, like stages were passed through. In the words of Maspero, Egypt was "divided at first into a great number of tribes, which at several points simultaneously began to establish small independent states, every one of which had its laws and its worship." The compound groups of Greeks first formed, were those minor ones resulting from the subjugation of weaker towns by stronger neighbouring towns. And in Northern Europe during pagan days, the numerous German tribes, each with its cantonal divisions, illustrated this second stage of aggregation. After such compound societies are consolidated, repetition of the process on a larger scale produces doubly-compound societies; which, usually cohering but feebly, become in some cases quite coherent. Maspero infers that the Egyptian nomes described above as resulting from integrations of tribes, coalesced into the two great principalities, Upper Egypt and Lower Egypt, which were eventually united: the small states becoming provinces. The boasting records of Mesopotamian kings similarly show us this union of unions going on. So, too, in Greece the integration at first occurring locally, began afterwards to combine the minor societies into two confederacies. During Roman days there arose for defensive purposes federations of tribes, which eventually consolidated; and subsequently these were compounded into still larger aggregates. Before and after the Christian era, the like happened throughout Northern Europe. Then after a period of vague and varying combinations, there came, in later times, as is well illustrated by French history, a massing of small feudal territories into provinces, and a subsequent massing of these into kingdoms.

So that in both organic and super-organic growths, we see a process of compounding and re-compounding carried to various stages. In both cases, after some consolidation of the smallest aggregates there comes the process of forming larger aggregates by union of them; and in both cases repetition of this process makes secondary aggregates into tertiary ones.

Organic growth and super-organic growth have yet another analogy. As above said, increase by multiplication of individuals in a group, and increase by union of groups, may go on simultaneously; and it does this in both cases.

The orginal clusters, animal and social, are not only small, but they lack density. Creatures of low types occupy large spaces considering the small quantities of animal substance they contain; and low-type societies spread over areas that are wide relatively to the numbers of their component individuals. But as integration in animals is shown by concentration as well as by increase of bulk; so that social integration which results from the clustering of clusters, is joined with augmentation of the number contained by each cluster. If we contrast the sprinklings in regions inhabited by wild tribes with the crowds filling equal regions in Europe; or if we contrast the density of population in England under the Heptarchy with its present density; we see that besides the growth produced by union of groups there has gone on interstitial growth. Just as the higher animal has become not only larger than the lower but more solid; so, too, has the higher society.

Social growth, then, equally with the growth of a living body, shows us the fundamental trait of evolution under a twofold aspect. Integration is displayed both in the formation of a larger mass, and in the progress of such mass towards that coherence due to closeness of parts.

It is proper to add, however, that there is a model of social growth to which organic growth affords no parallel—that caused by the migration of units from one society to another. Among many primitive groups and a few developed ones, this is a considerable factor; but, generally, its effect bears so small a ratio to the effects of growth by increase of population and coalescence of groups, that it does not much qualify the analogy.

E. B. Tylor

The Science of Culture

One of the most important figures in nineteenth-century anthropology was the Englishman, E. B. Tylor. Tylor established the anthropological meaning of culture and gave anthropology its subject matter. Tylor, too, believed that the study of human cultural behavior could be a science. In order to overcome his subjective biases, he always gathered as much data as he could before attempting to make generalizations about human behavior. Tylor was an armchair anthropologist who depended upon the descriptions and data of others. He envisioned anthropology as a comparative science and used comparative methods to help himself understand the similarities that appeared to exist among peoples all over the world. Tylor recognized that many cultural similarities were due to contact, or to diffusion of ideas. Nevertheless, he believed that similar evolutionary processes were the principal source of similar cultural traits. Tylor's reputation and influence in anthropology did not lie in any particularly novel view of evolution, but in his insistence that evolutionary explanations be used only after all evidence for contact and diffusion had been exhausted.

CULTURE OR CIVILIZATION, TAKEN in its wide ethnographic sense, is that complex whole which includes knowledge, belief, art, morals, law, custom, and any other capabilities and habits acquired by man as a member of society. The condition of culture among the various societies of mankind, in so far as it is capable of being investigated on general principles, is a subject apt for the study of laws of human thought and action. On the one hand, the uniformity which so largely pervades civilization may be ascribed, in great measure, to the uniform

47

action of uniform causes: while on the other hand its various grades may be regarded as stages of development or evolution, each the outcome of previous history, and about to do its proper part in shaping the history of the future. To the investigation of these two great principles in several departments of ethnography, with especial consideration of the civilization of the lower tribes as related to the civilization of the higher nations, the present volumes are devoted.

Our modern investigators in the sciences of inorganic nature are foremost to recognize, both within and without their special fields of work, the unity of nature, the fixity of its laws, the definite sequence of cause and effect through which every fact depends on what has gone before it, and acts upon what is to come after it. They grasp firmly the Pythagorean doctrine of pervading order in the universal Kosmos. They affirm, with Aristotle, that nature is not full of incoherent episodes, like a bad tragedy. They agree with Leibnitz in what he calls "my axiom, that nature never acts by leaps (*la nature n'agit jamais par saut*)," as well as in his "great principle, commonly little employed, that nothing happens without sufficient reason." Nor again, in studying the structure and habits of plants and animals, or in investigating the lower functions even of man, are these leading ideas unacknowledged. But when we come to talk of the higher processes of human feeling and action, of thought and language, knowledge and art, a change appears in the prevalent tone of opinion. The world at large is scarcely prepared to accept the general study of human life as a branch of natural science, and to carry out, in a large sense, the poet's injunction to "Account for moral as for natural things." To many educated minds there seems something presumptuous and repulsive in the view that the history of mankind is part and parcel of the history of nature, that our thoughts, wills, and actions accord with laws as definite as those which govern the motion of waves, the combination of acids and bases, and the growth of plants and animals.

The main reasons of this state of the popular judgment are not far to seek. There are many who would willingly accept a science of history if placed before them with substantial definiteness of principle and evidence, but who not unreasonably reject the systems offered to them, as falling too far short of a scientific standard. Through resistance such as this, real knowledge always sooner or later makes its way, while the habit of opposition to novelty does such excellent service against the invasions of speculative dogmatism, that we may

sometimes even wish it were stronger than it is. But other obstacles
to the investigation of laws of human nature arise from considerations
of metaphysics and theology. The popular notion of free human will
involves not only freedom to act in accordance with motive, but also
a power of breaking loose from continuity and acting without cause—
a combination which may be roughly illustrated by the simile of a
balance sometimes acting in the usual way, but also possessed of the
faculty of turning by itself without or against its weights. This view
of an anomalous action of the will, which it need hardly be said is
incompatible with scientific argument, subsists as an opinion patent
or latent in men's minds, and strongly affecting their theoretic views
of history, though it is not, as a rule, brought prominently forward in
systematic reasoning. Indeed the definition of human will as strictly
according with motive, is the only possible scientific basis in such
enquiries. Happily, it is not needful to add here yet another to the list
of dissertations on supernatural intervention and natural causation,
on liberty, predestination, and accountability. We may hasten to
escape from the regions of transcendental philosophy and theology, to
start on a more hopeful journey over more practicable ground. None
will deny that, as each man knows by the evidence of his own consciousness, definite and natural cause does, to a great extent, determine
human action. Then, keeping aside from considerations of extra-
natural interference and causeless spontaneity, let us take this admitted
existence of natural cause and effect as our standing-ground, and
travel on it so far as it will bear us. It is on this same basis that
physical science pursues, with ever-increasing success, its quest of laws
of nature. Nor need this restriction hamper the scientific study of
human life, in which the real difficulties are the practical ones of
enormous complexity of evidence, and imperfection of methods of
observation.

Now it appears that this view of human will and conduct as subject
to definite law, is indeed recognised and acted upon by the very
people who oppose it when stated in the abstract as a general principle,
and who then complain that it annihilates man's free will, destroys
his sense of personal responsibility, and degrades him to a soulless
machine. He who will say these things will nevertheless pass much
of his own life in studying the motives which lead to human action,
seeking to attain his wishes through them, framing in his mind
theories of personal character, reckoning what are like to be the effects

of new combinations, and giving to his reasoning the crowning character of true scientific enquiry, by taking it for granted that in so far as his calculation turns out wrong, either his evidence must have been false or incomplete, or his judgment upon it unsound. Such a one will sum up the experience of years spent in complex relations with society, by declaring his persuasion that there is a reason for everything in life, and that where events look unaccountable, the rule is to wait and watch in hope that the key to the problem may some day be found. This man's observation may have been as narrow as his inferences are crude and prejudiced, but nevertheless he has been an inductive philosopher "more than forty years without knowing it." He has practically acknowledged definite laws of human thought and action, and has simply thrown out of account in his own studies of life the whole fabric of motiveless will and uncaused spontaneity. It is assumed here that they should be just so thrown out of account in wider studies, and that the true philosophy of history lies in extending and improving the methods of the plain people who form their judgments upon facts, and check them upon new facts. Whether the doctrine be wholly or but partly true, it accepts the very condition under which we search for new knowledge in the lessons of experience, and in a word the whole course of our rational life is based upon it.

"One event is always the son of another, and we must never forget the parentage," was a remark made by a Bechuana chief to Casalis the African missionary. Thus at all times historians, so far as they have aimed at being more than mere chroniclers, have done their best to show not merely succession, but connexion, among the events upon their record. Moreover, they have striven to elicit general principles of human action, and by these to explain particular events, stating expressly or taking tacitly for granted the existence of a philosophy of history. Should any one deny the possibility of thus establishing historical laws, the answer is ready with which Boswell in such a case turned on Johnson: "Then, sir, you would reduce all history to no better than an almanack." That nevertheless the labours of so many eminent thinkers should have as yet brought history only to the threshold of science, need cause no wonder to those who consider the bewildering complexity of the problems which come before the general historian. The evidence from which he is to draw his conclusions is at once so multifarious and so doubtful, that a full and distinct view of its bearing on a particular question is hardly to be attained, and thus the temptation becomes all but irresistible to garble it in support of some rough and ready theory of the course of events. The philosophy of history at large, explaining the past and predicting the future phenomena of man's life in the world by reference to general laws, is in fact a subject with which, in the present state of knowledge, even genius aided by wide research seems but hardly able to cope. Yet there are departments of it which, though difficult enough, seem comparatively accessible. If the field of enquiry be narrowed from History as a whole to that branch of it which is here called Culture, the history, not of tribes or nations, but of the condition of knowledge, religion, art, custom, and the like among them, the task of investigation proves to lie within far more moderate compass. We suffer still from the same kind of difficulties which beset the wider argument, but they are much diminished. The evidence is no longer so wildly heterogeneous, but may be more simply classified and compared, while the power of getting rid of extraneous matter, and treating each issue on its own proper set of facts, makes close reasoning on the whole more available than in general history. This may appear from a brief preliminary examination of the problem, how the phenomena of Culture may be classified and arranged, stage by stage, in a probable order of evolution.

Surveyed in a broad view, the character and habit of mankind at once display that similarity and consistency of phenomena which led the Italian proverb-maker to declare that "all the world is one country," (*tutto il mondo è paese*). To general likeness in human nature on the one hand, and to general likeness in the circumstances of life on the other, this similarity and consistency may no doubt be traced, and they may be studied with especial fitness in comparing races near the same grade of civilization. Little respect need be had in such comparisons for date in history or for place on the map; the ancient Swiss lake-dweller may be set beside the mediaeval Aztec, and the Ojibwa of North America beside the Zulu of South Africa, as Dr. Johnson contemptuously said when he had read about Patagonians and South Sea Islanders in Hawkesworth's Voyages, "one set of savages is like another." How true a generalization this really is, any Ethnological Museum may show. Examine for instance the edged and pointed instruments in such a collection; the inventory includes hatchet, adze, chisel, knife, saw, scraper, awl, needle, spear and arrow-head, and of these most or all belong with only differences of detail to races the most various. So it is with savage occupations; the wood-chopping, fishing with net and line, shooting and spearing game, fire-making, cooking, twisting cord and plaiting baskets, repeat themselves with wonderful uniformity in the museum shelves which illustrate the life of the lower races from Kamchatka to Tierra del Fuego, and from Dahome to Hawaii. Even when it comes to comparing barbarous hordes with civilized nations, the consideration thrusts itself upon our minds, how far item after item of the life of the lower races passes into analogous proceedings of the higher, in forms not too far changed to be recognized, and sometimes hardly changed at all. Look at the modern European peasant using his hatchet and his hoe, see his food boiling or roasting over the log-fire, observe the exact place which beer holds in his calculation of happiness, hear his tale of the ghost in the nearest haunted house, and of the farmer's niece who was bewitched with knots in her inside till she fell into fits and died. If we choose out in this way things which have altered little in a long course of centuries, we may draw a picture where there shall be scarce a hand's breadth difference between an English ploughman and a Negro of Central Africa. These pages will be so crowded with evidence of such correspondence among mankind, that there is no need to dwell upon its details here, but it may be used at once to override a problem which would complicate the argument, namely, the question of race. For the present purpose it appears both possible and desirable to eliminate considerations of hereditary varieties or races of man, and to treat mankind as homogeneous in nature, though placed in different grades of civilization. The details of the enquiry will, I think, prove that stages of culture may be compared without taking into account how far tribes who use the same implement, follow the same custom, or believe the same myth, may differ in their bodily configuration and the colour of their skin and hair.

A first step in the study of civilization is to dissect it into details, and to classify these in their proper groups. Thus, in examining weapons, they are to be classed under spear, club, sling, bow and arrow, and so forth; among textile arts are to be ranged matting, netting, and several grades of making and weaving threads; myths are divided under such headings as myths of sunrise and sunset, eclipse-myths, earthquake-myths, local myths which account for the names of places by some fanciful tale, eponymic myths which account for the parentage of a tribe by turning its name into the name of an imaginary ancestor; under rites and ceremonies occur such practices as the various kinds of sacrifice to the ghosts of the dead and to other spiritual beings, the turning to the east in worship, the purification of ceremonial or moral uncleanness by means of water or fire. Such are a few miscellaneous examples from a list of hundreds, and the ethnographer's business is to classify such details with a view to making out their distribution in geography and history, and the relations which exist among them. What this task is like, may be almost perfectly illustrated by comparing these details of culture with the species of plants and animals as studied by the naturalist. To the ethnographer the bow and arrow is a species, the habit of flattening children's skulls is a species, the practice of reckoning numbers by tens is a species. The geographical distribution of these things, and their transmission from region to region, have to be studied as the naturalist studies the geography of his botanical and zoological species. Just as certain plants and animals are peculiar to certain districts, so it is with such instruments as the Australian boomerang, the Polynesian stick-and-groove for fire-making, the tiny bow and arrow used as a lancet or phleme by tribes about the Isthmus of Panama, and in like manner with many an art, myth, or custom, found isolated in a particular field. Just as the catalogue of all the species of plants and animals of a district represents its Flora and Fauna, so the list of all the items of the general life of a people represents that whole which we call its culture. And just as distant regions so often produce vegetables and animals which are analogous, though by no means identical, so it is with the details of the civilization of their inhabitants. How good a working analogy there really is between the diffusion of plants and animals and the diffusion of civilization, comes well into view when we notice how far the same causes have produced both at once. In district after district, the same causes which have introduced the cultivated plants and domesticated animals of civilization, have brought in with them a corresponding art and knowledge. The course of events which carried horses and wheat to America carried with them the use of the gun and the iron hatchet, while in return the whole world received not only maize, potatoes, and turkeys, but the habit of tobacco-smoking and the sailor's hammock.

It is a matter worthy of consideration, that the accounts of similar phenomena of culture, recurring in different parts of the world, actually supply incidental proof of their own authenticity. Some years since, a question which brings out this point was put to me by a great historian—"How can a statement as to customs, myths, beliefs, &c., of a savage tribe be treated as evidence where it depends on the testimony of some traveller or missionary, who may be a superficial observer, more or less ignorant of the native language, a careless retailer of unsifted talk, a man prejudiced or even wilfully deceitful?" This question is, indeed, one which every ethnographer ought to keep clearly and constantly before his mind. Of course he is bound to use his best judgment as to the trustworthiness of all authors he quotes, and if possible to obtain several accounts to certify each point in each locality. But it is over and above these measures of precaution that the test of recurrence comes in. If two independent visitors to different countries, say a mediaeval Mohammedan in Tartary and a modern Englishman in Dahome, or a Jesuit missionary in Brazil and a Wesleyan in the Fiji Islands, agree in describing some analogous art or rite or myth among the people they have visited, it becomes difficult or impossible to set down such correspondence to accident or wilful fraud. A story by a bushranger in Australia may, perhaps, be objected to as a mistake or an invention, but did a Methodist minister in Guinea conspire with him to cheat the public by telling the same story there? The possibility of intentional or unintentional mystification is often barred by such a state of things as that a similar statement is made in two remote lands, by two witnesses, of whom A lived a century before B, and B appears never to have heard of A. How distant are the countries, how wide apart the dates, how different the creeds and characters of the observers, in the catalogue of facts of civilization, needs no farther showing to any one who will even glance at the footnotes of the present work. And the more odd the statement, the less likely that several people in several places should have made it wrongly. This being so, it seems reasonable to judge that the statements are in the main truly given, and that their close and regular coincidence is due to the cropping up of similar facts in various districts of culture. Now the most important facts of ethnography are vouched for in this way. Experience leads the student after a while to expect and find that the phenomena of culture, as resulting from widely-acting similar causes, should recur again and again in the world. He even mistrusts isolated statements to which he knows of no parallel elsewhere, and waits for their genuineness to be shown by corresponding accounts from the other side of the earth, or the other end of history. So strong, indeed, is this means of authentication, that the ethnographer in his library may sometimes presume to decide, not only whether a particular explorer is a shrewd, honest observer, but also whether what he reports is comfortable to the general rules of civilization. *"Non quis, sed quid."*

To turn from the distribution of culture in different countries, to its diffusion within these countries. The quality of mankind which tends most to make the systematic study of civilization possible, is that remarkable tacit consensus or agreement which so far induces whole populations to unite in the use of the same language, to follow the same religion and customary law, to settle down to the same general level of art and knowledge. It is this state of things which makes it so far possible to ignore exceptional facts and to describe nations by a sort of general average. It is this state of things which makes it so far possible to represent immense masses of details by a few typical facts, while, these once settled, new cases recorded by new observers simply fall into their places to prove the soundness of the classification. There is found to be such regularity in the composition of societies of men, that we can drop individual differences out of sight, and thus can generalize on the arts and opinions of whole nations, just as, when looking down upon an army from a hill, we forget the individual soldier, whom, in fact, we can scarce distinguish in the mass, while we see each regiment as an organized body, spreading or concentrating, moving in advance or in retreat. In some branches of the study of social laws it is now possible to call in the aid of statistics, and to set apart special actions of large mixed communities of men by means of taxgatherers' schedules, or the tables of the insurance office. Among modern arguments on the laws of human action, none have had a deeper effect than generalizations such as those of M. Quetelet, on the regularity, not only of such matters as average stature and the annual rates of birth and death, but of the recurrence, year after year, of such obscure and seemingly incalculable products of national life as the numbers of murders and suicides, and the proportion of the very weapons of crime. Other striking cases are the annual regularity of persons killed accidentally in the London streets, and of undirected letters dropped into post-office letter-boxes. But in examining the culture of the lower races, far from having at command the measured arithmetical facts of modern statistics, we may have to judge of the condition of tribes from the imperfect accounts supplied by travellers or missionaries, or even to reason upon relics of prehistoric races of whose very names and languages we are hopelessly ignorant. Now these may seem at the first glance sadly indefinite and unpromising materials for scientific enquiry. But in fact they are neither indefinite nor unpromising, but give evidence that is good and definite so far as it goes. They are data which, for the distinct way in which they severally denote the condition of the tribe they belong to, will actually bear comparison with the statistician's returns. The fact is that a stone arrow-head, a carved club, an idol, a grave-mound where slaves and property have been buried for the use of the dead, an account of a sorcerer's rites in making rain, a table of numerals, the conjugation of a verb, are things which each express the state of a people as to one particular point of culture, as truly as the tabulated numbers of deaths by poison, and of chests of tea imported, express in a different way other partial results of the general life of a whole community.

That a whole nation should have a special dress, special tools and weapons, special laws of marriage and property, special moral and religious doctrines, is a remarkable fact, which we notice so little because we have lived all our lives in the midst of it. It is with such general qualities of organized bodies of men that ethnography has especially to deal. Yet, while generalizing on the culture of a tribe or nation, and setting aside the peculiarities of the individuals composing it as unimportant to the main result, we must be careful not to forget what makes up this main result. There are people so intent on the separate life of individuals that they cannot grasp a notion of the action of a community as a whole—such an observer, incapable of a wide view of society, is aptly described in the saying that he "cannot see the forest for the trees." But, on the other hand, the philosopher may be so intent upon his general laws of society as to neglect the individual actors of whom that society is made up, and of him it may be said that he cannot see the trees for the forest. We know how arts, customs, and ideas are shaped among ourselves by the combined actions of many individuals, of which actions both motive and effect often come quite distinctly within our view. The history of an invention, an opinion, a ceremony, is a history of suggestion and modification, encouragement and opposition, personal gain and party prejudice, and the individuals concerned act each according to his own motives, as determined by his character and circumstances. Thus sometimes we watch individuals acting for their own ends with little thought of their effect on society at large, and sometimes we have to study movements of national life as a whole, where the individuals co-operating in them are utterly beyond our observation. But seeing that collective social action is the mere resultant of many individual actions, it is clear that these two methods of enquiry, if rightly followed, must be absolutely consistent.

In studying both the recurrence of special habits or ideas in several districts, and their prevalence within each district, there come before us ever-reiterated proofs of regular causation producing the phenomena of human life, and of laws of maintenance and diffusion according to which these phenomena settle into permanent standard conditions of society, at definite stages of culture. But, while giving full importance to the evidence bearing on these standard conditions of society, let us be careful to avoid a pitfall which may entrap the unwary student. Of course the opinions and habits belonging in common to masses of mankind are to a great extent the results of sound judgment and practical wisdom. But to a great extent it is not so. That many numerous societies of men should have believed in the influence of the evil eye and the existence of a firmament, should have sacrificed slaves and goods to the ghosts of the departed, should have handed down traditions of giants slaying monsters and men turning into beasts—all this is ground for holding that such ideas were indeed produced in men's minds by efficient causes, but it is not ground for holding that the rites in question are profitable, the beliefs sound, and the history authentic. This may seem at the first glance a truism, but, in fact, it is the denial of a fallacy which deeply affects the minds of all but a small critical minority of mankind. Popularly, what everybody says must be true, what everybody does must be right—"*Quod ubique, quod semper, quod ab omnibus creditum est, hoc est vere proprieque Catholicum*"—and so forth. There are various topics, especially in history, law, philosophy, and theology, where even the educated people we live among can hardly be brought to see that the cause why men do hold an opinion, or practise a custom, is by no means necessarily a reason why they ought to do so. Now collections of ethnographic evidence bringing so prominently into view the agreement of immense multitudes of men as to certain traditions, beliefs, and usages, are peculiarly liable to be thus improperly used in

direct defence of these institutions themselves, even old barbaric nations being polled to maintain their opinions against what are called
modern ideas. As it has more than once happened to myself to find
my collections of traditions and beliefs thus set up to prove their own
objective truth, without proper examination of the grounds on which
they were actually received, I take this occasion of remarking that
the same line of argument will serve equally well to demonstrate,
by the strong and wide consent of nations, that the earth is flat, and
nightmare the visit of a demon.

It being shown that the details of Culture are capable of being
classified in a great number of ethnographic groups of arts, beliefs,
customs, and the rest, the consideration comes next how far the facts
arranged in these groups are produced by evolution from one another.
It need hardly be pointed out that the groups in question, though held
together each by a common character, are by no means accurately
defined. To take up again the natural history illustration, it may be
said that they are species which tend to run widely into varieties.
And when it comes to the question what relations some of these
groups bear to others, it is plain that the student of the habits of
mankind has a great advantage over the student of the species of
plants and animals. Among naturalists it is an open question whether
a theory of development from species to species is a record of transitions which actually took place, or a mere ideal scheme serviceable in
the classification of species whose origin was really independent. But
among ethnographers there is no such question as to the possibility
of species of implements or habits or beliefs being developed one out
of another, for development in Culture is recognized by our most
familiar knowledge. Mechanical invention supplies apt examples of
the kind of development which affects civilization at large. In the
history of fire-arms, the clumsy wheel-lock, in which a notched steel
wheel revolved by means of a spring against a piece of pyrites till a
spark caught the priming, led to the invention of the more serviceable
flint-lock, of which a few still hang in the kitchens of our farm-houses
for the boys to shoot small birds with at Christmas; the flint-lock in
time passed by modification into the percussion-lock, which is just now
changing its old-fashioned arrangement to be adapted from muzzle-
loading to breech-loading. The mediaeval astrolabe passed into the
quadrant, now discarded in its turn by the seaman, who uses the more
delicate sextant, and so it is through the history of one art and instru-

ment after another. Such examples of progression are known to us as direct history, but so thoroughly is this notion of development at home in our minds, that by means of it we reconstruct lost history without scruple, trusting to general knowledge of the principles of human thought and action as a guide in putting the facts in their proper order. Whether chronicle speaks or is silent on the point, no one comparing a long-bow and a cross-bow would doubt that the cross-bow was a development arising from the simpler instrument. So among the fire-drills for igniting by friction, it seems clear on the face of the matter that the drill worked by a cord or bow is a later improvement on the clumsier primitive instrument twirled between the hands. That instructive class of specimens which antiquaries sometimes discover, bronze celts modelled on the heavy type of the stone hatchet, are scarcely explicable except as first steps in the transition from the Stone Age to the Bronze Age, to be followed soon by the next stage of progress, in which it is discovered that the new material is suited to a handier and less wasteful pattern. And thus, in the other branches of our history, there will come again and again into view series of facts which may be consistently arranged as having followed one another in a particular order of development, but which will hardly bear being turned round and made to follow in reversed order. Such for instance are the facts . . . which tend to prove that as to this point of culture at least, savage tribes reached their position by learning and not by unlearning, by elevation from a lower rather than by degradation from a higher state.

Among evidence aiding us to trace the course which the civilization of the world has actually followed, is that great class of facts to denote which I have found it convenient to introduce the term "survivals." These are processes, customs, opinions, and so forth, which have been carried on by force of habit into a new state of society different from that in which they had their original home, and they thus remain as proofs and examples of an older condition of culture out of which a newer has been evolved. Thus, I know an old Somersetshire woman whose hand-loom dates from the time before the introduction of the "flying shuttle," which new-fangled appliance she has never even learnt to use, and I have seen her throw her shuttle from hand to hand in true classic fashion; this old woman is not a century behind her times, but she is a case of survival. Such examples often lead us back to the habits of hundreds and even thousands of years ago. The ordeal of the Key and Bible, still in use, is a survival; the Midsummer bonfire is a survival; the Breton peasants' All Souls' supper for the spirits of the dead is a survival. The simple keeping up of ancient habits is only one part of the transition from old into new and changing times. The serious business of ancient society may be seen to sink into the sport of later generations, and its serious belief to linger on in nursery folklore, while superseded habits of old-world life may be modified into new-world forms still powerful for good and evil. Sometimes old thoughts and practices will burst out afresh, to the amazement of a world that thought them long since dead or dying; here survival passes into revival, as has lately happened in so remarkable a way in the history of modern spiritualism, a subject full of instruction from the ethnographer's point of view. The study of the principles of survival has, indeed, no small practical importance, for most of what we call superstition is included within survival, and in this way lies open to the attack of its deadliest enemy, a reasonable explanation. Insignificant, moreover, as multitudes of the facts of survival are in themselves, their study is so effective for tracing the course of the historical development through which alone it is possible to understand their meaning, that it becomes a vital point of ethnographic research to gain the clearest possible insight into their nature. This importance must justify the detail here devoted to an examination of survival, on the evidence of such games, popular sayings, customs, superstitions, and the like, as may serve well to bring into view the manner of its operation.

Progress, degradation, survival, revival, modification, are all modes of the connexion that binds together the complex network of civilization. It needs but a glance into the trivial details of our own daily life to set us thinking how far we are really its originators, and how far but the transmitters and modifiers of the results of long past ages. Looking round the rooms we live in, we may try here how far he who only knows his own time can be capable of rightly comprehending even that. Here is the "honeysuckle" of Assyria, there the fleur-de-lis of Anjou, a cornice with a Greek border runs round the ceiling, the style of Louis XIV and its parent the Renaissance share the looking-glass between them. Transformed, shifted, or mutilated, such elements of art still carry their history plainly stamped upon them; and if the history yet farther behind is less easy to read, we are not to say that because we cannot clearly discern it there is therefore no history there. It is thus even with the fashion of the clothes men wear. The ridiculous little tails of the German postilion's coat show of themselves how they came to dwindle to such absurd rudiments; but the English clergyman's bands no longer so convey their history to the eye, and look unaccountable enough till one has seen the intermediate stages through which they came down from the more serviceable wide collars, such as Milton wears in his portrait, and which gave their name to the "band-box" they used to be kept in. In fact, the books of costume, showing how one garment grew or shrank by gradual stages and passed into another, illustrate with much force and clearness the nature of the change and growth, revival and decay, which go on from year to year in more important matters of life. In books, again, we see each writer not for and by himself, but occupying his proper place in history; we look through each philosopher, mathematician, chemist, poet, into the background of his education—through Leibnitz into Descartes, through Dalton into Priestley, through Milton into Homer. The study of language has, perhaps, done more than any other in removing from our view of human thought and action the ideas of chance and arbitrary invention, and in substituting for them a theory of development by the co-operation of individual men, through processes ever reasonable and intelligible where the facts are fully known. Rudimentary as the science of culture still is, the symptoms are becoming very strong that even what seem its most spontaneous and motiveless phenomena will, nevertheless, be shown to come within the range of distinct cause and effect as certainly as the facts of mechanics. What would be popularly thought more indefinite and uncontrolled than the products of the imagination in myths and fables? Yet any systematic investigation of mythology, on the basis of a wide collection of evidence, will show plainly enough in such efforts of fancy at once a development from stage to stage, and a production of uniformity of result from uniformity of cause. Here, as elsewhere, causeless spontaneity is seen to recede farther and farther into shelter within the dark precincts of ignorance; like chance, that still holds its place among the vulgar as a real cause of events otherwise unaccountable, while to educated men it has long consciously meant nothing but this ignorance itself. It is only when men fail to see the line of connexion in events, that they are prone to fall upon the notions of arbitrary impulses, causeless freaks, chance and nonsense and indefinite unaccountability. If childish games, purposeless

customs, absurd superstitions, are set down as spontaneous because
no one can say exactly how they came to be, the assertion may remind
us of the like effect that the eccentric habits of the wild rice-plant
had on the philosophy of a Red Indian tribe, otherwise disposed to
see in the harmony of nature the effects of one controlling personal
will. The Great Spirit, said these Sioux theologians, made all things
except the wild rice; but the wild rice came by chance.

"Man," said Wilhelm von Humboldt, "ever connects on from what
lies at hand *(der Mensch knüpft immer an Vorhandenes an)*." The
notion of the continuity of civilization contained in this maxim is no
barren philosophic principle, but is at once made practical by the
consideration that they who wish to understand their own lives ought
to know the stages through which their opinions and habits have
become what they are. Auguste Comte scarcely overstated the necessity of this study of development when he declared at the beginning
of his "Positive Philosophy" that "no conception can be understood
except through its history," and his phrase will bear extension to
culture at large. To expect to look modern life in the face and comprehend it by mere inspection, is a philosophy whose weakness can
easily be tested. Imagine any one explaining the trivial saying, "a
little bird told me," without knowing of the old belief in the language
of birds and beasts, to which Dr. Dasent, in the introduction to the
Norse Tales, so reasonably traces its origin. Attempts to explain by
the light of reason things which want the light of history to show
their meaning, may be instanced from Blackstone's Commentaries.
To Blackstone's mind, the very right of the commoner to turn his
beast out to graze on the common, finds its origin and explanation
in the feudal system. "For, when lords of manors granted out parcels
of land to tenants, for services either done or to be done, those tenants
could not plough or manure the land without beasts; these beasts
could not be sustained without pasture; and pasture could not be
had but in the lord's wastes, and on the uninclosed fallow grounds of
themselves and the other tenants. The law therefore annexed this
right of common, as inseparably incident, to the grant of the lands;
and this was the original of common appendant," &c. Now though
there is nothing irrational in this explanation, it does not agree at all
with the Teutonic land-law which prevailed in England long before
the Norman Conquest, and of which the remains have never wholly
disappeared. In the old village-community even the arable land, lying

in the great common fields which may still be traced in our country, had not yet passed into separate property, while the pasturage in the fallows and stubbles and on the waste belonged to the householders in common. Since those days, the change from communal to individual ownership has mostly transformed this old-world system, but the right which the peasant enjoys of pasturing his cattle on the common still remains, not as a concession to feudal tenants, but as possessed by the commoners before the lord ever claimed the ownership of the waste. It is always unsafe to detach a custom from its hold on past events, treating it as an isolated fact to be simply disposed of by some plausible explanation.

In carrying on the great task of rational ethnography, the investigation of the causes which have produced the phenomena of culture, and of the laws to which they are subordinate, it is desirable to work out as systematically as possible a scheme of evolution of this culture along its many lines. . . . By comparing the various stages of civilization among races known to history, with the aid of archaeological inference from the remains of prehistoric tribes, it seems possible to judge in a rough way of an early general condition of man, which from our point of view is to be regarded as a primitive condition, whatever yet earlier state may in reality have lain behind it. This hypothetical primitive condition corresponds in a considerable degree to that of modern savage tribes, who, in spite of their difference and distance, have in common certain elements of civilization, which seem remains of an early state of the human race at large. If this hypothesis be true, then, notwithstanding the continual interference of degeneration, the main tendency of culture from primaeval up to modern times has been from savagery towards civilization. . . . Survival in Culture, placing all along the course of advancing civilization way-marks full of meaning to those who can decipher their signs, even now sets up in our midst primaeval monuments of barbaric thought and life. Its investigation tells strongly in favour of the view that the European may find among the Greenlanders or Maoris many a trait for reconstructing the picture of his own primitive ancestors. Next comes the problem of the Origin of Language. Obscure as many parts of this problem still remain, its clearer positions lie open to the investigation whether speech took its origin among mankind in the savage state, and the result of the enquiry is that consistently with all known evidence, this may have been the case. From the examination of the

Art of Counting a far more definite consequence is shown. It may be
confidently asserted, that not only is this important art found in a
rudimentary state among savage tribes, but that satisfactory evidence
proves numeration to have been developed by rational invention from
this low stage up to that in which we ourselves possess it. The examination of Mythology . . . is for the most part made from a special
point of view, on evidence collected for a special purpose, that of
tracing the relation between the myths of savage tribes and their
analogues among more civilized nations. The issue of such enquiry
goes far to prove that the earliest myth-maker arose and flourished
among savage hordes, setting on foot an art which his more cultured
successors would carry on, till its results came to be fossilized in superstition, mistaken for history shaped and draped in poetry, or cast
aside as lying folly.

Nowhere, perhaps, are broad views of historical development more
needed than in the study of religion. Notwithstanding all that has
been written to make the world acquainted with the lower theologies,
the popular ideas of their place in history and their relation to the
faiths of higher nations are still of the mediaeval type. It is wonderful to contrast some missionary journals with Max Müller's Essays,
and to set the unappreciating hatred and ridicule that is lavished by
narrow hostile zeal on Brahmanism, Buddhism, Zoroastrianism, besides the catholic sympathy with which deep and wide knowledge
can survey those ancient and noble phases of man's religious consciousness; nor, because the religions of savage tribes may be rude and
primitive compared with the great Asiatic systems, do they lie too
low for interest and even for respect. The question really lies between
understanding and misunderstanding them. Few who will give their
minds to master the general principles of savage religion will ever
again think it ridiculous, or the knowledge of it superfluous to the
rest of mankind. Far from its beliefs and practices being a rubbish-
heap of miscellaneous folly, they are consistent and logical in so high
a degree as to begin, as soon as even roughly classified, to display
the principles of their formation and development; and these principles prove to be essentially rational, though working in a mental
condition of intense and inveterate ignorance. It is with a sense of
attempting an investigation which bears very closely on the current
theology of our own day, that I have set myself to examine systematically, among the lower races, the development of Animism; that is

to say, the doctrine of souls and other spiritual beings in general. More than half of the present work is occupied with a mass of evidence from all regions of the world, displaying the nature and meaning of this great element of the Philosophy of Religion, and tracing its transmission, expansion, restriction, modification, along the course of history into the midst of our own modern thought. Nor are the questions of small practical moment which have to be raised in an attempt to trace the development of certain prominent Rites and Ceremonies—customs so full of instruction as to the inmost powers of religion, whose outward expression and practical result they are.

In these investigations, however, made rather from an ethnographic than a theological point of view, there has seemed little need of entering into direct controversial argument, which indeed I have taken pains to avoid as far as possible. The connexion which runs through religion, from its rudest forms up to the status of an enlightened Christianity, may be conveniently treated of with little recourse to dogmatic theology. The rites of sacrifice and purification may be studied in their stages of development without entering into questions of their authority and value, nor does an examination of the successive phases of the world's belief in a future life demand a discussion of the arguments adduced for or against the doctrine itself. The ethnographic results may then be left as materials for professed theologians, and it will not perhaps be long before evidence so fraught with meaning shall take its legitimate place. To fall back once again on the analogy of natural history, the time may soon come when it will be thought as unreasonable for a scientific student of theology not to have a competent acquaintance with the principles of the religions of the lower races, as for a physiologist to look with the contempt of past centuries on evidence derived from the lower forms of life, deeming the structure of mere invertebrate creatures matter unworthy of his philosophic study.

Not merely as a matter of curious research, but as an important practical guide to the understanding of the present and the shaping of the future, the investigation into the origin and early development of civilization must be pushed on zealously. Every possible avenue of knowledge must be explored, every door tried to see if it is open. No kind of evidence need be left untouched on the score of remoteness or complexity, of minuteness or triviality. The tendency of modern enquiry is more and more towards the conclusion that if law is anywhere, it is everywhere. To despair of what a conscientious collection and study of facts may lead to, and to declare any problem insoluble because difficult and far off, is distinctly to be on the wrong side in science; and he who will choose a hopeless task may set himself to discover the limits of discovery. One remembers Comte starting in his account of astronomy with a remark on the necessary limitation of our knowledge of the stars: we conceive, he tells us, the possibility of determining their form, distance, size, and movement, whilst we should never by any method be able to study their chemical composition, their mineralogical structure, &c. Had the philosopher lived to see the application of spectrum analysis to this very problem, his proclamation of the dispiriting doctrine of necessary ignorance would perhaps have been recanted in favour of a more hopeful view. And it seems to be with the philosophy of remote human life somewhat as with the study of the nature of the celestial bodies. The processes to be made out in the early stages of our mental evolution lie distant from us in time as the stars lie distant from us in space, but the laws of the universe are not limited with the direct observation of our senses. There is vast material to be used in our enquiry; many workers are now busied in bringing this material into shape, though little may have yet been done in proportion to what remains to do; and already it seems not too much to say that the vague outlines of a philosophy of primaeval history are beginning to come within our view.

Sigmund Freud

Obsessive Acts and Religious Practices

Although many social scientists look with disfavor upon Sigmund
Freud's attempt to explain social events in terms of individual psychology, Freud's models of the human mental structure have been
invaluable to students of culture and society. Those who have called
Totem and Taboo a masterpiece of ethnological illiteracy—on the
grounds that no human group ever known conformed to its picture
of a primal horde—must reckon today with studies of ethology and
of animal social behavior which provide some support for the Freudian
picture. Ethology suggests that ritual behavior in animals is a normal
reaction to ambivalently conceived or anxiety-provoking situations.
The notion that religious ritual is a cultural reaction to group anxiety
is hardly as absurd as some social scientists believe. Perhaps the major
objection that can be made to the Freudian view of religious acts
and obsessive practices is the implication that ritual is pathological
and that religion is, therefore, a collective neurosis. Religious behavior
does seem to have an analogue in ritual behavior in animals; moreover, ritual seems to be a normal process, an adaptive mechanism to
a stress situation.

I AM CERTAINLY NOT THE first to be struck by the resemblance
between what are called obsessive acts in neurotics and those religious
observances by means of which the faithful give expression to their
piety. The name "ceremonial," which has been given to certain of
these obsessive acts, is evidence of this. The resemblance, however,
seems to me to be something more than superficial, so that an insight

into the origin of neurotic ceremonial may embolden us to draw by analogy inferences about the psychological processes of religious life.

Persons who are addicted to obsessive acts or ceremonials belong to the same class as those who suffer from obsessive thoughts and ideas, obsessive impulses and the like, and form with them a definite clinical group, the customary term for which is obsessional neurosis.[1] But one should not attempt to deduce the character of the disease from its name, for, strictly speaking, there are other morbid psychological phenomena which have an equal claim to the "obsessional character," as it is called. In place of a definition we must for the present be content with a detailed description of these conditions, for it has not yet been possible to demonstrate the essential feature which probably lies at the root of the obsessional neurosis, though one seems to find indications of it at every turn in clinical manifestations of the disorder.

The neurotic ceremonial consists of little prescriptions, performances, restrictions, and arrangements in certain activities of every-day life which have to be carried out always in the same or in a methodically varied way. These performances make the impression that they are mere "formalities"; they appear quite meaningless to us. Nor do they appear otherwise to the patient himself; yet he is quite incapable of renouncing them, for every neglect of the ceremonial is punished with the most intolerable anxiety, which forces him to perform it instantly. Just as trivial as the ceremonial performances themselves are the occasions which give rise to them, and the kind of actions which are thereby caricatured, hindered, and invariably also delayed, *e.g.* dressing and undressing, going to bed, and the satisfaction of bodily needs. The carrying out of a ceremonial may be described as the fulfillment of a series of unwritten rules; for example, in the bed ceremonial the chair must stand in a particular place by the bed, and the clothes must be folded and laid upon it in a particular order; the coverlet must be tucked in at the bottom, and the bedclothes evenly spread; the pillows must be arranged in such and such a manner, and the body must lie in a particular position—only when all is correct is it permissible to go to sleep. In slight cases, the ceremonial appears to be only an exaggeration of an ordinary and justifiable orderliness, but the remarkable conscientiousness with which it is carried out, and the anxiety which follows its neglect gives the ceremonial the character of a sacred rite. Any disturbance of it is tolerated with difficulty, and the presence of other persons during the performance of it is almost always out of the question.

Any activities whatsoever may become obsessive acts in a wide sense if they become elaborated by petty modifications or develop a rhythmic character by pauses and repetitions. A sharp distinction between "obsessive acts" and "ceremonials" is not to be expected; as a rule an obsessive act develops from a ceremonial. Besides these, prohibitions and hindrances (*aboulia*) complete the picture of the disorder; the latter only carry further the work of the obsessive acts, for in the one case a certain activity is interdicted altogether, and in the other it is only possible when the patient follows the prescribed ceremonial.

It is remarkable that both compulsions and prohibitions (that one thing must be done and another may not be done) originally relate only to the solitary activities of the persons affected, so that for many years such patients can treat their affliction as a private matter and hide it from others. Moreover, far more persons suffer from these forms of the obsessional neurosis than ever come to the knowledge of physicians. For many patients, too, concealment is not a difficult matter, because it is quite possible for them to fulfill their social duties during part of the day, after having devoted several hours to their secret performances in Melusina-like seclusion.

It is easy to see wherein lies the resemblance between neurotic ceremonial and religious rites; it is in the fear of pangs of conscience after their omission, in the complete isolation of them from all other activities (the feeling that one must not be disturbed), and in the conscientiousness with which the details are carried out. But equally obvious are the differences, some of which are so startling that they make the comparison into a sacrilege: the greater individual variability of neurotic ceremonial in contrast with the stereotyped character of rites (prayer, orientation, etc.); its private nature as opposed to the public and communal character of religious observances; especially, however, the distinction that the little details of religious ceremonies are full of meaning and are understood symbolically, while those of neurotics furnishes a tragi-comic travesty of a private religion. But this, the sharpest distinction between neurotic and religious ceremonials, disappears as soon as one penetrates by means of psychoanalytic investigation to insight into obsessive actions. By this process the outward appearance of being foolish and meaningless, which is characteristic of obsessive acts, is completely demolished, and the fact of their having this appearance is explained. It is found that obsessive acts are throughout and in all their details full of meaning, that they serve important interests of the personality, and that they give expression both to persisting impressions of previous experiences and to thoughts about them which are strongly charged with affect. This they do in two ways, either by direct or by symbolic representation, so that they are to be interpreted either historically or symbolically.

I must here give a few examples to illustrate these remarks. Those who are familiar with the results of the psychoanalytic investigation of the psychoneuroses will not be surprised to learn that what is expressed in an obsessive act or ceremonial is derived from the most intimate, and for the most part from the sexual, experiences of the patient.

(a) A girl of my acquaintance was under the compulsion to rinse out the basin many times after washing. The significance of this ceremonial lay in the proverbial saying, "Don't throw away dirty water until you have clean." The action had the meaning of a warning to her sister, to whom she was much attached, not to separate from her unsatisfactory husband until she had established a relationship with a better man.

(b) A woman who was living apart from her husband was subject to a compulsion to leave the best of whatever she ate; for example, she would only take the outside of a piece of roast meat. It appeared the day after she had refused marital relations with her husband, that is to say, had given up the best.

(c) The same patient could only sit on one particular chair, and could leave it again only with difficulty. In connection with certain details of her married life the chair symbolized to her her husband, to whom she remained faithful. She found the explanation of her compulsion in the sentence, "It is so hard to part from anything (chair or husband) in which one has once settled oneself."

(d) For a long time she used to repeat a very curious and senseless obsessive act. She ran out of her room into the next, in the middle of which stood a table with a cloth upon it. This she pulled straight in a particular manner, rang for the housemaid, who had to approach the table, and then sent her off again on some indifferent errand.

During her efforts to explain this compulsion it occurred to her that at one place on the tablecloth there was a stain and that she always arranged the cloth so that the housemaid was bound to see it. The whole scene proved to be a reproduction of an incident in her marriage. On the wedding-night her husband had met with a not unusual mishap. He found himself impotent, and "many times in the course of the night came hurrying from his room to hers" in order to try again. In the morning he said he would be shamed in the eyes of the hotel chambermaid who made the bed, so he took a bottle of red ink and poured its contents over the sheet; but he did it so clumsily that the stain came in a place most unsuitable for his purpose. With her obsessive act, therefore, she was reproducing the bridal night. ("Bed and board" indeed comprise marriage.)

(e) She started a compulsion to note the number of each currency-note before parting with it, and this also was to be interpreted historically. At a time when she had still had an intention to leave her husband if she could find a more trust-worthy man, she allowed herself to become the object of the attentions of a man she met at a watering-place, but was in doubt whether he was altogether in earnest. One day, as she was short of small change, she asked him to change a 5-kronen piece for her. He did so, and put the large coin in his pocket, saying with a gallant air that he would never part with it since it had passed through her hands. At their later meetings she was frequently tempted to challenge him to show her the 5-kronen piece, as if to convince herself that she could believe in his attentions. But she refrained, for the good reason that one cannot distinguish coins of the same value. Her doubts therefore remained unsolved; they left her with a compulsion to note the number of each currency-note by which each one can be distinguished from others of the same value.

These few examples, selected from many I have met with, are intended merely to illustrate the statement that in obsessive acts everything has its meaning and interpretation. The same is true of ceremonials in the strict sense, only that the evidence for this would require a more detailed presentation. I quite realize however, how far we seem to be getting from any connection between this interpretation of obsessive acts and the line of thought peculiar to religious practices.

It is one of the features of the disease that the person who is affected with a compulsion submits to it without understanding its meaning—or at any rate its chief meaning. It is only under the influence of psychoanalytic treatment that the meaning of the obsessive act, and therewith of the impelling motive underlying it, becomes conscious. We express this important fact by saying that the obsessive act serves to express *unconscious* motives and ideas. Here we seem to find a further departure from religious rites; but we must remember that as a rule the ordinary religious observer carries out a ceremonial without concerning himself with its significance, although priests and investigators may be familiar with its meaning which is usually symbolic. In all believers, however, the *motives* impelling them to religious practices are unknown, or are replaced in consciousness by others which are advanced in their stead.

The analysis of obsessive acts has already given us some sort of insight into their causes and into the network of motives which bring them to effect. One may say that a sufferer from compulsions and prohibitions behaves as if he were dominated by a sense of guilt, of which, however, he is ignorant—an unconscious sense of guilt, as one must call it in spite of the apparent contradiction in terms. The sense of guilt has its origin in certain early psychological occurrences, but is constantly revived by temptations which are renewed at every present opportunity; it gives rise, moreover, to a state of anxious expectation, or anticipation of misfortune, which through the idea of punishment is linked with the inner perception of temptation. When the compulsion is first being formed, the patient is conscious that he must do this or that lest misfortune occur, and as a rule the nature of the expected misfortune is also recognized in consciousness. But the relation between the occasion which gives rise to this anxiety and the danger to which it refers is already hidden from him, though it is always capable of demonstration. Thus a ceremonial begins as an act of defence or security—as a *protective measure*.

The protestations of the pious that they know they are miserable sinners in their hearts correspond to the sense of guilt of the obsessional neurotic; while the pious observances (prayers, invocations, etc.) with which they begin every act of the day, and especially every unusual undertaking, seem to have the significance of defensive and protective measures.

Deeper insight into the mechanism of the obsessional neurosis is gained when the primary factor underlying it is taken into account:

this is always the repression of an impulse (one component of the sexual instinct) which is inherent in the constitution of the person, and which for a while found expression in his childhood but succumbed later to suppression. In course of this repression a special type of conscientiousness directed towards opposing the aim of the impulse is developed; but this mental reaction is felt to be insecure and constantly threatened by the impulse which lurks in the unconscious. The influence of the repressed impulse is felt as a temptation, and anxiety is produced by the process of repression itself, which is dealt with by directing it towards the future in the form of anxious expectation. The process of repression which leads to the obsessional neurosis must be described as imperfectly carried through and as constantly threatening to break down. It may be compared, consequently, with an insoluble conflict; fresh mental efforts are continually required to counterbalance the constant forward pressure of the impulse. Thus the ceremonial and obsessive acts arise partly as a defense against temptation and partly as a protection against the misfortune expected. Against the temptation the protective measures seem to become rapidly ineffective; then the prohibitions come into play, for these are intended to keep at a distance situations which give rise to temptation. We thus see that prohibitions replace obsessive acts just as a phobia serves to hold off an hysterical attack. From another point of view a ceremonial represents the sum of all the conditions under which something not yet absolutely forbidden becomes permissible, just as the marriage ceremony of the Church signifies a sanction of sexual enjoyment, which is otherwise sinful. It is in the nature, moreover, of the obsessional neurosis—as of all similar affections—that its manifestations (symptoms, including also the obsessive acts) fulfil the condition of a compromise between the opposing forces in the mind. Thus they always reproduce something of the identical pleasure they were designed to prevent; they serve the repressed impulse no less than the repressing element. Indeed, as the disease develops the performances which at first were concerned chiefly with defence approximate ever more and more nearly to those proscribed actions in which the impulse was able to find an outlet in childhood.

This state of things has some counterparts in the sphere of religious life, as follows: the structure of a religion seems also to be founded on the suppression or renunciation of certain instinctual trends; these trends are not, however, as in the neurosis, exclusively components of the sexual instinct, but are egoistic, antisocial instincts, though even these for the most part are not without a sexual element. The sense of guilt in consequence of continual temptation, and the anxious expectation in the guise of fear of divine punishment, have indeed been familiar to us in religion longer than in neurosis. Possibly on account of the sexual elements which are also involved, possibly on account of some characteristic of instincts in general, the suppression active in religion proves here also to be neither completely effective nor final. Unredeemed back-slidings into sin are even more common among the pious than among neurotics, and these give rise to a new form of religious activity, namely, the acts of penance of which one finds counterparts in the obsessional neurosis.

We saw a curious feature of the obsessional neurosis, one that seems to render it unworthy and trivial, in the fact that these ceremonials are concerned with such petty performances of daily life, and are expressed in foolish regulations and restrictions in regard to them. One first understands this remarkable feature of the clinical picture when one finds that the mechanism of the psychical displacement, which I first discovered in the formation of dreams,[2] dominates the mental processes in the obsessional neurosis. It is already clear from the few examples of obsessive acts given above that their symbolism and the details of their execution are effected as if by a displacement from the actual important thing on to an insignificant one which replaces it, *e.g.* from the husband to the chair. It is this tendency to displacement which progressively changes the clinical picture of the symptoms, and eventually succeeds in turning apparently trivial matters into those of great and urgent importance. It cannot be denied that in the religious sphere also there is a similar tendency to a displacement of psychical values, and indeed in the same direction, so that petty ceremonials gradually become the essence of religious practices, and replace the ideas underlying them. It is for this reason that religions are subject to retroactive reforms which aim at the re-establishment of the original relative values.

The element of compromise in those obsessive acts which we find as neurotic symptoms is the feature least easy to find reproduced in corresponding religious observances. Yet here, too, one is reminded of this trait in the neurosis when one recalls how commonly all those acts which religion forbids—expressions of the instincts it represses—

are yet committed precisely in the name of, and ostensibly in the cause of, religion.

In view of these resemblances and analogies one might venture to regard the obsessional neurosis as a pathological counterpart to the formation of a religion, to describe this neurosis as a private religious system, and religion as a universal obsessional neurosis. The essential resemblance would lie in the fundamental renunciation of the satisfaction of inherent instincts, and the chief difference in the nature of these instincts, which in the neurosis are exclusively sexual, but in religion are of egoistic origin.

A progressive renunciation of inherent instincts, the satisfaction of which is capable of giving direct pleasure to the ego, appears to be one of the foundations of human civilization. Some part of this repression is effected by means of the various religions, in that they require individuals to sacrifice the satisfaction of their instincts to the divinity. "Vengeance is mine, saith the Lord." In the development of the ancient religions one seems to find that many things which mankind had renounced as wicked were surrendered in favour of the god, and were still permitted in his name; so that a yielding up of evil and asocial impulses to the divinity was the means by which man freed himself from them. For this reason it is surely no accident that all human characteristics—along with the crimes they prompt— were freely attributed to the ancient gods, and no anomaly that it was nevertheless not permissible to justify one's own misdeeds by reference to divine example.

NOTES

[1] *Cf.* Lowenfeld, *Die psychische Zwangserscheinungen*, 1904.
[2] *Cf.* Freud, *Die Traumdeutung.*

Karl Marx

The Class Struggle

The concept of Social Darwinism—"nature red in tooth and claw"—
underlay much evolutionary thinking of the nineteenth century.
Spencer's laissez-faire notions and Comte's Utopian technology simply
represented two approaches to what all men believed was a basic tenet
of human nature. A long line of thinkers, stretching from Machiavelli
through Thomas Hobbes to Karl Marx, had suggested that the source
of the state lay in man's attempts to control his "natural" aggressive
instincts. Darwin's biological formulations lent weight and support to
their argument. For Marx, evolutionary processes existed in society just
as they did among animals: competition and selection resulted in the
survival of the fittest. Marx justified the need for social action—as
opposed to laissez-faire—on the grounds of the historical inevitabilty of
the ascendancy of the proletariat.

Marx's great contribution to human thought, however, did not lie
so much in his evolutionism but in his concept of economic determinism. The economic superstructure, which conformed to evolutionary
imperatives, was a creation of human interaction. His economic determinism formed a bridge between those who believed that human social
behavior was explicable in evolutionary terms, and those who insisted
that social structures, rather than natural aspects of human behavior,
were determinative of society.

THE HISTORY OF ALL hitherto existing society [1] is the history of class
struggles.

Freeman and slave, patrician and plebeian, lord and serf, guild-
master [2] and journeyman, in a word, oppressor and oppressed, stood

in constant opposition to one another, carried on an uninterrupted, now hidden, now open fight, a fight that each time ended, either in a revolutionary re-constitution of society at large, or in the common ruin of the contending classes.

In the earlier epochs of history, we find almost everywhere a complicated arrangement of society into various orders, a manifold gradation of social rank. In ancient Rome we have patricians, knights, plebeians, slaves; in the middle ages, feudal lords, vassals, guild-masters, journeymen, apprentices, serfs; in almost all of these classes, again, subordinate gradations.

The modern bourgeois [3] society that has sprouted from the ruins of feudal society, has not done away with class antagonisms. It has but established new classes, new conditions of oppression, new forms of struggle in place of the old ones.

Our epoch, the epoch of the bourgeoisie, possesses, however, this distinctive feature; it has simplified the class antagonisms. Society as a whole is more and more splitting up into two great hostile camps, into two great classes directly facing each other: Bourgeoisie and Proletariat.

From the serfs of the Middle Ages sprang the chartered burghers of the earliest towns. From these burgesses the first elements of the bourgeoisie were developed.

The discovery of America, the rounding of the Cape, opened up fresh ground for the rising bourgeoisie. The East-Indian and Chinese markets, the colonisation of America, trade with colonies, the increase in the means of exchange and in commodities generally, gave to commerce, to navigation, to industry, an impulse never before known, and thereby, to the revolutionary element in the tottering feudal society, a rapid development.

The feudal system of industry, under which industrial production was monopolized by closed guilds, now no longer sufficed for the growing wants of the new markets. The manufacturing system took its place. The guild-masters were pushed on one side by the manufacturing middle-class; division of labour between different corporate guilds vanished in the face of division of labour in each single workshop.

Meantime the markets kept ever growing, the demand, ever rising. Even manufacture no longer sufficed. Thereupon, steam and machinery revolutionized industrial production. The place of manufacture was taken by the giant, Modern Industry, the place of the industrial middle-class, by industrial millionaires, the leaders of whole industrial armies, the modern bourgeois.

Modern industry has established the world-market, for which the discovery of America paved the way. This market has given an immense development to commerce, to navigation, to communication by land. This development has, in its turn, reacted on the extension of industry; and in proportion as industry, commerce, navigation, railways extended, in the same proportion the bourgeoisie developed, increased its capital, and pushed into the background every class handed down from the Middle Ages.

We see, therefore, how the modern bourgeoisie is itself the product of a long course of development, of a series of revolutions in the modes of production and of exchange.

Each step in the development of the bourgeoisie was accompanied by a corresponding political advance of that class. An oppressed class under the sway of the feudal nobility, an armed and self-governing association in the mediaeval commune,[4] here independent urban republic (as in Italy and Germany), there taxable "third estate" of the monarchy (as in France), afterwards, in the period of manufacture proper, serving either the semi-feudal or the absolute monarchy as a counterpoise against the nobility, and, in fact, corner stone of the great monar hies in general, the bourgeoisie has at last, since the establishment of Modern Industry and of the world-market, conquered for itself, in the modern representative State, exclusive political sway. The executive of the modern State is but a committee for managing the common affairs of the whole bourgeoisie.

The bourgeoisie, historically, has played a most revolutionary part.

The bourgeoisie, wherever it has got the upper hand, has put an end to all feudal patriarchal, idyllic relations, It has pitilessly torn asunder the motley feudal ties that bound man to his "natural superiors," and has left remaining no other nexus between man and man than naked self-interest, than callous "cash payment." It has drowned the most heavenly ecstacies of religious fervour, of chivalrous enthusiasm, of philistine sentimentalism in the icy water of egotistical calculation. It has resolved personal worth into exchange value, and in place of the numberless indefeasible chartered freedoms, has set us that single, unconscionable freedom—Free Trade. In one word, for political exploitation, veiled by religious and political illusions, it has substituted naked, shameless, direct, brutal exploitation.

The bourgeoisie has stripped of its halo every occupation hitherto honoured and looked up to with reverent awe. It has converted the physician, the lawyer, the priest, the poet, the man of science, into its paid wage-labourers.

The bourgeoisie has torn away from the family its sentimental veil, and has reduced the family relation to a mere money relation.

The bourgeoisie has disclosed how it came to pass that the brutal display of vigour in the Middle Ages, which Reactionists so much admire, found its fitting complement in the most slothful indolence. It has been the first to shew what man's activity can bring about. It has accomplished wonders far surpassing Egyptian pyramids, Roman aqueducts, and Gothic cathedrals; it has conducted expeditions that put in the shade all former Exoduses of nations and crusades.

The bourgeoisie cannot exist without constantly revolutionising the instruments of production, and thereby the relations of production, and with them the whole relations of society. Conservation of the old modes of production in unaltered form, was, on the contrary, the first condition of existence for all earlier industrial classes. Constant revolutionising of production, uninterrupted disturbance of all social conditions, everlasting uncertainty and agitation distinguish the bourgeois epoch from all earlier ones. All fixed, fast-frozen relations, with their train of ancient and venerable prejudices and opinions, are swept away, all new-formed ones become antiquated before they can ossify. All that is solid melts into air, all that is holy is profaned, and man is at last compelled to face with sober senses, his real conditions of life, and his relations with his kind.

The need of a constantly expanding market for its products chases the bourgeoisie over the whole surface of the globe. It must nestle everywhere, settle everywhere, establish connexions everywhere.

The bourgeoisie has through its exploitation of the world-market given a cosmopolitan character to production and consumption in every country. To the great chagrin of Reactionists, it has drawn from under the feet of industry the national ground on which it stood. All old-established national industries have been destroyed or are daily being destroyed. They are dislodged by new industries, whose introduction becomes a life and death question for all civilised nations, by industries that no longer work up indigenous raw material, but raw material drawn from the remotest zones; industries whose products are consumed, not only at home, but in every quarter of the globe. In place of the old wants, satisfied by the productions of the country, we find new wants, requiring for their satisfaction the products of distant lands and climes. In place of the old local and national seclusion and self-sufficiency, we have intercourse in every direction, universal inter-dependence of nations. And as in material, so also in intellectual production. The intellectual creations of individual nations become common property. National one-sidedness and narrow-mindedness become more and more impossible, and from the numerous national and local literatures there arises a world-literature.

The bourgeoisie, by the rapid improvement of all instruments of production, by the immensely facilitated means of communication, draws all, even the most barbarian, nations into civilisation. The cheap prices of its commodities are the heavy artillery with which it batters down all Chinese walls, with which it forces the barbarians' intensely obstinate hatred of foreigners to capitulate. It compels all nations, on pain of extinction, to adopt the bourgeois mode of production; it compels them to introduce what it calls civilisation into their midst, i.e., to become bourgeois themselves. In a word, it creates a world after its own image.

The bourgeoisie has subjected the country to the rule of the towns. It has created enormous cities, has greatly increased the urban population as compared with the rural, and has thus rescued a considerable part of the population from the idiocy of rural life. Just as it has made the country dependent on the towns, so it has made barbarian and semi-barbarian countries dependent on the civilised ones, nations of peasants on nations of bourgeois, the East on the West.

The bourgeoisie keeps more and more doing away with the scattered state of the population, of the means of production, and of property. It has agglomerated population, centralised means of production, and has concentrated property in a few hands. The necessary consequence of this was political centralisation. Independent, or but loosely connected provinces, with separate interests, laws, governments and systems of taxation, became lumped together in one nation, with one government, one code of laws, one national class-interest, one frontier and one customs-tariff.

The bourgeoisie, during its rule of scarce one hundred years, has created more massive and more colossal productive forces than have all preceding generations together. Subjection of Nature's forces to man, machinery, application of chemistry to industry and agriculture, steam-navigation, railways, electric telegraphs, clearing of whole continents for cultivation, canalisation of rivers, whole populations conjured out of the ground—what earlier century had even a presentiment that such productive forces slumbered in the lap of social labour?

We see then: the means of production and of exchange on whose foundation the bourgeoisie built itself up, were generated in feudal society. At a certain stage in the development of these means of production and of exchange, the conditions under which feudal society produced and exchanged, the feudal organisation of agriculture and manufacturing industry, in one word, the feudal relations of property became no longer compatible with the already developed productive forces; they became so many fetters. They had to burst asunder; they were burst asunder.

Into their places stepped free competition, accompanied by a social and political constitution adapted to it, and by the economical and political sway of the bourgeois class.

The weapons with which the bourgeoisie felled feudalism to the ground are now turned against the bourgeoisie itself.

But not only has the bourgeoisie forged the weapons that bring death to itself; it has also called into existence the men who are to wield those weapons—the modern working-class—the proletarians.

In proportion as the bourgeoisie, i.e., capital, is developed, in the same proportion is the proletariat, the modern working-class, developed, a class of labourers, who live only so long as they find work, and who find work only so long as their labour increases capital. These labourers, who must sell themselves piecemeal, are a commodity, like every other article of commerce, and are consequently exposed to all the vicissitudes of competition, to all the fluctuations of the market.

Owing to the extensive use of machinery and to division of labour, the work of the proletarians has lost all individual character, and, consequently, all charm for the workman. He becomes an appendage of the machine, and it is only the most simple, most monotonous, and most easily acquired knack that is required of him. Hence, the cost of production of a workman is restricted, almost entirely, to the means of subsistence that he requires for his maintenance, and for the propagation of his race. But the price of a commodity, and also of labour, is equal to its cost of production. In proportion, therefore, as the repulsiveness of the work increases, the wage decreases. Nay more, in proportion as the use of machinery and division of labour increases, in the same proportion the burden of toil also increases, whether by prolongation of the working hours, by increase of the work enacted in a given time, or by increased speed of the machinery, etc.

Modern industry has converted the little workshop of the patriarchal master into the great factory of the industrial capitalist. Masses of labourers crowded into the factory, are organised like soldiers. As privates of the industrial army they are placed under the command of a perfect hierarchy of officers and sergeants. Not only are they the slaves of the bourgeois class, and of the bourgeois State, they are daily and hourly enslaved by the machine, by the over-looker, and, above all, by the individual bourgeois manufacturer himself. The more openly this despotism proclaims gain to be its end and aim, the more petty, the more hateful and the more embittering it is. . . .

But with the development of industry the proletariat not only increases in number; it becomes concentrated in greater masses, its strength grows, and it feels that strength more. The various interests and conditions of life within the ranks of the proletariat are more and more equalised, in proportion as machinery obliterates all distinctions of labour, and nearly everywhere reduces wages to the same low level. The growing competition among the bourgeois, and the resulting commercial crises, make the wages of the workers even more fluctuating. The unceasing improvement of machinery, ever more rapidly developing, makes their livelihood more and more precarious; the collisions between individual workmen and individual bourgeois take more and more the character of collisions between two classes. Thereupon the workers begin to form combinations (Trades' Unions) against the bourgeois; they club together in order to keep up the rate of wages; they found permanent associations in order to make provisions beforehand for these occasional revolts. Here and there the contest breaks out into riots.

Now and then the workers are victorious, but only for a time. The real fruit of their battles lies, not in the immediate result, but in the ever expanding union of the workers. This union is helped on by the improved means of communication that are created by modern industry, and that place the workers of different localities in contact with one another. It was just this contact that was needed to centralise the numerous local struggles, all of the same character, into one national struggle between classes. But every class struggle is a political struggle. And that union, to attain which the burghers of the Middle Ages, with their miserable highways, required centuries, the modern proletarians, thanks to railways, achieve in a few years. . . .

Of all the classes that stand face to face with the bourgeoisie to-day, the proletariat alone is a really revolutionary class. The other classes decay and finally disappear in the face of modern industry; the proletariat is its special and essential product.

The lower middle-class, the small manufacturer, the shopkeeper, the artisan, the peasant, all these fight against the bourgeoisie, to save from extinction their existence as fractions of the middle class. They are therefore not revolutionary, but conservative. Nay more, they are reactionary, for they try to roll back the wheel of history. If by chance they are revolutionary, they are so, only in view of their impending transfer into the proletariat, they thus defend not their present, but their future interests, they desert their own standpoint to place themselves at that of the proletariat.

The "dangerous class," the social scum, that passively rotting mass thrown off by the lowest layers of old society, may, here and there, be swept into the movement by a proletarian revolution; its conditions of life, however, prepare it far more for the part of a bribed tool of reactionary intrigue.

In the conditions of the proletariat, those of old society at large are already virtually swamped. The proletarian is without property; his relation to his wife and children has no longer anything in common with the bourgeois family-relations; modern industrial labour, modern subjection to capital, the same in England as in France, in America as in Germany, has stripped him of every trace of national character. Law, morality, religion, are to him so many bourgeois prejudices, behind which lurk in ambush just as many bourgeois interests.

All the preceding classes that got the upper hand sought to fortify their already acquired status by subjecting society at large to their conditions of appropriation. The proletarians cannot become masters of the productive forces of society, except by abolishing their own previous mode of appropriation, and thereby also every other previous mode of appropriation. They have nothing of their own to secure and to fortify; their mission is to destroy all previous securities for, and insurances of, individual property.

All previous historical movements were movements of minorities, or in the interest of minorities. The proletarian movement is the self-conscious independent movement of the immense majority in the interest of the immense majority. The proletariat, the lowest stratum of our present society, cannot stir, cannot raise itself up, without the whole superincumbent strata of official society being sprung into the air.

Though not in substance, yet in form, the struggle of the proletariat with the bourgeoisie is at first a national struggle. The proletariat of each country must, of course, first of all settle matters with its own bourgeoisie.

In depicting the most general phases of the development of the proletariat, we traced the more or less veiled civil war, raging within existing society, up to the point where that war breaks out into open revolution, and where the violent overthrow of the bourgeoisie, lays the foundation for the sway of the proletariat.

Hitherto, every form of society has been based, as we have already seen, on the antagonism of oppressing and oppressed classes. But in order to oppress a class, certain conditions must be assured to it under which it can, at least, continue its slavish existence. The serf, in the period of serfdom, raised himself to membership in the commune, just as the petty bourgeois, under the yoke of feudal absolutism, managed to develop into bourgeois. The modern labourer, on the contrary, instead of rising with the progress of industry, sinks deeper and deeper below the conditions of existence of his own class. He becomes a pauper, and pauperism develops more rapidly than population and wealth. And here it becomes evident, that the bourgeoisie is unfit any longer to be the ruling class in society, and to impose its conditions of existence upon society as an over-riding law. It is unfit to rule, because it is incompetent to assure an existence to its slave within his slavery, because it cannot help letting him sink into such a state, that it has to feed him, instead of being fed by him. Society can no longer live under this bourgeoisie, in other words, its existence is no longer compatible with society.

The essential condition for the existence, and for the sway of the bourgeois class, is the formation and augmentation of capital; the condition for capital is wage-labour. Wage-labour rests exclusively on competition between the labourers. The advance of industry, whose involuntary promoter is the bourgeoisie, replaces the isolation of the labourers, due to competition, by their involuntary combination, due to association. The development of Modern Industry, therefore, cuts from under its feet the very foundation on which the bourgeoisie produces and appropriates products. What the bourgeoisie therefore produces, above all, are its own gravediggers. Its fall and the victory of the proletariat are equally inevitable.

NOTES

[1] That is, all written history. In 1847, the pre-history of society, the social organisation existing previous to recorded history, was all but unknown. Since then Haxthausen discovered common ownership of land in Russia, Maurer proved it to be the social foundation from which all Teutonic races started in history, and by and by village communities were found to be, or to have been, the primitive form of society everywhere from India to Ireland. The inner organisation of this primitive Communistic society was laid bare, in its typical form, by Morgan's crowning discovery of the true nature of the gens and its relation to tribe. With the dissolution of these primaeval communities society begins to be differentiated into separate and finally antagonistic classes. I have attempted to retrace this process of dissolution in "Der Ursprung der Familie des Privateigenthums und des Staats," 2nd edit., Stuttgart 1886.

[2] Guild-master, that is a full member of a guild, a master within, not a head of, a guild.

[3] By bourgeoisie is meant the class of modern Capitalists, owners of the means of social production and employers of wage-labour. By proletariat, the class of modern wage-labourers who, having no means of production of their own, are reduced to selling their labour-power in order to live.

[4] "Commune" was the name, taken in France, by the nascent towns even before they had conquered from their feudal lords and masters, local self-government; and political rights as "the Third Estate." Generally speaking for the economical development of the bourgeoisie, England is here taken as the typical country, for its political development, France.

Lewis Henry Morgan

General Observations Upon Systems of Relationship

Lewis Henry Morgan was a first-hand observer of aboriginal cultures. His observations of American Indian life brought anthropology into the field and out of the library. By a freak of fortune, however, he, of all anthropologists, enjoys an international reputation. His *Ancient Society* was picked up and popularized by Marx and Engels because it conformed in many ways to their own evolutionary thought. In *Ancient Society* Morgan had proposed a three-stage scheme that began with savagery, went on to barbarism, and ended with civilization. His stages had economic correlates, and like most of his contemporaries Morgan believed that his own society was the most progressive, and those most unlike it were the least advanced. Morgan's importance to anthropology, however, did not lie in his evolutionary scheme but in his establishment of the study of kinship systems. His *Systems of Consanguinity and Affinity* indicated that kinship terms were not random developments but in fact were correlated with social and economic factors. Analysis of kinship systems could yield vital data about social relationships—and, Morgan believed, could provide clues to past social arrangements as well. Morgan made numerous errors—explaining, for example, that a kinship system in which cousins called each other by the terms used for brothers or sisters indicated the existence of a stage in which group marriage took place. Nevertheless, his work gave anthropologists and sociologists a marvelous tool for understanding the functional relationships which are reflected in kinship terminology.

In CONSIDERING THE ELEMENTS of a system of consanguinity the exist-ence of marriage between single pairs must be assumed. Marriage forms the basis of relationships. In the progress of the inquiry it may become necessary to consider a system with this basis fluctuating, and, perhaps, altogether wanting. The alternative assumption of each may be essential to include all the elements of the subject in its practical relations. The natural and necessary connection of consanguinei with each other would be the same in both cases; but with this difference, that in the former the lines of descent from parent to child would be known, while in the latter they would, to a greater or less extent, be incapable of ascertainment. These considerations might affect the form of the system of consanguinity.

The family relationships are as ancient as the *family*. They exist in virtue of the law of derivation, which is expressed by the perpetuation of the species through the marriage relation. A system of consanguin-ity, which is founded upon a community of blood, is but the formal expression and recognition of these relationships. Around every person there is a circle or group of kindred of which such person is the centre, the *Ego,* from whom the degree of the relationship is reckoned, and to whom the relationship itself returns. Above him are his father and his mother and their ascendants, below him are his children and their descendants; while upon either side are his brothers and sisters and their descendants, and the brothers and sisters of his father and of his mother and their descendants, as well as a much greater number of collateral relatives descended from common ancestors still more remote. To him they are nearer in degree than other individuals of the nation at large. A formal arrangement of the more immediate blood kindred into lines of descent, with the adoption of some method to distinguish one relative from another, and to express the value of the relationship, would be one of the earliest acts of human intelligence.

Should the inquiry be made how far nature suggests a uniform method or plan for the discrimination of the several relationships, and for the arrangement of kindred into distinct lines of descent, the answer would be difficult, unless it was first assumed that marriage between single pairs had always existed, thus rendering definite the lines of parentage. With this point established or assumed, a natural system, numerical in its character, will be found underlying any form which man may contrive; and which, resting upon an ordinance of nature, is both universal and unchangeable. All of the descendants of an original pair, through intermediate pairs, stand to each other in fixed degrees of proximity, the nearness or remoteness of which is a mere matter of computation, if we ascend from ancestor to ancestor in the lineal line, and again descend through the several collateral lines until the widening circle of kindred circumscribes millions of the living and the dead, all of these individuals, in virtue of their descent from common ancestors, are bound to the *"Ego"* by the chain of consanguinity.

The blood relationships, to which specific terms have been assigned, under the system of the Aryan family, are few in number. They are grandfather and grandmother, father and mother, brother and sister, son and daughter, grandson and granddaughter, uncle and aunt, nephew and niece, and cousin. Those more remote in degree are described either by an augmentation or by a combination of these terms. After these are the affineal or marriage relationships, which are husband and wife, father-in-law and mother-in-law, son-in-law and daughter-in-law, brother-in-law and sister-in-law, step-father and step-mother, step-son and step-daughter, and step-brother and step-sister: together with such of the husbands and wives of blood relatives as receive the corresponding designation by courtesy. These terms are barely sufficient to indicate specifically the nearest relationships, leaving much the largest number to be described by a combination of terms.

So familiar are these ancient household words, and the relationships which they indicate, that a classification of kindred by means of them according to their degrees of nearness, would seem to be not only a simple undertaking, but, when completed, to contain nothing of interest beyond its adaptation to answer a necessary want. But, since these specific terms are entirely inadequate to designate a person's kindred, they contain in themselves only the minor part of the system. An arrangement into lines, with descriptive phrases to designate such relatives as fall without the specific terms, becomes necessary to its completion. In the mode of arrangement and of description diversities may exist. Every system of consanguinity must be able to ascend and descend in the lineal line through several degrees from any given person, and to specify the relationship of each to *Ego;* and also from the lineal, to enter the several collateral lines and follow and describe the collateral relatives through several generations. When spread out in detail and examined, every scheme of consanguinity and affinity will be found to rest upon definite ideas, and to be framed, so far as it contains any plan, with reference to particular ends. In fine, a system of relationship, originating in necessity, is a domestic institution, which serves to organize a family by the bond of consanguinity. As such it possesses a degree of vitality and a power of self-perpetuation commensurate with its nearness to the primary wants of man.

In a general sense, as has elsewhere been stated, there are but two radically distinct forms of consanguinity. . . . One of these is descriptive and the other classificatory. The first, which is that of the Aryan, Semitic, and Uralian families, rejecting the classification of kindred, except so far as it is in accordance with the numerical system, describes collateral consanguinei, for the most part, by an augmentation or combination of the primary terms of relationship. These terms, which are those for husband and wife, father and mother, brother and sister, and son and daughter, to which must be added, in such languages as possess them, grandfather and grandmother, and grandson and granddaughter, are thus restricted to the primary sense in which they are here employed. All other terms are secondary. Each relationship is thus made independent and distinct from every other. But the second, which is that of the Turanian, American Indian, and Malayan families, rejecting descriptive phrases in every instance, and reducing consanguinei to great classes by a series of apparently arbitrary generalizations, applies the same terms to all the members of the same class. It thus confounds relationships, which, under the descriptive system, are distinct, and enlarges the signification both of the primary and secondary terms beyond their seemingly appropriate sense.

Although a limited number of generalizations have been developed in the system of the first-named families, which are followed by the introduction of additional special terms to express in the concrete the relationships thus specialized, yet the system is properly characterized as descriptive, and was such originally. It will be seen in the sequel that the partial classification of kindred which it now contains is in harmony with the principle of the descriptive form, and arises from it legitimately to the extent to which it is carried; and that it is founded upon conceptions entirely dissimilar from those which govern in the classificatory form. These generalizations, in some cases, are imperfect when logically considered; but they were designed to realize in the concrete the precise relationships which the descriptive phrases suggest by implication. In the Erse, for example, there are no terms for uncle or aunt, nephew or niece, or cousin; but they were described as *father's brother, mother's brother, brother's son,* and so on. These forms of the Celtic are, therefore, purely descriptive. In most of the Aryan languages terms for these relationships exist. My father's brothers and my mother's brothers, in English, are generalized into one class, and the term *uncle* is employed to express the relationship. The relationships to *Ego* of the two classes of persons are equal in their degree of nearness, but not the same in kind; wherefore, the Roman method is preferable, which employed *patruus* to express the former, and *avunculus* to indicate the latter. The phrase "father's brother" describes a person, but it likewise implies a bond of connection which *patruus* expresses in the concrete. In like manner, my father's brother's son, my father's sister's son, my mother's brother's son, and my mother's sister's son are placed upon an equality by a similar generalization, and the relationship is expressed by the term *cousin.* They stand to me in the same degree of nearness, but they are related to me in four different ways. The use of these terms, however, does not invade the principles of the descriptive system, but attempts to realize the implied relationships in a simpler manner. On the other hand, in the system of the last-named families, while corresponding terms exist, their application to particular persons is founded upon very different generalizations, and they are used in apparently arbitrary manner. In Seneca-Iroquois, for example, my father's brother is my father. Under the system he stands to me in that relationship and no other. I address him by the same term *Hä-niĥ,* which I apply to my own father. My mother's brother, on the contrary, is my uncle, *Hoc-nó-seh,* to whom, of the two, this relationship is restricted. Again, with myself a male, my brother's son is my son, *Ha-aĥ-wuk,* the same as my own son; while my sister's son is my nephew, *Ha yă-wan-da;* but with myself a female, these relationships are reversed. My brother's son is then my nephew; while my sister's son is my son. Advancing to the second collateral line, my father's brother's son and my mother's sister's son are my brothers, and they severally stand to me in the same relationship as my own brother; but my father's sister's son and my mother's brother's son are my cousins. The same relationships are recognized under the two forms, but the generalizations upon which they rest are different.

In the system of relationship of the Aryan, Semitic, and Uralian families, the collateral lines are maintained distinct and perpetually divergent from the lineal, which results, theoretically as well as practically, in a dispersion of the blood. The value of the relationships of collateral consanguinei is depreciated and finally lost under the burdensomeness of the descriptive method. This divergence is one of the characteristics of the descriptive system. On the contrary, in that of the Turanian, American Indian, and Malayan families, the several collateral lines, near and remote, are finally brought into, and merged in the lineal line, thus theoretically, if not practically, preventing a dispersion of the blood. The relationships of collaterals by this means is both appreciated and preserved. This mergence is, in like manner, one of the characteristics of the classificatory system.

How these two forms of consanguinity, so diverse in their fundamental conceptions and so dissimilar in their structure, came into existence it may be wholly impossible to explain. The first question to be considered relates to the nature of these forms and their ethnic distribution, after the ascertainment of which their probable origin may be made a subject of investigation. While the existence of two radically distinct forms appears to separate the human family . . . into two great divisions, the Indo-European and the Indo-American, the same testimony seems to draw closer together the several families of which these divisions are composed, without forbidding the supposition that a common point of departure between the two may yet be discovered. If the evidence deposited in these systems of relationship tends, in reality, to consolidate the families named into two great divisions, it is a tendency in the direction of unity of origin of no inconsiderable importance.

After the several forms of consanguinity and affinity, which now prevail in the different families of mankind, have been presented and discussed, the important question will present itself, how far these forms become changed with the progressive changes of society. The uses of systems of relationship to establish the genetic connection of nations will depend, first, upon the structure of the system, and, secondly, upon the stability of its radical forms. In form and feature they must be found able, when once established, to perpetuate themselves through indefinite periods of time. The question of their use must turn upon that of the stability of their radical features. Development and modification, to a very considerable extent, are revealed in the tables in which the comparison of forms is made upon an extended scale, but it will be observed, on further examination, that these changes are further developments of the fundamental conceptions which lie, respectively, at the foundation of the two original systems.

There is one powerful motive which might, under certain circumstances, tends [sic] to the overthrow of the classificatory form and the substitution of the descriptive, but it would arise after the attainment of civilization. This is the inheritance of estates. It may be promised that the bond of kindred, among uncivilized nations, is a strong influence for the mutual protection of related persons. Among nomadic stocks, especially, the respectability of the individual was measured, in no small degree, by the number of his kinsmen. The wider the circle of kindred the greater the assurance of safety, since they were the natural guardians of his rights and the avengers of his wrongs. Whether designedly or otherwise, the Turanian form of consanguinity organized the family upon the largest scale of numbers. On the other hand, a gradual change from a nomadic to a civilized condition would prove the severest test to which a system of consanguinity could be subjected. The protection of the law, or of the State, would become substituted for that of kinsmen; but with more effective power the rights of property might influence the system of relationship. This last consideration, which would not arise until after a people had emerged from barbarism, would be adequate beyond any other known cause to effect a radical change in a pre-existing system, if [it] recognized relationships which would defeat natural justice in the inheritance of property. In Tamilian society, where my brother's son and my cousin's son are both my sons, a useful purpose may have been subserved by drawing closer, in this manner, the kindred bond; but in a civilized sense it would be manifestly unjust to place either of these collateral sons upon an equality with my own son for the inheritance of my estate. Hence the growth of property and the settlement of its distribution might be expected to lead to a more precise discrimination of the several degrees of consanguinity if they were confounded by the previous system.

Where the original system, anterior to civilization, was descriptive, the tendency to modification, under the influence of refinement, would be in the direction of a more rigorous separation of the several lines of descent, and of a more systematic description of the persons or relationships in each. It would not necessarily lead to the abandonment of old terms nor to the invention of new. This latter belongs, usually, to the formative period of a language. When that is passed, compound terms are resorted to if the descriptive phrases are felt to be inconvenient. Wherever these compounds are found it will be known at once that they are modern in the language. The old terms are not necessarily radical, but they have become so worn down by long-continued use as to render the identification of their component parts impossible. While the growth of nomenclatures of relationship tends to show the direction in which existing systems have been modified, it seems to be incapable of throwing any light upon the question whether a classificatory form ever becomes changed into a descriptive, or the reverse. It is more difficult, where the pimitive system was classificatory, to ascertain the probable direction of the change. The uncivilized nations have remained substantially stationary in their condition through all the centuries of their existence, a circumstance eminently favorable to the permanency of their domestic institutions. It is not supposable, however, that they have resisted all modifications of their system of consanguinity. The opulence of the nomenclature of relationships, which is characteristic of the greater portion of the nations whose form is classificatory, may tend to show that, if it changed materially, it would be in the direction of a greater complexity of classification. It is extremely difficult to arrive at any general conclusions upon this question with reference to either form. But it may be affirmed that if an original system changes materially, after it has been adopted into use, it is certain to be done in harmony with the ideas and conceptions which it embodies, of which the changes will be further and logical developments.

It should not be inferred that forms of consanguinity and affinity are either adopted, modified, or laid aside at pleasure. The tables entirely dispel such a supposition. When a system has once come into practical use, with its nomenclature adopted, and its method of description or of classification settled, it would, from the nature of the case, be very slow to change. Each person, as has elsewhere been observed, is the centre around whom a group of consanguinei is arranged. It is my father, my mother, my brother, my son, my uncle, my cousin, with each and every human being; and, therefore, each one is compelled to understand, as well as to use, the prevailing system. It is an actual necessity to all alike, since each relationship is personal to *Ego*. A change of any of these relationships, or a subversion of any of the terms invented to express them would be extremely difficult if not impossible; and it would be scarcely less difficult to enlarge or contract the established use of the terms themselves. The possibility of this permanence is increased by the circumstance that these systems exist by usage rather than legal enactment, and therefore the motive to change must be as universal as the usage. Their use and preservation are intrusted to every person who speaks the common language, and their channel of transmission is the blood. Hence it is that, in addition to the natural stability of domestic institutions, there are special reasons which contribute to their permanence, by means of which it is rendered not improbable that they might survive changes of social condition sufficiently radical to overthrow the primary ideas in which they originated.

Émile Durkheim

Social Order and Anomie

If Auguste Comte gave sociology its name, Émile Durkheim provided much of its method and philosophy. Durkheim's theories derive to some extent from the Marxian notion of the superstructure. They can be understood only within the context of the intellectual climate of the late nineteenth century. Durkheim's insistence that sociology study a social level of behavior was at least in part a reaction to the premature reductionisms of the past, which saw human behavior as the result of geographical, biological, or psychological forces. Durkheim focused his attention on what he called the *conscience collective*—the social structures or arrangements that he believed were the principal determinants of behavior. He saw society as a constraining force and insisted that even such apparently individual phenomena as suicides were, in fact, socially determined and predictable statistically. Although Durkheim himself is strangely ambivalent about the extent of human freedom, and although he appeared somewhat reluctant to admit that individual will and desire were subject to social controls, his emphasis upon the group mind was transformed in the hands of successors into the objectification of man. The Durkheimian view thus paved the way for the sociological view of man as an object whose behavior was determined by the laws of a society that stood somewhat apart from him.

No LIVING THING CAN be contented, or even go on living, unless its wants are sufficiently harmonized with the means at its disposal. If these wants require more or something different than is available, they will constantly be thwarted and will be unable to function without pain. Now, a movement which cannot occur without pain tends not to be repeated. Tendencies which fail of fulfilment atrophy, and, since the urge to live is merely the resultant of all other tendencies, it cannot but weaken if these other tendencies lose their force.

In the case of an animal, at least under normal circumstances, this equilibrium between wants and resources is established automatically and spontaneously because it depends upon purely material conditions. The organism requires only that the quantities of matter and energy which are endlessly consumed in the maintenance of life be periodically replaced by equivalent amounts, i.e., that replacement be equal to wear and tear. When the hole which living digs in its own resources has been filled up again, the animal is satisfied and asks for nothing more. Its reflective powers are not sufficiently well developed to conceive of aims other than those implicit in its physical structure. On the other hand, as the work required of each organ itself depends on the general condition of the life processes and on the necessities of organic equilibrium, the wear and tear involved in the use of the organ is regulated by its replacement and thus a balance is struck automatically. The limits of the one are the limits of the other; they are both alike registered in the very constitution of the living organism, which has no way of going beyond them.

The situation of man is different, however, for most of his wants are not at all, or at least not to the same degree, dependent upon his body. At the most, one can conceive as determinable the physical quantity of material nourishment that is essential for the maintenance of a human life. However, even this determination would be less precise and the scope for variable combinations of desires greater than in the preceding case of lower animals. For, beyond the indispensable minimum with which nature is willing to content herself when she functions instinctively, reflective thought, being more vigorous in man than in animals, leads man to imagine better conditions which then appear as desirable goals and incite his activity. However, we may admit that desires of this kind [bodily desires] sooner or later reach a limit beyond which they cannot pass. Yet how is one to determine exactly the amount of well-being, of comfort, of luxury, to which a human being can legitimately aspire? In neither the organic nor the psychological constitution of man is anything to be found which sets a boundary to such propensities. The operation of the individual's life process does not require that those wants stop at one point rather than at another. This is proved by the fact that they have grown periodically since the beginning of history, that progressively fuller satisfaction has been given to them, and that, in spite of these changes, the average level of health has not declined. Above all, how is one to determine the manner in which these wants should vary according to social conditions, occupation, relative importance of services, etc.? There is no society in which they are satisfied equally at the different levels of the social hierarchy. And yet, in its essential characteristics, human nature obviously is the same for all members of society. Thus, it is not human nature which would be capable of setting such a variable limit to human desires [for well-being, comfort and luxury] as they require. Therefore, insofar as they depend upon the individual alone, these desires are boundless. In itself, disregarding all external forces which control it, our capacity for feeling *(sensibilité)* is a bottomless abyss which nothing could fill.

But then, if no external force limits our feeling, it can be by itself nothing but a source of pain. For unlimited desires are insatiable by definition, and it is not without reason that insatiability is regarded as a sign of morbidity. Since nothing restricts them, such wants are forever and infinitely outdistancing the means available for their satisfaction; hence nothing can appease them. An unquenchable thirst is a perpetually renewed agony. To be sure, the saying goes that it is characteristic of human activity to unfold without assignable end and to set up for itself aims which it cannot realize. But it is impossible to see how such a state of indeterminateness can be reconciled any more readily with the conditions of mental life than with the exigencies of physical life. Whatever pleasure man may experience in acting, moving, exerting effort, he still needs to feel that his efforts are not futile and that as he travels he gets somewhere. But one does not progress when one is moving toward no goal, or, what comes to the same thing, when the goal toward which one is moving is infinitely far away. If one's distance from the goal remains always the same, however far one has gone, the result is the same as if one were running on a treadmill. Even backward glances, and the feeling of pride which one may have as one looks over the ground already covered, can bring only an illusory satisfaction, since the distance still to be covered has not been reduced correspondingly. To pursue a goal that is by hypothesis unattainable is thus to condemn oneself to a perpetual state of discontent. No doubt man does hope against all reason; and, even when it is irrational, hope has its joys. Hence, it may sustain him for a while; but it cannot indefinitely survive the repeated disillusionments of experience. Now, what more can the future possibly offer than the past, since it is forever impossible to reach a place where a stand can be made, and since one cannot even approach the ideal at which one aims? Thus, the more one has and the more one wants, the more the satisfactions already attained have the effect only of stimulating, never of appeasing, one's wants. But in the first place, that is true only if one closes one's eyes sufficiently to remain unaware of the action's futility. Then, too, if this pleasure is to be felt and if it is even partly to assuage and disguise the painful anxiety by which it is accompanied, this endless striving must at least go on easily and without any obstacles. Let it be thwarted, and only the anxiety is left, together with the discomfort which it induces. Now, it would be miraculous if no insurmountable obstacle ever arose. Under these circumstances, one holds onto life only by an extremely slender thread, which may snap at any moment.

If the outcome is to be different, the first requisite is that bounds be set to the passions. Only then can they be harmonized with one's powers and consequently gratified. But since there is nothing within the individual which can set a limit to his propensities, any such limitation must come from a source outside himself. Some regulating power must play the same role with reference to the social wants that the physical organism plays with reference to the biological wants. In other words, this power must itself be a moral [social] force. For it was the awakening of the mind which began to upset the equilibrium in which the animal lay sleeping; thus mind alone can provide the means for restoring it. Physical checks would be useless here; human passions cannot be changed by physico-chemical forces. To the extent that appetites are not curbed automatically by physiological mechanisms, they cannot be halted except by a limitation which they themselves recognize as just. Men would not consent to limit their desires if they believed themselves justified in overriding the assigned boundaries. Yet they cannot prescribe this rule of justice to themselves, for the reasons we have indicated. They must receive it from an authority which they respect and before which they bow spontaneously. Only society, whether directly and as a whole, or indirectly through one of its agencies, is in a position to play this restraining role; for it is the only moral power which is superior to the individual and which he acknowledges as superior. Society alone has the authority necessary to say what is right, and set for the passions the point beyond which they are not to go. Furthermore, society alone can act as judge to determine what reward should be offered to each group for the performance of its particular social function, for the sake of the common interest.

And in fact, at every moment in history there exists in the mores (*conscience des sociétés*) a vague notion of what the various social functions are worth, of the relative remuneration due each of them, and, consequently, of the degree of comfort appropriate to the average worker in each occupation. The various functions are ranked by public opinion into a sort of hierarchy, and a certain coefficient of welfare is assigned to each according to the place it occupies in the hierarchy. Traditionally, for example, there is a certain mode of life which is regarded as the upper limit to which the manual worker may aspire in his efforts to improve his lot, and a lower limit below which we can hardly bear to see him fall unless he has forfeited our respect. Both these limits differ as between the urban and the rural worker, the domestic servant and the journeyman, the commercial employee and the public official, etc., etc. Similarly, again, people find fault with the rich man who lives as if he were poor, but they condemn him also if he tries to acquire too many of the refinements of luxury. In vain do the economists protest; it will always offend public sentiment that any single person may consume in utterly needless waste an over-large amount of wealth, and in fact it seems that this intolerance is relaxed only in periods of moral confusion.[1]

There is, consequently, a very real set of rules which, though it does not always have a legal form, nonetheless sets more or less precisely the maximum standard of living which each class may legitimately seek to attain. Yet the scale thus set up is by no means unalterable. It changes as the total social income grows or diminishes, and in accordance with the changes which occur in the mores of the society.

So it happens that things which look like luxury to one age no longer looks so to another; that a level of comfort which for a long time was granted to a particular class only as an exceptional and superfluous right, now is regarded as absolutely necessary and a matter of strict equity.

Under this pressure, each person in his own orbit takes account in a general way of the extreme point to which his ambitions may go, and aspires to nothing beyond it. At least, if he respects the rule and submits to group authority—that is, if he is of sound moral make-up— he feels that it is not right to demand more. An objective and a limit are thus marked out for human passions. To be sure, this determination has nothing either rigid or absolute about it. The economic ideal assigned to each category of citizens is defined by certain upper or lower limits between which there is a large area within which their desires may move about freely. But this area is not unlimited. It is just this relative limitation and the resulting moderation which make men content with their lot and at the same time spur them on moderately to improve it; and it is this contentment which gives birth to that feeling of serene yet active delight, to that enjoyment of being and living which, in societies as well as in individuals, is the sign of health. Generally speaking, everyone is then well adjusted to his station in life and desires only those things for which he can legitimately hope as the normal reward for his efforts. Moreover, a man is not thereby condemned to immobility. He can try to embellish or improve his life; but such attempts may fail without leaving him despondent. For, as he enjoys what he has, and does not put his whole soul into seeking what he has not, he may not succeed in getting all the new things he desired and hoped to acquire, without feeling that he has lost everything at the same time. The essentials he still has. The equilibrium of his happiness is stable because it is determinate and a few disappointments are not enough to upset it.

However, it would not be sufficient that everyone accept as equitable the hierarchy of functions as it is set up by the mores, if he did not also consider equally equitable the manner in which the individuals who are to perform these social functions are recruited. The worker is not adjusted to his social position if he is not convinced that he really has the position he deserves. If he believes he should in justice hold some other rank, the one he occupies cannot satisfy him. Thus it is not enough that the general level of wants for each social rank should be regulated by public sentiment; there must exist along with this another, more precise system of regulation which determines the manner in which the various ranks are to be opened up to individuals. And as a matter of fact, there is no society in which such regulation does not exist. It varies with time and place. Formerly it made birth the almost exclusive principle of social stratification; today it recognizes no native inequalities but those which stem from inherited wealth or personal worth. Yet beneath these widely varying forms this type of regulation has the same purport everywhere. Everywhere, too, it is effective only if imposed upon individuals by an authority which is superior to them—that is, by collective authority. For this control cannot operate without requiring sacrifices and concessions from one group or another—or more generally from all groups—in the name of public interest.

Certain writers, to be sure, have argued that this social pressure would become useless as soon as economic position ceased to be transmitted by inheritance. If, they have said, the inheritance system has been abolished and each person begins life with the same resources, if, therefore, the competitive struggle is joined under conditions of perfect equality, no one could consider the results of this struggle unjust. Everyone would recognize spontaneously that things are as they ought to be.

As a matter of fact, there is no doubt that, the closer we approach to that ideal equality, the less necessary social control will be. But this is only a question of degree. For one kind of heritage will always remain, namely that of natural endowments. Intelligence, taste, scientific or artistic or literary or industrial ability, courage, manual dexterity are powers which each of us receives at birth, just as the property-owner by inheritance receives his capital, or as the noble used to receive his title and feudal office. A moral discipline will still be needed to induce those least favored by nature to accept the inferior station in life which they owe to the accidents of birth. Some will go so far as to insist that everyone's share should be identical, that no advantage should be given to the more productive and deserving. But if that is to be the case, a very different yet equally vigorous discipline will be required to get these latter to accept treatment no better than that accorded to the mediocre and inefficient.

However, this discipline, like the type mentioned earlier, can be socially useful only if the people subjected to it believe it to be fair. When it is maintained only by habit and force, peace and harmony continue to exist only outwardly; the spirit of restlessness and discontent are latent; appetites, only superficially held in check, will soon break loose. This is what happened in Rome and in Greece when the beliefs on which rested the ancient organization of patriciate and plebs were shaken, and in our modern societies when the traditional aristocratic principles began to lose their former ascendancy. But this state of disturbance is unusual; it occurs only when society is passing through some abnormally disturbed period of transition (*crise maladive*). Normally, the social order is acknowledged as equitable by the vast majority of its subjects. Thus, when we say that an authority is required to impose this order upon the individuals, we do not imply at all that violence is the only means by which it can be imposed. Because this control is to restrain the passions of individuals, it must emanate from a power which can master these individuals; but it is equally true that this power must be obeyed from respect and not from fear.

Accordingly, it is not true that human activity can be freed of every restraint. Nothing in this world can enjoy such a privilege. For every being, since it is part of the universe, is relative to the rest of the universe; its nature and the way in which it manifests that nature depend not only upon itself, but also upon the other beings, which as a natural consequence, restrain and control it. In this respect, the only differences between inorganic matter and thinking beings are differences of degree and form. The unique characteristic of man is the fact that the check to which he is subjected is not physical but moral, that is, social. He receives his law not from a material environment which imposes itself upon him by brute force, but from a mind that is superior to his own, and whose superiority he realizes. Because the greater and better part of his life transcends the life of the body, he escapes the yoke of the body but becomes subject to that of society.

NOTE

[1] This condemnation nowadays is entirely of an informal moral character, and seems to be scarcely capable of legal enforcement. We do not believe that any re-introduction of sumptuary laws would be desirable or even possible.

Georg Simmel

The Dyad and the Triad

A major departure from the system-building approach of social thinkers that preceded him was the work of Georg Simmel. The founder of "formal" sociology, he advocated an approach to social data that is somewhat analogous to geometry. Simmel insisted that sociology must deal with forms of sociation, and he believed that these forms—not their content—were determinative. Like Durkheim, Boas, and the "functional" anthropologists, Simmel insisted that sociology attend first to specific problems rather than broad generalizations. Simmel's abstractions helped pave the way for sociological studies based upon separation of the social from the biological and psychological aspects of human behavior.

The Non-Partisan and the Mediator

It is sociologically very significant that isolated elements are unified by their common relation to a phenomenon which lies outside of them. This applies as much to the alliance between states for the purpose of defense against a common enemy as to the "invisible church" which unifies all the faithful in their equal relation to the one God. The group-forming, mediation function of a third element will be discussed in a later context. In the cases under examination now, the third element is at such a distance from the other two that there exist no properly sociological interactions which concern all three elements alike. Rather, there are configurations of two. In the center of sociological attention, there is either the relation between the two joining elements, the relation between them as a unit and the center of interest that confronts them. At the moment, however, we are concerned with three elements which are so closely related or so closely approach one another that they form a group, permanent or momentary.

In the most significant of all dyads, monogamous marriage, the child or children, as the third element, often has the function of holding the whole together. Among many "nature peoples," only childbirth makes a marriage perfect or insoluble. And certainly one of the reasons why developing culture makes marriages deeper and closer is that children become independent relatively late and therefore need longer care. Perfection of marriage through childbirth rests, of course, on the value which the child has for the husband, and on his inclination, sanctioned by law and custom, to expel a childless wife. But the actual result of the third element, the child, is that it alone really closes the circle by tying the parents to one another. This can occur in two forms. The existence of the third element may directly start or strengthen the union of the two, as for instance, when the birth of a child increases the spouses' mutual love, or at least the husband's for his wife. Or the relation of each of the spouses to the child may produce a new and indirect bond between them. In general, the common preoccupations of a married couple with the child reveal that their union passes through the child, as it were; the union often consists of sympathies which could not exist without such a point of mediation. This emergence of the inner socialization of three elements, which the two elements by themselves do not desire, is the reason for . . . the tendency of unhappily married couples not to wish children. They instinctively feel that the child would close a circle within which they would be nearer one another, not only externally but also in their deeper psychological layers, than they are inclined to be.

When the third element functions as a non-partisan, we have a different variety of mediation. The non-partisan either produces the concord of two colliding parties, whereby he withdraws after making the effort of creating direct contact between the unconnected or quarreling elements; or he functions as an arbiter who balances, as it were, their contradictory claims against one another and eliminates what is incompatible in them. Differences between labor and management, especially in England, have developed both forms of unification. There are boards of conciliation where the parties negotiate their conflicts under the presidency of a non-partisan. The mediator, of course, can achieve reconciliation in this form only if each party believes that the proportion between the reasons for the hostility, in short, the objective situation justifies the reconciliation and makes peace advantageous. The very great opportunity that non-partisan mediation has to produce this belief lies not only in the obvious elimination of misunderstandings or in appeals to good will, etc. It may also be analyzed as follows. The non-partisan shows each party the claims and arguments of the other; they thus lose the tone of subjective passion which usually provokes the same tone on the part of the adversary. What is so often regrettable here appears as something wholesome, namely, that the feeling which accompanies a psychological content when one individual has it, usually weakens greatly when it is transferred to a second. This fact explains why recommendations and testimonies that have to pass several mediating persons before reaching the deciding individual, are so often ineffective, even if their objective content arrives at its destination without any change. In the course of these transfers, affective imponderables get lost; and these not only supplement insufficient objective qualifications, but, in practice, they alone cause sufficient ones to be acted upon.

Here we have a phenomenon which is very significant for the development of purely psychological influences. A third mediating social element deprives conflicting claims of their affective qualities because it neutrally formulates and presents these claims to the two parties involved. Thus this circle that is fatal to all reconciliation is avoided: the vehemence of the one no longer provokes that of the other, which in turn intensifies that of the first, and so forth, until the whole relationship breaks down. Furthermore, because of the non-partisan, each party to the conflict not only listens to more objective terms than it would if it confronted the other without mediation. For now it is important for each to win over even the mediator. This, however, can be hoped for only on purely objective grounds, because the mediator is not the arbitrator, but only guides the process of coming to terms; because, in other words, he must always keep out of any decision—whereas the arbitrator ends up by taking sides. Within the realm of sociological techniques, there is nothing that serves the reconciliation of conflicting parties so effectively as does objectivity, that is, the attempt at limiting all complaints and requests to their objective contents. Philosophically speaking, the conflict is reduced to the objective spirit of each partial standpoint, so that the personalities involved appear as the mere vehicles of objective conditions. In case of conflict, the personal form in which objective contents become subjectively alive must pay for its warmth, color, and depth of feeling with the sharpness of the antagonism that it engenders. The diminution of this personal tone is the condition under which the understanding and reconciliation of the adversaries can be attained, particularly because it is only under this condition that each of the two parties actually realizes what the other must insist upon. To put it psychologically, antagonism of the will is reduced to intellectual antagonism. Reason is everywhere the principle of understanding; on its basis can come together what on that of feeling and ultimate decision of the will is irreconcilably in conflict. It is the function of the mediator to bring this reduction about, to represent it, as it were, in himself; or to form a transformation point where, no matter in what form the conflict enters from one side, it is transmitted to the other only in an objective form; a point where all is retained which would merely intensify the conflict in the absence of mediation.

It is important for the analysis of social life to realize clearly that the constellation thus characterized constantly emerges in all groups of more than two elements. To be sure, the mediator may not be specifically chosen, nor be known or designated as such. But the triad here serves merely as a type or scheme; ultimately all cases of mediation can be reduced to this form. From the conversation among three persons that lasts only an hour, to the permanent family of three, there is no triad in which a dissent between any two elements does not occur from time to time—a dissent of a more harmless or more pointed, more momentary or more lasting, more theoretical or more practical nature—and in which the third member does not play a mediating role. This happens innumerable times in a very rudimentary and inarticulate manner, mixed with other actions and interactions, from which the purely mediating function cannot be isolated. Such mediations do not even have to be performed by means of words. A gesture, a way of listening, the mood that radiates from a particular person, are enough to change the difference between two individuals so that they can seek understanding, are enough to make them feel their essential commonness which is concealed under their acutely differing opinions, and to bring this divergence into the shape in which it can be ironed out the most easily. The situation does not have to involve a real conflict or fight. It is rather the thousand insignificant differences of opinion, the allusions to an antagonism of personalities, the emergence of quite momentary contrasts of interest or feeling, which continuously color the fluctuating forms of all living together; and this social life is constantly determined in its course by the presence of the third person, who almost inevitably exercises the function of mediation. This function makes the round among the three elements, since the ebb and flow of social life realizes the form of conflict in every possible combination of two members.

The non-partisanship that is required for mediation has one of two presuppositions. The third element is non-partisan either if he stands above the contrasting interest and opinions and is actually not concerned with them, or if he is equally concerned with both. The first case is the simpler of the two and involves fewest complications. In conflicts between English laborers and entrepreneurs, for instance, the non-partisan called in could be neither a laborer nor an entrepreneur. It is notable how decisively the separation of objective from personal elements in the conflict (mentioned earlier) is realized here. The idea is that the non-partisan is not attached by personal interest to the objective aspects of either party position. Rather, both come to be weighed by him as by a pure, impersonal intellect, without touching the subjective sphere. But the mediator must be subjectively interested in the persons or groups themselves who exemplify the contents of the quarrel which to him are merely theoretical, since otherwise he would not take over his function. It is, therefore, as if subjective interest set in motion a purely objective mechanism. It is the fusion of personal distance from the objective significance of the quarrel with personal interest in its subjective significance which characterizes the non-partisan position. This position is the more perfect, the more distinctly each of these two elements is developed and the more harmoniously, in its very differentiation, each cooperates with the other.

The situation becomes more complicated when the non-partisan owes his position, not to his neutrality but to his equal participation in the interests in conflict. This case is frequent when a given individual belongs to two different interest groups, one local, and the other objective, especially occupational. In earlier times, bishops could sometimes intervene between the secular ruler of their diocese and the pope. The administrator who is thoroughly familiar with the special interests of his district will be the most suitable mediator in the case of a collision between these special interests and the general interests of the state which employs him. The measure of the combination between impartiality and interest which is favorable to the mediation between two locally separate groups, is often found in persons who come from one of these groups but live with the other. The difficulty of positions of this kind in which the mediator may find himself, usually derives from the fact that his equal interests in both parties, that is, his inner equilibrium, cannot be definitely ascertained and is, in fact, doubted often enough by both parties.

Yet an even more difficult and, indeed, often tragic situation occurs when the third is tied to the two parties, not by specific interests, but by his total personality; and this situation is extreme when the whole matter of the conflict cannot be clearly objectified, and its objective aspect is really only a pretext or opportunity for deeper personal irreconcilabilities to manifest themselves. In such a case, the third, whom love or duty, fate or habit have made equally intimate with both, can be crushed by the conflict—much more so than if he himself took sides. The danger is increased because the balance of his interests, which does not lean in either direction, usually does not lead to successful mediation, since reduction to a merely objective contrast fails. This is the type instanced by a great many family conflicts. The mediator, whose equal distance to both conflicting parties assures his impartiality, can accommodate both with relative ease. But the person who is impartial because he is equally close to the two, will find this much more difficult and will personally get into the most painful dualism of feelings. Where the mediator is chosen, therefore, the equally uninterested will be preferred (other things being equal) to the equally interested. Medieval Italian cities, for instance, often obtained their judges from the outside in order to be sure that they were not prejudiced by inner party frictions.

This suggests the second form of accommodation by means of an impartial third element, namely, arbitration. As long as the third properly operates as a mediator, the final termination of the conflict lies exclusively in the hands of the parties themselves. But when they choose an arbitrator, they relinquish this final decision. They project, as it were, their will to conciliation, and this will becomes personified in the arbitrator. He thus gains a special impressiveness and power over the antagonistic forces. The voluntary appeal to an arbitrator, to whom they submit from the beginning, presupposes a greater subjective confidence in the objectivity of judgment than does any other form of decision. For, even in the state tribunal, it is only the action of the complaint that results from confidence in just decision, since the complainant considers the decision that is favorable to him the just decision. The defendant, on the other hand, must enter the suit whether or not he believes in the impartiality of the judge. But arbitration results only when both parties to the conflict have this belief. This is the principle which sharply differentiates mediation from arbitration; and the more official the act of conciliation, the more punctiliously is this differentiation observed.

This statement applies to a whole range of conflicts; from those between capitalist and worker, which I mentioned earlier, to those of great politics, where the "good services" of a government in adjusting a conflict between two others are quite different from the arbitration occasionally requested of it. The trivialities of daily life, where the typical triad constantly places one into a clear or latent, full or partial difference from two others, offer many intermediary grades between these two forms. In the inexhaustibly varying relations, the parties' appeal to the third person, to his voluntarily or even forcibly seized initiative to conciliate, often gives him a position whose mediating and arbitrating elements it is impossible to separate. If one wants to understand the real web of human society with its indescribable dynamics and fullness, the most important thing is to sharpen one's eyes for such beginnings and transitions, for forms of relationship which are merely hinted at and are again submerged, for their embryonic and fragmentary articulations. Illustrations which exemplify in its purity any one of the concepts denoting these forms, certainly are indispensable sociological tools. But their relation to actual social life is like that of the approximately exact space forms, that are used to illustrate geometrical propositions, to the immeasurable complexity of the actual formations of matter.

After all that has been said, it is clear that from an over-all viewpoint, the existence of the impartial third element serves the perpetuation of the group. As the representative of the intellect, he confronts the two conflicting parties, which for the moment are guided more by will and feeling. He thus, so to speak, complements them in the production of that psychological unity which resides in group life. On the one hand, the non-partisan tempers the passion of the others. On the other hand, he can carry and direct the very movement of the whole group if the antagonism of the other two tends to paralyze their forces. Nevertheless, this success can change into its opposite. We thus understand why the most intellectually disposed elements of a group lean particularly toward impartiality: the cool intellect usually finds lights and shadows in either quarter; its objective justice does not easily side unconditionally with either. This is the reason why sometimes the most intelligent individuals do not have much influence on the decisions in conflicts, although it would be very desirable that such decisions come from them. Once the group has to choose between "yes" and "no" they, above all others, ought to throw their weight into the balance, for then the scale will be more likely to sink in favor of the right side. If, therefore, impartiality does not serve practical mediation directly, in its combination with intellectuality it makes sure that the decision is not left to the more stupid, or at least more prejudiced, group forces. And in fact, ever since Solon, we often find disapproval of impartial behavior. In the social sense, this disapproval is something very healthy: it is based on a much deeper instinct for the welfare of the whole than on mere suspicion of cowardice—an attack which is frequently launched against impartiality, though often quite unjustifiably.

Whether impartiality consists in the equal distance or in the equal closeness that connects the non-partisan and the two conflicting parties, it is obvious that it may be mixed with a great many other relations between him and each of the two others and their group as a whole. For instance, if he constitutes a group with the other two but is remote from their conflicts, he may be drawn into them in the very name of independence from the parties which already exist. This may greatly serve the unity and equilibrium of the group, although the equilibrium may be highly unstable. It was this sociological form in which the third estate's participation in state matters occurred in England. Ever since Henry III, state matters were inextricably dependent on the cooperation of the great barons who, along with the prelates, had to grant the monies; and their combination had power, often superior power, over the king. Nevertheless, instead of the fruitful collaboration between estates and crown, there were incessant splits, abuses, power shifts, and clashes. Both parties came to feel that these could be ended only by resort to a third element which, until then, had been kept out of state matters: lower vassals, freemen, counties, and cities. Their representatives were invited to councils; and this was the beginning of the House of Commons. The third element thus exerted a double function. First, it helped to make an actuality of government as the image of the state in its comprehensiveness. Secondly, it did so as an agency which confronted hitherto existing government parties objectively, as it were, and thus contributed to the more harmonious employment of their reciprocally exhausted forces for the over-all purpose of the state.

Alfred Kroeber

The Superorganic

It is somewhat difficult to define the differences between Kroeber's concept of the *superorganic* and Durkhim's concept of the *conscience collective*. Both saw society as constraining and determinative forces and both turned the attention of their respective disciplines to analysis of social and cultural regularities rather than to the search for causal factors in biology, geography, or psychology. Kroeber's definition of culture, however, stemmed from Tylor and included art, artifacts, patterns, and ideas. Durkheim's notion of society was more structural and less concerned with either artifacts or ideas. Both provided a necessary corrective to the reductionist determinisms of the past. But both suffered somewhat from their unwillingness to admit the individual human mind as a factor in the understanding of cultural or social affairs.

A WAY OF THOUGHT CHARACTERISTIC of our western civilization has been the formation of complementary antitheses, a balancing of exclusive opposites. One of these pairs of ideas with which our world has been laboring for some two thousand years is expressed in the words *body* and *soul*. Another couplet that has served its useful purpose, but which science is now often endeavoring to rid itself of, at least in certain aspects, is the distinction of the *physical* from the *mental*. A third discrimination is that of the *vital* from the *social*, or in other phraseology, of the *organic* from the *cultural*. The implicit recognition of the difference between organic qualities and processes and social qualities and processes is of long standing. The formal

112

distinction is however recent. In fact the full import of the significance of the antithesis may be said to be only dawning upon the world. For every occasion on which some human mind sharply separates organic and social forces, there are dozens of other times when the distinction between them is not thought of, or an actual confusion of the two ideas takes place.

One reason for this current confusion of the organic and social is the predominance, in the present phase of the history of thought, of the idea of evolution. This idea, one of the earliest, simplest, and also vaguest ever attained by the human mind, has received its strongest ground and fortification in the domain of the organic; in other words, through biological science. At the same time, there is an evolution, or growth, or gradual development, apparent also in other realms than that of plant and animal life. We have theories of stellar or cosmic evolution; and there is obvious, even to the least learned, a growth or evolution of civilization. In the nature of things there is little danger of the carrying over of the Darwinian or post-Darwinian principles of the evolution of life into the realm of burning suns and lifeless nebulae. Human civilization or progress, on the other hand, which exists only in and through living members of the species, is outwardly so similar to the evolution of plants and animals, that it has been inevitable that there should have been sweeping applications of the principles of organic development to the facts of cultural growth. This of course is reasoning by analogy, or arguing that because two things resemble each other in one point they will also be similar in others. In the absence of knowledge, such assumptions are justifiable as assumptions. Too often, however, their effect is to predetermine mental attitude, with the result that when the evidence begins to accumulate which could prove or disprove the assumption based on analogy, this evidence is no longer viewed impartially and judiciously, but is merely distributed and disposed of in such a way as not to interfere with the established conviction into which the original tentative guess has long since turned.

This is what has happened in the field of organic and social evolution. This distinction between them, which is so obvious that to former ages it seemed too commonplace to remark upon, except incidentally and indirectly, has been largely obscured in the last fifty years through the hold which thoughts connected with the idea of organic evolution have had on minds of the time. It even seems fair to say that this confusion has been greater and more general among those to whom study and scholarship are a daily pursuit than to the remainder of the world.

And yet many aspects of the difference between the organic and that in human life which is not organic, are so plain that a child can grasp them, and that all human beings, including the veriest savages, constantly employ the distinction. Everyone is aware that we are born with certain powers and that we acquire others. There is no need of argument to prove that we derive some things in our lives and make-up from nature through heredity, and that other things come to us through agencies with which heredity has nothing to do. No one has yet been found to assert that any human being is born with an inherent knowledge of the multiplication table; nor, on the other hand, to doubt that the children of a Negro are born Negroes through the operation of hereditary forces. Some qualities in every individual are however clearly debatable ground; and when the development of civilization as a whole and the evolution of life as a whole are compared, the distinction of the processes involved has too often been allowed to lapse.

Some millions of years ago, it is currently taught, natural selection, or some other evolutionary agency, first caused birds to appear in the world. They sprang from reptiles. Conditions were such that the struggle for existence on the earth was hard; while in the air there were safety and room. Gradually, either by a series of almost imperceptible gradations through a long line of successive generations, or by more marked and sudden leaps in a shorter period, the group of birds was evolved from its reptilian ancestors. In this development, feathers were acquired and scales lost; the grasping faculty of the front legs was converted into an ability to sustain the body in the air. The advantages of resistance enjoyed by a cold-blooded organization were given up for the equivalent or greater compensation of the superior activity that goes with warm-bloodedness. The net result of this chapter of evolutionary history was that a new power, that of aerial locomotion, was added to the sum total of faculties possessed by the highest group of animals, the vertebrates. The vertebrate animals as a whole, however, were not affected. The majority of them are without the power of flight as their ancestors were millions of years ago. The birds, in turn, had lost certain faculties which they once possessed, and presumably would still possess were it not for the acquisition of their wings.

In the last few years human beings have also attained the power of aerial locomotion. But the process by which this power was attained, and its effects on the species, are as different from those which characterized the acquisition of flight by the first birds as it is possible for them to be. Our means of flying are outside of our bodies. A bird is born with a pair of wings, but we have invented the aeroplane. The bird renounced a potential pair of hands to get his wings; we, because our new faculty is not part of our congenital make-up, keep all the organs and capacities of our forefathers but add to them the new ability. The process of the development of civilization is clearly one of accumulation: the old is retained, in spite of the incoming of the new. In organic evolution, the introduction of new features is generally possible only through the loss or modification of existing organs or faculties.

In short, the growth of new species of animals takes place through, and in fact consists of, changes in their organic constitution. As regards the growth of civilization, on the other hand, the one example cited is sufficient to show that change and progress can take place through an invention without any such constitutional alteration of the human species.

There is another way of looking at this difference. It is clear that as a new species originates, it is derived wholly from the individual or individuals that first showed the particular traits distinguishing the new species. When we say that it is derived from these individuals we mean, literally, that it is descended. In other words, the species is composed only of such individuals as contain the "blood"—the germ-plasm—of particular ancestors. Heredity is thus the indispensable means of transmission. When however an invention is made, the entire human race is capable of profiting thereby. People who have not the slightest blood kinship to the first designers of aeroplanes can fly and are flying today. Many a father has used, enjoyed, and profited by the invention of his son. In the evolution of animals, the descendant can build upon the inheritance transmitted to him from his ancestors, and may rise to higher powers and more perfect development; but the ancestor is, in the very nature of things, precluded from thus profiting from his descendant. In short, organic evolution is essentially and inevitably connected with hereditary processes; the social evolution which characterizes the progress of civilization, on the other hand, is not, or not necessarily, tied up with hereditary agencies.

The whale is not only a warm-blooded mammal, but is recognized as the remote descendant of carnivorous land animals. In some few million years, as such genealogies are usually reckoned, this animal lost his legs for running, his claws for holding and tearing, his original hair and external ears that would be useless or worse in water, and acquired fins and fluke, a cylindrical body, a layer of fat, and the power of holding his breath. There was much that the species gave up; more, on the whole, perhaps than it gained. Certainly some of its parts have degenerated. But there was one new power that it did achieve: that of roaming the ocean indefinitely.

The parallel and also contrast is in the human acquisition of the identical faculty. We do not, in gradual alteration from father to son, change our arms into flippers and grow a tail. We do not enter the water at all to navigate it. We build a boat. And what this means is that we preserve our bodies and our natal faculties intact, unaltered from those of our fathers and remotest ancestors. Our means of marine travel is outside of our natural endowment. We make it and use it: the original whale had to turn himself into a boat. It took him countless generations to attain to his present condition. All individuals that failed to conform to type left no offspring; or none that went into the blood of the whales of today.

Again, we may compare human and animal beings when groups of them reach a new and arctic environment, or when the climate of the tract where the race is established slowly becomes colder and colder. The non-human mammal species comes to have heavy hair. The polar bear is shaggy; his Sumatran relative sleek. The arctic hare is enveloped in soft fur; the jack-rabbit in comparison is shabbily thin and moth-eaten. Good furs come from the far north, and they lose in richness, in quality, and in value, in proportion as they are stripped from animals of the same species that inhabit milder regions. And this difference is racial, not individual. The jack-rabbit would quickly perish with the end of summer in Greenland; the caged polar bear suffers from temperature warmth within the massive coat which nature has fastened on him.

Now there are people who look for the same sort of inborn peculiarities in the Arctic Eskimo and Samoyed; and find them, because they look for them. That the Eskimo is furry, no one can assert: in fact, we are hairier than he. But it is asserted that he is fat-protected—like the blubber-covered seal that he lives on; and that he devours quantities of meat and oil because he needs them. The true amount of his fat, compared with that of other human beings, remains to be ascertained. He probably has more than the European; but probably no more than the normal full-blooded Samoan and Hawaiian from under the tropics. And as to his diet, if this is seal and seal and seal all winter long, it is not from any congenital craving of his stomach, but because he does not know how to get himself anything else. The Alaskan miner, and the arctic and antarctic explorer, do not guzzle blubber. Wheat-flour, eggs, coffee, sugar, potatoes, canned vegetables—whatever the exigencies of their vocation and the cost of transportation permit—make up their fare. The Eskimo is only too anxious to join them; and both he and they can thrive on the one diet as on the other.

In fact, what the human inhabitant of intemperate latitudes does, is not to develop a peculiar digestive system, any more than he grows hair. He changes his environment, and thereby is able to retain his original body unaltered. He builds a closed house, which keeps out the wind and retains the heat of his body. He makes a fire or lights a lamp. He skins a seal or a caribou of the furry hide with which natural selection or other processes of organic evolution have endowed these beasts; he has his wife make him a shirt and trousers, boots and gloves, or two sets of them; he puts them on; and in a few years, or days, he is provided with the protection which it took the polar bear and the arctic hare, the sable and the ptarmigan, untold periods to acquire. What is more, his baby, and his baby's baby, and his hundredth descendant are born as naked, and unarmed physically, as he and his hundredth ancestor were born.

That this difference in method of resisting a difficult environment, as followed respectively by the polar bear species and the human Eskimo race, is absolute, need not be asserted. That the difference is deep, is unquestionable. That it is as important as it is often neglected, it is the object of this essay to establish.

It has long been the custom to say that the difference is that between body and mind; that animals have their physiques adapted to their circumstances, but that man's superior intelligence enables him to rise superior to such lowly needs. But this is not the most significant point of difference. It is true that without the much greater mental faculties of man, he could not achieve the attainments the lack of which keeps the brute chained to the limitations of his anatomy. But the greater human intelligence in itself does not cause the differences that exist. This psychic superiority is only the indispensable condition of what is peculiarly human: civilization. Directly, it is the civilization in which every Eskimo, every Alaskan miner or arctic discoverer is reared, and not any greater inborn faculty, that leads him to build houses, ignite fire, and wear clothing. The distinction between animal and man which counts is not that of the physical and mental, which is one of relative degree, but that of the organic and social which is one of kind. The beast has mentality, and we have bodies; but in civilization man has something that no animal has.

That this distinction is actually something more than that of the physical and mental, appears from an example that may be chosen from the non-bodily: speech.

On the surface, human and animal speech, in spite of the enormously greater richness and complexity of the former, are much alike. Both express emotions, possibly ideas, in sounds formed by bodily organs and understood by the hearing individual. But the difference between the so-called language of brutes and that of men is infinitely great; as a homely illustration will set forth.

A newly-born pup is brought up in a litter of kittens by a fostering cat. Familiar anecdotes and newspaper paragraphs to the contrary, the youngster will bark and growl, not purr or miaow. He will not even try to do the latter. The first time his toe is stepped on, he will whine, not squeal, just as surely as when thoroughly angered he will bite as his never-beheld mother did, and not even attempt to claw as he has seen his foster-mother do. For half his life seclusion may keep him from sight or sound or scent of another dog. But then let a bark or a snarl reach him through the restraining wall, and he will be all attention—more than at any voice ever uttered by his cat associates. Let the bark be repeated, and interest will give way to excitement, and he will answer in kind, as certainly as, put with a bitch, the sexual impulses of his species will manifest themselves. It cannot be doubted that dog speech is ineradicably part of dog nature, as fully contained in it without training or culture, as wholly part of the dog organism, as are teeth or feet or stomach or motions or instincts. No degree of contact with cats, or deprivation of association with his own kind, can make a dog acquire cat speech, or lose his own, any more than it can cause him to switch his tail instead of wagging it, to rub his sides against his master instead of leaping against him, or to grow whiskers and carry his drooping ears erect.

Let us take a French baby, born in France of French parents, themselves descended for numerous generations from French-speaking ancestors. Let us, at once after birth, entrust the infant to a mute nurse, with instructions to let no one handle or see her charge, while she travels by the directest route to the interior heart of China. There she delivers the child to a Chinese couple, who legally adopt it, and rear it as their son. Now suppose three or ten or thirty years passed. Is it needful to discuss what the growing or grown Frenchman will speak? Not a word of French; pure Chinese, without a trace of accent and with Chinese fluency; and nothing else.

It is true that there is a common delusion, frequent even among educated people, that some hidden influence of his French-talking ancestors will survive in the adopted Chinaman: that it is only necessary to send him to France with a batch of real Chinamen, and he will acquire his mother's tongue with appreciably greater facility, fluency, correctness, and naturalness than his Mongolian companions. That a belief is common, however, is as likely to stamp it a common superstition as a common truth. And a reasonable biologist, in other words, an expert qualified to speak of heredity, will pronounce this answer to this problem in heredity, superstition. He might merely choose a politer phrase.

Now there is something deep-going here. No amount of association with Chinese would turn our young Frenchman's eyes from blue to black, or slant them, or flatten his nose, or coarsen or stiffen his wavy, oval-sectioned hair; and yet his speech is totally that of his associates, in no measure that of his blood kin. His eyes and his nose and his hair are his from heredity; his language is non-hereditary—as much so as the length to which he allows his hair to grow, or the hole which, in conformity to fashion, he may or may not bore in his ears. It is not so much that speech is mental and facial proportions are physical; the distinction that has meaning and use is that human language is non-hereditary and social, eye-color and nose-shape hereditary and organic. By the same criterion, dog speech, and all that is vaguely called the language of animals, is in a class with men's noses, the proportions of their bones, the color of their skin, and the slope of their eyes, and not in a class with any human idiom. It is inherited, and therefore organic. By a human standard, it is not really language at all, except by the sort of metaphor that speaks of the language of the flowers.

It is true that now and then a French child would be found that under the conditions of the experiment assumed, would learn Chinese more slowly, less idiomatically, and with less power of expression, than the average Chinaman. But there would also be French babies, and as many, that would acquire the Chinese language more quickly, more fluently, with richer power of revealing their emotions and defining their ideas, than the normal Chinese. These are individual differences, which it would be absurd to deny, but which do not affect the average, and are not to the point. One Englishman speaks better English, and more of it, than another, and he may also through precocity, learn it much sooner; but one talks English no more and no less truly than the other.

There is one form of animal expression in which the influence of association has sometimes been alleged to be greater than that of heredity. This is the song of birds. There is a good deal of conflicting opinion, and apparently of evidence, on this point. Many birds have a strong inherent impulse to imitate sounds. It is also a fact that the singing of one individual stimulates the other—as with dogs, wolves, cats, frogs, and most noisy animals. That in certain species of birds capable of a complex song the full development will not often be reached in individuals raised out of hearing of their kind, may probably be admitted. But it seems to be clear that every species has a song or call distinctively its own; that this minimum is attainable without association by every normal member of the singing sex, as soon as conditions of age, food, and warmth are proper, and the requisite stimulus of noise, or silence, or sex development, is present. That there has been serious conflict of opinion as to the nature of bird song, will ultimately be found to be chiefly due to the pronouncement of opinions on the matter by those who read their own mental states and activities into animals—a common fallacy that every biological student is now carefully trained against at the outset of his career. In any event, whether one bird does or does not in some degree "learn" from another, there is no fragment of evidence that bird song is a tradition, that like human speech or human music it accumulates and develops from age to age, that it is inevitably altered from generation to generation by fashion or custom, and that it is impossible for it ever to remain the same: in other words, that it is a social thing or due to a process even remotely akin to those affecting the constituents of human civilization.

It is also true that there is in human life a series of utterances that are of the type of animal cries. A man in pain moans without purpose of communication. The sound is literally pressed from him. A person in supreme fright may shriek. We know that his cry is unintended, what the physiologist calls a reflex action. The true shriek is as liable to escape the victim pinned before the approching engineerless train, as him who is pursued by thinking and planning enemies. The woodsman crushed by a rock forty miles from the nearest human being, will moan like the run-over city dweller surrounded by a crowd waiting for the speeding ambulance. Such cries are of a class with those of animals. In fact, really to understand the "speech" of brutes, we must think ourselves into a condition in which our utterances would be totally restricted to such instinctive cries—"inarticulate" is their general though often inaccurate designation. In an exact sense, they are not language at all.

This is precisely the point. We undoubtedly have certain activities of utterance, certain faculties and habits of sound production, that are truly parallel with those of animals; and we also have something more that is quite different and without parallel among the animals. To deny that something purely animal underlies human speech, is fatuous; but it would be equally narrow to believe that because our speech springs from an animal foundation, and originated in this foundation, it therefore is nothing but animal mentality and utterances greatly magnified. A house may be built on rock; without this base it might be impossible for it to have been erected; but no one will maintain that therefore the house is nothing but improved and glorified stone.

As a matter of fact, the purely animal element in human speech is small. Apart from laughter and crying, it finds rare utterance. Our interjections are denied by philologists as true speech, or at best but half admitted. It is a fact that they differ from full words in not being voiced, generally, to convey a meaning—nor to conceal one. But even these particles are shaped and dictated by fashion, by custom, by the type of civilization to which we belong, in short by social and not by organic elements. When I drive the hammer on my thumb instead of on the head of the nail, an involuntary "damn" may escape me as readily if I am alone in the house, as if companions stand on each side. Perhaps more readily. So far, the exclamation does not serve the purpose of speech and is not speech. But the Spaniard will say "carramba" and not "damn"; and the Frenchman, the German, the Chinaman, will avail himself of still different expression. The American says "ouch" when hurt. Other nationalities do not understand this syllable. Each people has its own sound; some even two— one used by men and the other by women. A Chinaman will understand a laugh, a moan, a crying child, as well as we understand it, and as well as a dog understands the snarl of another dog. But he must learn "ouch," or it is meaningless. No dog, on the other hand, ever has given utterance to a new snarl, unintelligible to other dogs, as a result of having been brought up in different associations. Even this lowest element of human speech, then, this involuntary half-speech of exclamations, is therefore shaped by social influences.

Herodotus tells of an Egyptian king, who, wishing to ascertain the parent tongue of humanity, had some infants brought up in isolation from their own kind, with only goats as companions and for sustenance. When the children, grown older, were revisited, they cried the word "bekos," or, subtracting the ending which the normalizing and sensitive Greek could not endure omitting from anything that passed his lips, more probably "bek." The king then sent to all countries to learn in what land this vocable meant something. He ascertained that in the Phrygian idiom it signified bread, and, assuming that the children were crying for food, concluded that they spoke Phrygian in voicing their "natural" human speech, and that this tongue must therefore be the original one of mankind. The king's belief in an inherent and congenital language of man, which only the blind accidents of time had distorted into a multitude of idioms, may seem simple; but naive as it is, inquiry would reveal crowds of civilized people still adhering to it.

This however is not our moral to the tale. That lies in the fact that the one and only word attributed to the children, "bek," was, if the story has any authenticity whatsoever, only a reflection or imitation— as the commentators of Herodotus long since conjectured—of the bleating of the goats that were the children's only associates and instructors. In short, if it is allowable to deduce any inference from so apocryphal an anecdote, what it proves is that there is no natural and therefore no organic human language.

Thousands of years later another sovereign, the Mogul emperor Akbar, repeated the experiment with the intent of ascertaining the "natural" religion of mankind. His band of children were shut up in a house. When, the necessary time having elapsed, the doors were opened in the presence of the expectant and enlightened ruler, his disappointment was great: the children trooped out as dumb as deaf-mutes. Faith dies hard, however; and we may suspect that it would take a third trial, under modern chosen and controlled conditions, to satisfy some natural scientists that speech, for the human individual and for the human race, is wholly an acquired and not a hereditary thing, entirely outward and not at all inward—a social product and not an organic growth.

Human and animal speech, then, though one roots in the other, are in the nature of a different order. They resemble each other only as the flight of a bird and of an aeronaut are alike. That the analogy between them has frequently deceived, proves only the guilelessness of the human mind. The operative processes are wholly unlike; and this, to him who is desirous of understanding, is far more important than the similarity of effect. The savage and the peasant who cure by cleaning the knife and leaving the wound unattended, have observed certain indisputable facts. They know that cleanness aids, dirt on the whole impedes recovery. They know the knife as the cause, the wound as the effect; and they grasp, too, the correct principle that treatment of the cause is in general more likely to be effective than treatment of the symptom. They fail only in not inquiring into the process that may be involved. Knowing nothing of the nature of sepsis, of bacteria, of the agencies of putrefaction and retardation of healing, they fall back on agencies more familiar to themselves, and use, as best they may, the process of magic intertwined with that of medicine. They carefully scrape the knife; they oil it; they keep it bright. The facts from which they work are correct; their logic is sound enough; they merely do not distinguish between two irreconcilable processes—that of magic and that of physiological chemistry—and apply one in place of another. The student of today who reads the civilizationally moulded mind of men into the mentality of a dog or ape, or who tries to explain civilization—that is, history—by organic factors, commits an error which is less antiquated and more in fashion, but of the same kind and nature.

A. R. Radcliffe-Brown

On the Concept of Function in Social Science

It is difficult to separate the concept of functionalism in anthropology from the name of Franz Boas. Boas was one of the most influential of all American anthropologists. Though he wrote very little, his wide-ranging mind seems, in retrospect, to have foreseen many of the developments that now seem so new and exciting to anthropologists. Boas not only insisted that anthropologists use a field method approach to the study of cultural groups, he believed that understanding could only be arrived at through the use of the informant's language itself and through participant observation. He added much to the science of linguistics; he suggested in a little-known paper the use of statistical method. But perhaps his most influential notion was the idea that cultures must be studied as functioning wholes.

It was this idea that lay behind much of the work of the British "functionalist" school. These men, who called themselves social anthropologists, were pessimistic about the possibilities of reconstructing human history, and they turned, instead, to the study of cultures as a whole. Like Durkheim, the functionalists insisted that explanation of a social trait lay in other social factors. For A. R. Radcliffe-Brown, understanding of a particular social trait was achieved when one could explain how that trait functioned to maintain a society or culture in operation.

Radcliffe-Brown wrote the following essay in response to some criticisms of functionalism by another anthropologist, Dr. Abraham Lesser. Lesser had criticized what he felt to be a conflict between functionalism and historical reconstruction. He was also unenthusiastic about the functionalist tendency to stress certain aspects of social behavior above others. Dr. Lesser believed that functionalism threatened the holistic approach that was anthropology's trademark. Though there was some truth to these assertions, Dr. Lesser's final criticism—that functionalism would tend to stress psychology—has been thoroughly disproven by subsequent developments. In fact, functionalism led to a stress on cultural determinism and a decreasing emphasis on psychology.

Today's functionalists are not in agreement about the nature of their approach, and anthropological literature is filled with arguments attesting to the validity or uselessness of particular varieties of functionalism. By and large, however, all agree that the model of society as a homeostatic mechanism, maintaining itself in a state of equilibrium, has been a useful one. Today's emphasis is placed largely on attempts to see societies as organisms interacting with the environment, rather than as discrete social units which maintain and transform themselves without reference to environment, biology, or psychology.

THE CONCEPT OF FUNCTION applied to human societies is based on an analogy between social life and organic life. The recognition of the analogy and of some of its important implications is at least as old as Protagoras and Plato. In the nineteenth centry the analogy, the concept of function, and the word itself appear frequently in social philosophy and sociology. So far as I know the first systematic formulation of the concept as applying to the strictly scientific study of society was that of Emile Durkheim in 1895.[1]

Durkheim's definition is that the "function" of a social institution is the correspondence between it and the needs of the social organism. This definition requires some elaboration. In the first place, to avoid possible ambiguity and in particular the possibility of a teleological interpretation, I would like to substitute for the term "needs" the term "necessary conditions of existence," or, if the term "need" is used, it is to be understood only in this sense. It may here be noted, as a point to be returned to, that any attempt to apply this concept of function in social science involves the assumption that there *are* necessary conditions of existence for human societies just as there are for animal organisms, and that they can be discovered by the proper kind of scientific enquiry.

For the further elucidation of the concept it is convenient to use the analogy between social life and organic life. Like all analogies it has to be used with care. An animal organism is an agglomeration of cells and interstitial fluids arranged in relation to one another not as an aggregate but as an integrated whole. For the bio-chemist, it is a complexly integrated system of complex molecules. The system of relations by which these units are related is the organic structure. As the terms are here used the organism *is not* itself the structure; it is a collection of units (cells or molecules) arranged in a structure, i.e., in a set of relations; the organism *has* a structure. Two mature animals of the same species and sex consist of similar units combined in a similar structure. The structure is thus to be defined as a set of relations between the entities. (The structure of a cell is in the same way a set of relations between complex molecules, and the structure of an atom is a set of relations between electrons and protons.) As long as it lives the organism preserves a certain continuity structure although it does not preserve the complete identity of its constituent parts. It loses some of its constituent molecules by respiration or excretion; it takes in others by respiration and alimentary absorption. Over a period its constituent cells do not remain the same. But the structural arrangement of the constituent units does remain similar. The process by which this structural continuity of the organism is maintained is called life. The life-process consists of the activities and interactions of the constituent units of the organism, the cells, and the organs into which the cells are united.

As the word function is here being used the life of an organism is conceived as the *functioning* of its structure. It is through and by the continuity of the functioning that the continuity of the structure is preserved. If we consider any recurrent part of the life-process, such as respiration, digestion, etc., its *function* is the part it plays in, the contribution it makes to, the life of the organism as a whole. As the terms are here being used a cell or an organ has an *activity* and that activity has a *function*. It is true that we commonly speak of the secretion of gastric fluid as a "function" of the stomach. As the words are here used we should say that this is an "activity" of the stomach, the "function" of which is to change the proteins of food into a form in which these are absorbed and distributed by the blood to the tissues.[2] We may note that the function of a recurrent physiological process is thus a correspondence between it and the needs (i.e., necessary conditions of existence) of the organism.

If we set out upon a systematic investigation of the nature of organisms and organic life there are three sets of problems presented to us. (There are, in addition, certain other sets of problems concerning aspects or characteristics of organic life with which we are not here concerned.) One is that of morphology—what kinds of organic structures are there, what similarities and variations do they show, and how can they be classified? Second are the problems of physiology—how, in general, do organic structures function, what, therefore, is the nature of the life-process? Third are the problems of development—how do new types of organisms come into existence?

To turn from organic life to social life, if we examine such a community as an African or Australian tribe we can recognize the existence of a social structure. Individual human beings, the essential units in this instance, are connected by a definite set of social relations into an integrated whole. The continuity of the social structure, like that of an organic structure, is not destroyed by changes in the units. Individuals may leave the society, by death or otherwise; others may enter it. The continuity of structure is maintained by the process of social life, which consists of the activities and interactions of the individual human beings and of the organized groups into which they are united. The social life of the community is here defined as the *functioning* of the social structure. The *function* of any recurrent activity, such as the punishment of a crime, or a funeral ceremony, is the part it plays in the social life as a whole and therefore the contribution it makes to the maintenance of the structural continuity.

The concept of function as here defined thus involves the notion of a *structure* consisting of a *set of relations* amongst *unit entities*, the *continuity* of the structure being maintained by a *life-process* made up of the *activities* of the constituent units.

If, with these concepts in mind, we set out on a systematic investigation of the nature of human society and of social life, we find presented to us three sets of problems. First, the problems of social morphology—what kinds of social structures are there, what are their similarities and differences, how are they to be classified? Second, the problems of social physiology—how do social structures function? Third, the problems of development—how do new types of social structure come into existence?

Two important points where the analogy between organism and society breaks down must be noted. In an animal organism it is possible to observe the organic structure to a large extent independently of its functioning. It is therefore possible to make a morphology which is independent of physiology. But in human society the social structure as a whole can only be *observed* in its functioning. Some of the features of social structure, such as the geographical distribution of individuals and groups can be directly observed, but most of the social relations which in their totality constitute the structure, such as relations of father and son, buyer and seller, ruler and subject, cannot be observed except in the social activities in which the relations are functioning. It follows that a social morphology cannot be established independently of a social physiology.

The second point is that an animal organism does not, in the course of its life, change its structural type. A pig does not become a hippopotamus. (The development of the animal from germination to maturity is not a change of type since the process in all its stages is typical for the species.) On the other hand a society in the course of its history can and does change its structural type without any breach of continuity.

By the definition here offered "function" is the contribution which a partial activity makes to the total activity of which it is a part. The function of a particular social usage is the contribution it makes to the total social life as the functioning of the total social system. Such a view implies that a social system (the total social structure of a society together with the totality of social usages, in which that structure appears and on which it depends for its continued existence) has a certain kind of unity, which we may speak of as a functional unity. We may define it as a condition in which all parts of the social system work together with a sufficient degree of harmony or internal consistency, i.e., without producing persistent conflicts which can neither be resolved nor regulated.[3]

This idea of the functional unity of a social system is, of course, a hypothesis. But it is one which, to the functionalist, it seems worth while to test by systematic examination of the facts.

There is another aspect of functional theory that should be briefly mentioned. To return to the analogy of social life and organic life, we recognize that an organism may function more or less efficiently and so we set up a special science of pathology to deal with all phenomena of disfunction. We distinguish in an organism what we call health and disease. The Greeks of the fifth century B.C. thought that one might apply the same notion to society, to the city-state, distinguishing conditions of *eunomia,* good order, social health, from *dysnomia,* disorder, social ill-health. In the nineteenth century Durkheim, in his application of the notion of function, sought to lay the basis for a scientific social pathology, based on a morphology and a physiology.[4] In his works, particularly those on suicide and on the division of labor, he attempted to find objective criteria by which to judge whether a given society at a given time is normal or pathological, eunomic or dysnomic. For example, he tried to show that the increase of the rate of suicide in many countries during part of the nineteenth century is symptomatic of a dysnomic or, in his terminology, anomic, social condition. Probably there is no sociologist who would hold that Durkheim really succeeded in establishing an objective basis for a science of social pathology.[5]

In relation to organic structures we can find strictly objective criteria by which to distinguish disease from health, pathological from normal, for disease is that which either threatens the organism with death (the dissolution of its structure) or interferes with the activities which are characteristic of the organic type. Societies do not die in the same sense that animals die and therefore we cannot define dysnomia as that which leads, if unchecked, to the death of a society. Further a society differs from an organism in that it can change its structural type, or can be absorbed as an integral part of a larger society. Therefore we cannot define dysnomia as a disturbance of the usual activities of a social type (as Durkheim tried to do).

Let us return for a moment to the Greeks. They conceived the health of an organism and the eunomia of a society as being in each instance a condition of the harmonious working together of its parts.[6] Now this, where society is concerned, is the same thing as what was considered above as the functional unity or inner consistency of a social system, and it is suggested that for the degree of functional unity of a particular society it may be possible to establish a purely objective criterion. Admittedly this cannot be done at present; but the science of human society is as yet in its extreme infancy. So that it may be that we should say that while an organism that is attacked by a virulent disease will react thereto, and, if its reaction fails, will die, a society that is thrown into a condition of functional disunity or inconsistency (for this we now provisionally identify with dysnomia) will not die, except in such comparatively rare instances as an Australian tribe overwhelmed by the white man's destructive force, but will continue to struggle toward some sort of eunomia, some kind of social health, and may, in the course of this, change its structural type. This process, it seems, the "functionalist" has ample opportunities of observing at the present day, in native peoples subjected to the domination of the civilized nations, and in those nations themselves.[7]

Space will not allow a discussion here of another aspect of functional theory, viz., the question whether change of social type is or is not dependent on function i.e., on the laws of social physiology. My own view is that there is such a dependence and that its nature can be studied in the development of the legal and political institutions, the economic systems and the religions of Europe through the last twenty-five centuries. For the pre-literate societies with which anthropology is concerned it is not possible to study the details of long processes of change of type. The one kind of change which the anthropologist can observe is the disintegration of social structures. Yet even here we can observe and compare spontaneous movements towards reintegration. We have, for instance, in Africa, in Oceania, and in America the appearance of new religions which can be interpreted on a functional hypothesis as attempts to relieve a condition of social dysnomia produced by the rapid modification of the social life through contact with white civilization.

The concept of function as defined above constitutes a "working hypothesis" by which a number of problems are formulated for investigation. No scientific enquiry is possible without some such formulation of working hypotheses. Two remarks are necessary here. One is that the hypothesis does not require the dogmatic assertion that everything in the life of every community has a function. It only requires the assumption that it *may* have one, and that we are justified in seeking to discover it. The second is that what appears to be the same social usage in two societies may have different functions in the two. Thus the practice of celibacy in the Roman Catholic Church of to-day has very different functions from those of celibacy in the early Christian church. In other words, in order to define a social usage, and therefore in order to make valid comparisons between the usages of different peoples or periods it is necessary to consider not merely the form of the usage but also its function. On this basis, for example, belief in a Supreme Being in a simple society is something different from such a belief in a modern civilized community.

The acceptance of the functional hypothesis or point of view outlined above results in the recognition of a vast number of problems for the solution of which there are required wide comparative studies of societies of many diverse types and also intensive studies of as many single societies as possible. In field studies of the simpler peoples it leads, first of all, to a direct study of the social life of the community as the functioning of a social structure, and of this there are several examples in recent literature. Since the function of a social activity is to be found by examining its effects upon individuals, these are studied, either in the average individual or in both average and exceptional individuals. Further the hypothesis leads to attempts to investigate directly the functional consistency or unity of a social system and to determine as far as possible in each instance the nature of that unity. Such field studies will obviously be different in many ways from studies carried out from other points of view, e.g., the ethnological point of view that lays emphasis on diffusion. We do not have to say that one point of view is better than another, but only that they are different, and any particular piece of work should be judged in reference to what it aims to do.

If the view here outlined is taken as one form of "functionalism," a few remarks on Dr. Lesser's paper become permissible. He makes reference to a difference of "content" in functional and non-functional anthropology. From the point of view here presented the "content" or subject-matter of social anthropology is the whole social life of a people in all its aspects. For convenience of handling it is often necessary to devote special attention to some particular part or aspect of the social life, but if functionalism means any thing at all it does mean the attempt to see the social life of a people as a whole, as a functional unity.

Dr. Lesser speaks of the functionalist as stressing "the psychological aspects of culture." I presume that he here refers to the functionalist's recognition that the usages of a society work or "function" only through their effects in the life, i.e., in the thoughts, sentiments and actions of individuals.

The "functionalist" point of view here presented does therefore imply that we have to investigate as thoroughly as possible all aspects of social life, considering them in relation to one another, and that an essential part of the task is the investigation of the individual and of the way in which he is moulded by or adjusted to the social life.

Turning from content to method Dr. Lesser seems to find some conflict between the functional point of view and the historical. This is reminiscent of the attempts formerly made to see a conflict between sociology and history. There need be no conflict, but there is a difference.

There is not, and cannot be, any conflict between the functional hypothesis and the view that any culture, any social system, is the end-result of a unique series of historical accidents. The process of development of the race-horse from its five-toed ancestor was a unique series of historical accidents. This does not conflict with the view of the physiologist that the horse of to-day and all the antecedent forms conform or conformed to physiological laws, i.e., to the necessary conditions of organic existence. Palaeontology and physiology are not in conflict. One "explanation" of the race-horse is to be found in its history—how it came to be just what it is and where it is. Another and entirely independent "explanation" is to show how the horse is a special exemplification of physiological laws. Similarly one "explanation" of a social system will be its history, where we know it—the detailed account of how it came to be what it is and where it is. Another "explanation" of the same system is obtained by showing (as the functionalist attempts to do) that it is a special exemplification of laws of social physiology or social functioning. The two kinds of explanation do not conflict, but supplement one another.[8]

The functional hypothesis is in conflict with two views that are held by some ethnologists, and it is probably these, held as they often are without precise formulation, that are the cause of the antagonism to that approach. One is the "shreds and patches" theory of culture, the designation being taken from a phrase of Professor Lowie [9] when he speaks of "that planless hodge-podge, that thing of shreds and patches called civilization." The concentration of attention on what is called the diffusion of culture-traits tends to produce a conception of culture as a collection of disparate entities (the so-called traits) brought together by pure historical accident and having only accidental relations to one another. The conception is rarely formulated and maintained with any precision, but as a half unconscious point of view it does seem to control the thinking of many ethnologists. It is, of course, in direct conflict with the hypothesis of the functional unity of social systems.

The second view which is in direct conflict with the functional hypothesis is the view that there are no discoverable significant sociological laws such as the functionalist is seeking. I know that some two or three ethnologists say that they hold this view, but I have found it impossible to know what they mean, or on what sort of evidence (rational or empirical) they would base their contention. Generalizations about any sort of subject matter are of two kinds: the generalizations of common opinion, and generalizations that have been verified or demonstrated by a systematic examination of evidence afforded by precise observations systematically made. Generalizations of the latter kind are called scientific laws. Those who hold that there are no laws of human society cannot hold that there are no generalizations about human society because they themselves hold such generalizations and even make new ones of their own. They must therefore hold that in the field of social phenomena, in contradistinction to physical and biological phenomena, any attempt at the systematic testing of existing generalizations or towards the discovery and verification of new ones, is, for some unexplained reason, futile, or, as Dr. Radin puts it, "crying for the moon." Argument against such a contention is unprofitable or indeed impossible.

NOTES

[1] *Règles de la Méthode Sociologique.*

[2] The insistence on this precise form of terminology is only for the sake of the analogy that is to be drawn. I have no objection to the use of the term function in physiology to denote both the activity of an organ and the results of that activity in maintaining life.

[3] Opposition, i.e., organized and regulated antagonism, is, of course, an essential feature of every social system.

[4] For what is here called dysnomia Durkheim used the term anomia (*anomie* in French). This is to my mind inappropriate. Health and disease, eunomia and dysnomia are essentially relative terms.

[5] I would personally agree in the main with the criticisms of Roger Lacombe (*La Méthode Sociologique de Durkheim,* 1926, Ch. IV) on Durkheim's general theory of social pathology, and with the criticisms of Durkheim's treatment of suicide presented by Halbwachs, *Les Causes du Suicide.*

[6] See, for example, the Fourth Book of Plato's *Republic.*

[7] To avoid misunderstanding it is perhaps necessary to observe that this distinction of eunomic and dysnomic social conditions does not give us any evaluation of these societies as "good" or "bad." A savage tribe practicing polygamy, cannibalism, and sorcery can possibly show a higher degree of functional unity or consistency than the United States of 1935. This objective judgment, for such it must be if it is to be scientific, is something very different from any judgment as to which of the two social systems is the better, the more to be desired or approved.

[8] I see no reason at all why the two kinds of study—the historical and the functional—should not be carried on side by side in perfect harmony. In fact, for

fourteen years I have been teaching both—the historical and geographical study of peoples under the name of ethnology in close association with archaeology, and the functional study of social systems under the name of social anthropology. I do think that there are many disadvantages in mixing the two subjects together and confusing them. See "The Methods of Ethnology and Social Anthropology" (*South African Journal of Science*, 1923, pp. 124–47).

[9] *Primitive Society*, 441. A concise statement of this point of view is the following passage from Dr. Ruth Benedict's "The Concept of the Guardian Spirit in North America" (*Memoirs*, American Anthropological Association, 29, 1923), page 84: "It is, so far as we can see, an ultimate fact of human nature that man builds up his culture out of disparate elements, combining and recombining them; and until we have abandoned the superstition that the result is an organism functionally interrelated, we shall be unable to see our cultural life objectively, or to control its manifestations." I think that probably neither Professor Lowie nor Dr. Benedict would, at the present time, maintain this view of the nature of culture.

Leslie A. White

The Science of Culture

Leslie White's view of culture represents a more self-conscious amalgam of Marxian and superorganic notions, coupled with an emphasis upon evolution that was altogether absent from both Durkheimian sociology and functionalist anthropology. White's attempts to synthesize these divergent tendencies led him to insist that, in fact, evolution of society does occur and that the mechanism of cultural evolution is to be understood in the study of purely cultural determinants.

IF PHILOSOPHY IS A mechanism of adjustment of the human animal to his cosmic setting, then man is at the bottom of philosophic concern. . . . We can trace the history and the growth of science from the standpoint of determinants of human behavior. Astrology was an attempt to appraise the role of heavenly bodies in human affairs and to predict the course of human events as determined by the stars. The philosophy of science found its first expression in astronomy because the heavenly bodies, being the least significant of determinants of human behavior, could be dislodged most easily from the anthropomorphic tradition in which self was confused with not-self. The point of view and the techniques of science, once established in the sector of the celestial, began to spread to other areas. The course of expansion of the scope of science was determined by this law: science will advance and develop in inverse ratio to the significance of phenomena as determinants of human behavior. Terrestrial physics and mechanics followed astronomy. The physical sciences took form before the biological because physical phenomena are less significant as determinants of human behavior than are biological phenomena. Within the biological realm, anatomy develops first, then physiology and psychology. The point upon which these three sciences focused was the individual organism. But it came eventually to be realized that there is a class of phenomena outside and beyond the individual that is nevertheless powerful and significant in the determination of his behavior. Sociology and social psychology were the organizations of scientific techniques to grapple with this class of meta-individual determinants. In the organization of these sciences it was assumed that the categories of determinants of human behavior had now been exhausted. Astronomy and terrestrial physics would take care of the inanimate determinants; anatomy, physiology, and psychology would encompass the individual determinants; and sociology, the science of society, would deal with the supra-individual determinants: what other determinants were there to be reckoned with?

As we have already shown, the assumption of the founders of sociology was far from adequate. True enough, a man behaves differently in the company of his fellows than when alone, just as roosters, dogs, ducks, and apes do. A sociology of man—or ape, rat, dog, or duck—is in order, therefore, in addition to a psychology. But to go no further would be to overlook a fundamental difference between man and all other species. A monkey, dog, or rat, as we have just noted, behaves differently when in the company of his fellows than when alone. We distinguish therefore individual and social aspects of this individual's behavior. We can go farther and recognize a social system of behavior in which the system as such is the focus of attention and interpretation. Thus we distinguish both individual and social systems. But—and here we come to the fundamental difference between man as a human being and all other species—whether we consider rat, dog, or ape behavior in its individual or social aspects, whether we regard it in the form of individual systems or social systems, the determinant is the biological organism. We find one type of social system or behavior in one species of animal, another type in another species; ducks will have one type of social system or behavior, eagles another; lions one type, bison another; sharks one kind, herring another, etc. Among the lower species, social systems are functions of their respective biological organisms: $S = f(O)$. But in the human species, on the level of symbolic behavior, this is not the case. Human behavior, either in its average individual or its social aspects, is nowhere a function of the organism. Human behavior does not vary as the organism varies; it varies with the extra-somatic factor of culture. Human behavior is a function of culture: $B = f(C)$. As the culture varies so will the behavior.

Thus it is not society, or the group, that constitutes the last of a series of categories of determinants of human behavior. Among the lower species, the group is properly regarded as a determinant of the behavior of any one of its members. But in the human species, the group is itself determined by the cultural tradition: whether we find a guild of artisans, a clan, a polyandrous household, or an order of knights in a human society will depend upon its culture. The discovery of this class of determinants and the isolation, in logical analysis, of these extra-somatic cultural determinants from the biological—in their group aspect as well as individual—has been one of the most significant advances in science in recent times. This assertion will no doubt strike some as extravagant. We are so accustomed to being regaled with accounts of the marvels of modern science—meaning physics, chemistry, and medicine—and so used to disparagements of social science, that to claim that the achievement of the concept of culture is one of the most significant advances in modern science may well seem preposterous to some. We have no desire whatever to minimize the significance of recent advances in physics, chemistry, genetics, or medicine. Some of them, such as quantum mechanics in physics and genetics in biology, may quite properly be called revolutionary. But such advances have taken place in fields that have been cultivated by science for generations or even centuries. But with the achievement of the concept of culture a whole new field was opened to science. The lack of significant achievement so far in the new science of culture is therefore not an indication of extravagance of claim on our part. The very newness of our science, the fact that this new sector of experience was discovered, isolated and defined only yesterday, in itself means that there has not yet been time for much accomplishment. It is the discovery of a new world that is so significant, not the relative magnitude or value of achievements won so far in this new world. We are so impressed with the achievements of physics and astronomy that it is hard for some to believe that the lowly "social" sciences can ever match them. This point of view is of course understandable in a day when science can map the distribution of galaxies in the cosmos and measure the mass and temperature of stars a million light years away, whereas in another field, science has no adequate answer to the question of the prohibition of polygamy in certain societies. But the lot and destiny of man on this planet embrace more than measuring galaxies, splitting atoms, or discovering a new wonder drug. The socio-political-economic systems—in short, the cultures—within which the human species lives and breathes and propagates have much to do with the future of Man. We are just beginning to realize this. And we may look forward to a time when the scientific comprehension of such cultural processes as polygamy and inflation will be considered quite as significant as the measurement of distant stars, the splitting of atoms, or the synthesis of organic compounds. The "discovery" of culture may one day rank in importance in the history of science with the heliocentric theory of Copernicus or the discovery of the cellular basis of all living forms.

This is not to say, as we have tried to make clear earlier, that man is going to win control over the course of cultural development through a scientific comprehension of its structure and processes, any more than we have won control over the sun or distant galaxies by coming to a considerable understanding of them. Understanding, scientific understanding, is itself a cultural process. The growth of science is a culture process just as the development of a musical style, a type of architecture, or forms of corporate organization in business are culture processes. The development of understanding in astronomy, in medicine, and in culturology alike will make possible a more realistic and effective adjustment of the human species to the earth and cosmos.

PART II ○ ○ ○

The Human Center

Charles Horton Cooley

Society and the Individual

The construction of a science of society which was to study abstract social processes required the introduction of a dynamic theory by which society as a thing could be transformed into society as a process. To some extent, Simmel had attempted to set up such a science, but his forms of sociation disregarded the interplay between internal and external processes by which individual behavior is controlled. Charles Horton Cooley succeeded in reintroducing into sociology some of the voluntaristic concepts that had informed much American thought. Seeing the individual and society both as equally real and equally abstract, Cooley helped to achieve a more balanced view of the interactive relationship that exists between the individual and the social group.

"Society and the individual" is really the subject of this whole book, and not merely of Chapter I. It is my general aim to set forth, from various points of view, what the individual is, considered as a member of a social whole; while the special purpose of this chapter is only to offer a preliminary statement of the matter, as I conceive it, afterward to be unfolded at some length and variously illustrated.

If we accept the evolutionary point of view we are led to see the relation between society and the individual as an organic relation. That is, we see that the individual is not separable from the human whole, but a living member of it, deriving his life from the whole through social and hereditary transmission as truly as if men were literally one body. He cannot cut himself off; the strands of heredity and education are woven into all his being. And, on the other hand, the social whole is in some degree dependent upon each individual, because each contributes something to the common life that no one else can contribute. Thus we have, in a broad sense of the word, an "organism" or living whole made up of differentiated members, each of which has a special function.

This is true of society in that large sense which embraces all humanity, and also of any specific social group. A university, for example, is an organic whole, made up of students, teachers, officials, and others. Every member is more or less dependent upon every other, because all contribute to the common life. And note that it is precisely his individuality, his functional difference from the rest, that gives each member his peculiar importance. The professor of Paleontology has a part that on one else can play; and so, less obviously, perhaps, has every teacher and student. The organic view stresses both the unity of the whole and the peculiar value of the individual, explaining each by the other. What is a football team without a quarterback? Almost as useless as a quarterback without a team. A well-developed individual can exist only in and through a well-developed whole, and *vice versa*.

This seems a simple idea, and so it is, but it is so opposed to some of our most cherished habits of thought that we may well ask time to look at it from various points of view.

A separate individual is an abstraction unknown to experience and so likewise a society when regarded as something apart from individuals. The real thing is Human Life, which may be considered either in an individual aspect or in a social, that is to say a general, aspect; but is always, as a matter of fact, both individual and general. In other words, "society" and "individuals" do not denote separable phenomena, but are simply collective and distributive aspects of the same thing, the relation between them being like that between other expressions, one of which denotes a group as a whole and the other the members of the group, such as the army and the soldiers, the class and the students, and so on. This holds true of any social aggregate, great or small; of a family, a city, a nation, a race; of mankind as a whole: no matter how extensive, complex, or enduring a group may be, no good reason can be given for regarding it as essentially different in this respect from the smallest, simplest, or most transient.

So far, then, as there is any difference between the two, it is rather in our point of view than in the object we are looking at: when we speak of society, or use any other collective term, we fix our minds upon some general view of the people concerned, while when we speak of individuals we disregard the general aspect and think of them as if they were separate. Thus "the Cabinet" may consist of President Lincoln, Secretary Stanton, Secretary Seward, and so on; but when I say "the Cabinet" I do not suggest the same idea as when I enumerate these gentlemen separately. Society, or any complex group, may, to ordinary observation, be a very different thing from all of its members viewed one by one—as a man who beheld General Grant's army from Missionary Ridge would have seen something other than he would by approaching every soldier in it. In the same way a picture is made up of so many square inches of painted canvas; but if you should look at these one at a time, covering the others, until you had seen them all, you would still not have seen the picture. There may, in all such cases, be a system or organization in the whole that is not apparent in the parts. In this sense, and in no other, is there a difference between society and the individuals of which it is composed; a difference not residing in the facts themselves but existing to the observer on account of the limits of his perception. A *complete* view of society would also be a complete view of all the individuals, and *vice versa;* there would be no difference between them.

And just as there is no society or group that is not a collective view of persons, so there is no individual who may not be regarded as a particular view of social groups. He has no separate existence; through both the hereditary and the social factors in his life a man is bound into the whole of which he is a member, and to consider him apart from it is quite as artificial as to consider society apart from individuals.

If this is true there is, of course, a fallacy in that not uncommon manner of speaking which sets the social and the individual over against each other as separate and antagonistic. The word "social" appears to be used in at least three fairly distinct senses, but in none of these does it mean something that can properly be regarded as opposite to individual or personal.

In its largest sense it denotes that which pertains to the collective aspect of humanity, to society in its widest and vaguest meaning. In this sense the individual and all his attributes are social, since they are all connected with the general life in one way or another, and are part of a collective development.

Again, social may mean what pertains to immediate intercourse, to the life of conversation and face-to-face sympathy—sociable, in short. This is something quite different, but no more antithetical to individual than the other; it is in these relations that individuality most obviously exists and expresses itself.

In a third sense the word means conducive to the collective welfare, and thus becomes nearly equivalent to moral, as when we say that crime or sensuality is unsocial or anti-social; but here again it cannot properly be made the antithesis of individual—since wrong is surely no more individual than right—but must be contrasted with immoral, brutal, selfish, or some other word with an ethical implication.

There are a number of expressions which are closely associated in common usage with this objectionable antithesis; such words, for instance, as individualism, socialism, particularism, collectivism.[1] These appear to be used with a good deal of vagueness, so that it is always in order to require that any one who employs them shall make it plain in what sense they are to be taken. I wish to make no captious objections to particular forms of expression, and so far as these can be shown to have meanings that express the facts of life I have nothing to say against them. Of the current use of individualism and socialism in antithesis to each other, about the same may be said as of the words without the *ism*. I do not see that life presents two distinct and opposing tendencies that can properly be called individualism and socialism, any more than that there are two distinct and opposing entities, society and the individual, to embody these tendencies. The phenomena usually called individualistic are always socialistic in the sense that they are expressive of tendencies growing out of the general life, and, cantrariwise, the so-called socialistic phenomena have always an obvious individual aspect. These and similar terms may be used, conveniently enough, to describe theories or programmes of the day, but whether they are suitable for purposes of careful study appears somewhat doubtful. If used, they ought, it seems to me, to receive more adequate definition than they have at present.

For example, all the principal epochs of European history might be, and most of them are, spoken of as individualistic on one ground or another, and without departing from the current usage of the word. The decaying Roman Empire was individualistic if a decline of public spirit and an every-man-for-himself feeling and practice constitute individualism. So also was the following period of political confusion. The feudal system is often regarded as individualistic, because of the relative independence and isolation of small political units—quite a different use of the word from the preceding—and after this come the Revival of Learning, the Renaissance, and the Reformation, which are all commonly spoken of, on still other grounds, as assertions of individualism. Then we reach the seventeenth and eighteenth centuries, sceptical, transitional, and, again, individualistic; and so to our own time, which may hold to be the most individualistic of all. One feels like asking whether a word which means so many things as this means anything whatever.

There is always some confusion of terms in speaking of opposition between an individual and society in general, even when the writer's meaning is obvious enough: it would be more accurate to say either that one individual is opposing many, or that one part of society is opposing other parts; and thus avoid confusing the two aspects of life in the same expression. When Emerson says that society is in a conspiracy against the independence of each of· its members, we are to understand that any peculiar tendency represented by one person finds itself more or less at variance with the general current of tendencies organized in other persons. It is no more individual, nor any less social, in a large sense, than other tendencies represented by more persons. A thousand persons are just as truly individuals as one, and the man who seems to stand alone draws his being from the general stream of life just as truly and inevitably as if he were one of a thousand. Innovation is just as social as conformity, genius as mediocrity. These distinctions are not between what is individual and what is social, but between what is usual or established and what is exceptional or novel. In other words, wherever you find life as society there you will find life as individuality, and *vice versa*.

I think, then, that the antithesis, society *versus* the individual, is false and hollow whenever used as a general or philosophical statement of human relations. Whatever idea may be in the minds of those who set these words and their derivatives over against each other, the notion conveyed is that of two separable entities or forces; and certainly such a notion is untrue to fact.

Most people not only think of individuals and society as more or less separate and antithetical, but they look upon the former as antecedent to the latter. That persons make society would be generally admitted as a matter of course; but that society makes persons would strike many as a startling notion, though I know of no good reason for looking upon the distributive aspect of life as more primary or causative than the collective aspect. The reason for the common impression appears to be that we think most naturally and easily of the individual phase of life, simply because it is a tangible one, the phase under which men appear to the senses, while the actuality of groups, of nations, of mankind at large, is realized only by the active and instructed imagination. We ordinarily regard society, so far as we conceive it at all, in a vaguely material aspect, as an aggregate of physical bodies, not as the vital whole which it is; and so, of course, we do not see that it may be as original or causative as anything else. Indeed, many look upon "society" and other general terms as somewhat mystical, and are inclined to doubt whether there is any reality back of them.

This naïve individualism of thought—which, however, does not truly see the individual any more than it does society—is reinforced by traditions in which all of us are brought up, and is so hard to shake off that it may be worth while to point out a little more definitely some of the prevalent ways of conceiving life which are permeated by it, and which any one who agrees with what has just been said may regard as fallacious. . . .

First, then, we have *mere individualism*. In this the distributive aspect is almost exclusively regarded, collective phases being looked upon as quite secondary and incidental. Each person is held to be a separate agent, and all social phenomena are thought of as originating in the action of such agents. The individual is the source, the independent, the only human source, of events. Although this way of looking at things has been much discredited by the evolutionary science and philosophy of recent years, it is by no means abandoned, even in theory, and practically it enters as a premise, in one shape or another, into most of the current thought of the day. It springs naturally from the established way of thinking, congenial, as I have remarked, to the ordinary material view of things and corroborated by theological and other traditions.

Next is *double causation,* or a partition of power between society and the individual, thought of as separate causes. This notion, in one shape or another, is the one ordinarily met with in social and ethical discussion. It is no advance, philosophically, upon the preceding. There is the same premise of the individual as a separate, unrelated agent; but over against him is set a vaguely conceived general or collective interest and force. It seems that people are so accustomed to thinking of themselves as uncaused causes, special creators on a small scale, that when the existence of general phenomena is forced upon their notice they are likely to regard these as something additional, separate, and more or less antithetical. Our two forces contend with varying fortunes, the thinker sometimes sympathizing with one, sometimes with the other, and being an individualist or a socialist accordingly. The doctrines usually understood in connection with these terms differ, as regards their conception of the nature of life, only in taking opposite sides of the same questionable antithesis. The socialist holds it desirable that the general or collective force should win; the individualist has a contrary opinion. Neither offers any change of ground, any reconciling and renewing breadth of view. So far as breadth of view is concerned a man might quite as well be an individualist as a socialist or collectivist, the two being identical in philosophy though antagonistic in programme. If one is inclined to neither party he may take refuge in the expectation that the controversy, resting as he may hold that it does, on a false conception of life, will presently take its proper place among the forgotten *débris* of speculation.

Thirdly we have *primitive individualism*. This expression has been used to describe the view that sociality follows individuality in time, is a later and additional product of development. This view is a variety of the preceding, and is, perhaps, formed by a mingling of individualistic preconceptions with a somewhat crude evolutionary philosophy. Individuality is usually conceived as lower in moral rank as well as precedent in time. Man *was* a mere individual, mankind a mere aggregation of such, but he had gradually become socialized, he is progressively merging into a social whole. Morally speaking, the individual is the bad, the social the good, and we must push on the work of putting down the former and bringing in the latter.

Of course the view which I regard as sound, is that individuality is neither prior in time nor lower in moral rank than sociality; but that the two have always existed side by side as complementary aspects of the same thing, and that the line of progress is from a lower to a higher type of both, not from the one to the other. If the word social is applied only to the higher forms of mental life it should, as already suggested, be opposed not to individual, but to animal, sensual, or some other word implying mental or moral inferiority. If we go back to a time when the state of our remote ancestors was such that we are not willing to call it social, then it must have been equally undeserving to be described as individual or personal; that is to say, they must have been just as inferior to us when viewed separately as when viewed collectively. To question this is to question the vital unity of human life.

The life of the human species, like that of other species, must always have been both general and particular, must always have had its collective and distributive aspects. The plane of this life has gradually risen, involving, of course, both the aspects mentioned. Now, as ever, they develop as one, and may be observed united in the highest activities of the highest minds. Shakespeare, for instance, is in one point of view a unique and transcendent individual; in another he is a splendid expression of the general life of mankind: the difference is not in him but in the way we choose to look at him.

Finally, there is *the social faculty view*. This expression might be used to indicate those conceptions which regard the social as including only a part, often a rather definite part, of the individual. Human nature is thus divided into individualistic or non-social tendencies or faculties, and those that are social. Thus, certain emotions, as love, are social; others, as fear or anger, are unsocial or individualistic. Some writers have even treated the intelligence as an individualistic faculty, and have found sociality only in some sorts of emotion or sentiment.

This idea of instincts or faculties that are peculiarly social is well enough if we use this word in the sense of pertaining to conversation or immediate fellow-feeling. Affection is certainly more social in this sense than fear. But if it is meant that these instincts or faculties are in themselves morally higher than others, or that they alone pertain to the collective life, the view is, I think, very questionable. At any rate the opinion I hold . . . is that man's psychical outfit is not divisible into the social and the non-social; but that he is all social in a large sense, is all a part of the common human life, and that his social or moral progress consists less in the aggrandizement of particular faculties or instincts and the suppression of others, than in the discipline of all with reference to a progressive organization of life which we know in thought as conscience.

Some instincts or tendencies may grow in relative importance, may have an increasing function, while the opposite may be true of others. Such relative growth and diminution of parts seems to be a general feature of evolution, and there is no reason why it should be absent from our mental development. But here as well as elsewhere most parts, if not all, are or have been functional with reference to a life collective as well as distributive; there is no sharp separation of faculties, and progress takes place rather by gradual adaptation of old organs to new functions than by disuse and decay.

To make it quite clear what the organic view involves, so far as ·regards theory, I will take several questions, such as I have found that people ask when discussing the relation of society and the individual, and will suggest how, as it seems to me, they may be answered.

1. Is not society, after all, made up of individuals, and of nothing else?

I should say, Yes. It is plain, every-day humanity, not a mysterious something else.

2. Is society anything more than the sum of the individuals?

In a sense, Yes. There is an organization, a life-process, in any social whole that you cannot see in the individuals separately. To study them one by one and attempt to understand society by putting them together will lead you astray. It is "individualism" in a bad sense of the word. Whole sciences, like political economy; great institutions, like the church, have gone wrong at this point. You must see your groups, your social processes, as the living wholes that they are.

3. Is the individual a product of society?

Yes, in the sense that everything human about him has a history in the social past. If we consider the two sources from which he draws his life, heredity and communication, we see that what he gets through the germ-plasm has a social history in that it has had to adapt itself to past society in order to survive: the traits we are born with are such as have undergone a social test in the lives of our ancestors. And what he gets from communication—language, education, and the like

—comes directly from society. Even physical influences, like food and climate, rarely reach us except as modified and adapted by social conditions.

4. Can we separate the individual from society?

Only in an external sense. If you go off alone into the wilderness you take with you a mind formed in society, and you continue social intercourse in your memory and imagination, or by the aid of books. This, and this only, keeps humanity alive in you, and just insofar as you lose the power of intercourse your mind decays. Long solitude, as in the case of sheepherders on the Western plains, or prisoners in solitary confinement, often produces imbecility. This is especially likely to happen with the uneducated, whose memories are not well stored with material for imaginative intercourse.

At times in the history of Christianity, and of other religions also, hermits have gone to dwell in desert places, but they have usually kept up some communication with one another and with the world outside, certain of them, like St. Jerome, having been famous letter-writers. Each of them, in fact, belonged to a social system from which he drew ideals and moral support. We may suspect that St. Simeon Stylites, who dwelt for years on top of a pillar, was not unaware that his austerity was visible to others.

A castaway who should be unable to retain his imaginative hold upon human society might conceivably live the life of an intelligent animal, exercising his mind upon the natural conditions about him, but his distinctively human faculties would certainly be lost, or in abeyance.

5. Is the individual in any sense free, or is he a mere piece of society?

Yes, he is free, as I conceive the matter, but it is an organic freedom, which he works out in co-operation with others, not a freedom to do things independently of society. It is team-work. He has freedom to function in his own way, like the quarter-back, but, in one way or another, he has to play the game as life brings him into it.

The evolutionary point of view encourages us to believe that life is a creative process, that we are really building up something new and worth while, and that the human will is a part of the creative energy that does this. Every individual has his unique share in the work, which no one but himself can discern and perform. Although his life flows into him from the hereditary and social past, his being as a whole is new, a fresh organization of life. Never any one before had the same powers and opportunities that you have, and you are free to use them in your own way.

It is, after all, only common sense to say that we exercise our freedom through co-operation with others. If you join a social group—let us say a dramatic club—you expect that it will increase your freedom, give your individual powers new stimulus and opportunity for expression. And why should not the same principle apply to society at large? It is through a social development that mankind has emerged from animal bondage into that organic freedom, wonderful though far from complete, that we now enjoy.

NOTE

[1] Also free-will, determinism, egoism, and altruism, which involve, in my opinion, a kindred misconception.

Edward Sapir

Language, an Introduction to the Study of Speech

Edward Sapir's contributions to anthropology straddled both linguistics and culture-personality. Sapir did not see psychology and
social structure or organization as diametrically opposed forces. Rather
he saw them as interacting processes. Sapir believed that language
could provide a bridge between psychology and sociology, and that
true understanding of man lay in an understanding of the processes by
which he affected his culture as well as those by which his culture
affected him.

THE QUESTION HAS OFTEN been raised whether thought is possible
without speech; further, if speech and thought be not but two facets
of the same psychic process. The question is all the more difficult
because it has been hedged about by misunderstandings. In the first
place, it is well to observe that whether or not thought necessitates
symbolism, that is speech, the flow of language itself is not always
indicative of thought. We have seen that the typical linguistic element
labels a concept. It does not follow from this that the use to which
language is put is always or even mainly conceptual. We are not in
ordinary life so much concerned with concepts as such as with concrete particularities and specific relations. When I say, for instance,
"I had a good breakfast this morning," it is clear that I am not in
the throes of laborious thought, that what I have to transmit is
hardly more than a pleasurable memory symbolically rendered in
the grooves of habitual expression. Each element in the sentence de-

fines a separate concept or conceptual relation or both combined, but the sentence as a whole has no conceptual significance whatever. It is somewhat as though a dynamo capable of generating enough power to run an elevator were operated almost exclusively to feed an electric doorbell. The parallel is more suggestive than at first sight appears. Language may be looked upon as an instrument capable of running a gamut of psychic uses. Its flow not only parallels that of the inner content of consciousness, but parallels it on different levels, ranging from the state of mind that is dominated by particular images to that in which abstract concepts and their relations are alone at the focus of attention and which is ordinarily termed reasoning. Thus the outward form only of language is constant; its inner meaning, its psychic value or intensity, varies freely with attention or the selective interest of the mind, also, needless to say, with the mind's general development. From the point of view of language, thought may be defined as the highest latent or potential content of speech, the content that is obtained by interpreting each of the elements in the flow of language as possessed of its very fullest conceptual value. From this it follows at once that language and thought are not strictly coterminous. At best language can but be the outward facet of thought on the highest, most generalized, level of symbolic expression. To put our viewpoint somewhat differently, language is primarily a pre-rational function. It humbly works up to the thought that is latent in, that may eventually be read into, its classifications and its forms; it is not, as is generally but naïvely assumed, the final label put upon the finished thought.

Most people, asked if they can think without speech, would probably answer, "Yes, but it is not easy for me to do so. Still I know it can be done." Language is but a garment! But what if language is not so much a garment as a prepared road or groove? It is, indeed, in the highest degree likely that language is an instrument originally put to uses lower than the conceptual plane and that thought arises as a refined interpretation of its content. The product grows, in other words, with the instrument, and thought may be no more conceivable, in its genesis and daily practice, without speech than is mathematical reasoning practicable without the lever of an appropriate mathematical symbolism. No one believes that even the most difficult mathematical proposition is inherently dependent on an arbitrary set of symbols, but it is impossible to suppose that the human mind is capable of arriving at or holding such a proposition without the symbolism. The writer, for one, is strongly of the opinion that the feeling entertained by so many that they can think, or even reason, without language is an illusion. The illusion seems to be due to a number of factors. The simplest of these is the failure to distinguish between imagery and thought. As a matter of fact, no sooner do we try to put an image into conscious relation with another than we find ourselves slipping into a silent flow of words. Thought may be a natural domain apart from the artificial one of speech, but speech would seem to be the only road we know of that leads to it. A still more fruitful source of the illusive feeling that language may be dispensed with in thought is the common failure to realize that language is not identical with its auditory symbolism. The auditory symbolism may be replaced, point for point, by a motor or by a visual symbolism (many people can read, for instance, in a purely visual sense, that is, without the intermediating link of an inner flow of the auditory images that correspond to the printed or written words) or by still other, more subtle and elusive, types of transfer that are not so easy to define. Hence the contention that one thinks without language merely because he is not aware of a coexisting auditory imagery is very far indeed from being a valid one. One may go so far as to suspect that the symbolic expression of thought may in some cases run along outside the fringe of the conscious mind, so that the feeling of a free, non-linguistic stream of thought is for minds of a certain type a relatively, but only a relatively, justified one. Psychophysically, this would mean that the auditory or equivalent visual or motor centers in the brain, together with the appropriate paths of association, that are the cerebral equivalent of speech, are touched off so lightly during the process of thought as not to rise into consciousness at all. This would be a limiting case—thought riding lightly on the submerged crests of speech, instead of jogging along with it, hand in hand. The modern psychology has shown us how powerfully symbolism is at work in the unconscious mind. It is therefore easier to understand at the present time than it would have been twenty years ago that the most rarefied thought may be but the conscious counterpart of an unconscious linguistic symbolism.

One word more as to the relation between language and thought. The point of view that we have developed does not by any means preclude the possibility of the growth of speech being in a high degree dependent on the development of thought. We may assume that language arose pre-rationally—just how and on what precise level of mental activity we do not know—but we must not imagine that a highly developed system of speech symbols worked itself out before the genesis of distinct concepts and of thinking, the handling of concepts. We must rather imagine that thought processes set in, as a kind of psychic overflow, almost at the beginning of linguistic expression; further, that the concept, once defined, necessarily reacted on the life of its linguistic symbol, encouraging further linguistic growth. We see this complex process of the interaction of language and thought actually taking place under our eyes. The instrument makes possible the product, the product refines the instrument. The birth of a new concept is invariably foreshadowed by a more or less strained or extended use of old linguistic material; the concept does not attain to individual and independent life until it has found a distinctive linguistic embodiment. In most cases, the new symbol is but a thing wrought from linguistic material already in existence in ways mapped out by crushingly despotic precedents. As soon as the word is at hand, we instinctively feel, with something of a sigh of relief, that the concept is ours for the handling. Not until we own the symbol do we feel that we hold a key to the immediate knowledge or understanding of the concept. Would we be so ready to die for "liberty," to struggle for "ideals," if the words themselves were not ringing within us? And the word, as we know, is not only a key; it may also be a fetter.

Max Weber

Subjective Meaning in the Social Situation

Of all sociological thinkers, Max Weber was, perhaps, one of those most acutely aware of the problems raised by the intrusion of values into the scientific study of society. In pointing out the difference between "real" and "ideal" systems (or between models and actuality) he suggested that the use of such "ideal" pictures, which referred to systems based largely upon subjective, Western, modes of thought, could yield only partial data. For Weber, no science of culture or society could exist without understanding of the real system that incorporated the meaning of the act to the subject himself. The Weberian view, by and large, is a sociological equivalent of the empirical and relativistic anthropological outlook. It has been invaluable in uncovering the limitations of such models as "classic" economic theory when these are imposed upon non-Western cultures. Classic economics is based upon the market or scarcity principle, and when imposed upon non-Western society it indicates that primitive behavior is wasteful and irrational. On the contrary, analysis of economic behavior in terms of the economic system as described by the people themselves, and in terms of data yielded by the society under study, has proven Weber's point: The models derived from attention to the subjective meaning of the social situation provide far more adequate predictions of primitive economic behavior than do so-called objective market models.

SOCIOLOGY (in the sense in which this highly ambiguous word is used here) is a science which attempts the interpretive understanding of social action in order thereby to arrive at a causal explanation of its course and effects. In "action" is included all human behaviour when and in so far as the acting individual attaches a subjective meaning to it. Action in this sense may be either overt or purely inward or subjective; it may consist of positive intervention in a situation, or of deliberately refraining from such intervention or passively acquiescing in the situation. Action is social in so far as, by virtue of the subjective meaning attached to it by the acting individual (or individuals), it takes account of the behaviour of others and is thereby oriented in its course.[1]

The Methodological Foundations of Sociology [2]

1. "Meaning" may be of two kinds. The term may refer first to the actual existing meaning in the given concrete case of a particular actor, or to the average or approximate meaning attributable to a given plurality of actors; or secondly to the theoretically conceived *pure type*[3] of subjective meaning attributed to the hypothetical actor or actors in a given type of action. In no case does it refer to an objectively "correct" meaning or one which is "true" in some metaphysical sense. It is this which distinguishes the empirical sciences of action, such as sociology and history, from the dogmatic disciplines in that area, such as jurisprudence, logic, ethics, and esthetics, which seek to ascertain the "true" and "valid" meanings associated with the objects of their investigation.

2. The line between meaningful action and merely reactive behaviour to which no subjective meaning is attached, cannot be sharply drawn empirically. A very considerable part of all sociologically relevant behaviour, especially purely traditional behaviour, is marginal between the two. In the case of many psychophysical processes, meaningful, i.e. subjectively understandable, action is not to be found at all; in others it is discernible only by the expert psychologist. Many mystical experiences which cannot be adequately communicated in words are, for a person who is not susceptible to such experiences, not fully understandable. At the same time the ability to imagine one's self performing a similar action is not a necessary prerequisite to understanding; "one need not have been Caesar in order to understand Caesar." For the verifiable accuracy[4] of interpretation of the meaning of a phenomenon, it is a great help to be able to put one's self imaginatively in the place of the actor and thus sympathetically to participate in his experiences, but this is not an essential condition of meaningful interpretation. Understandable and non-under-

standable components of a process are often intermingled and bound up together.

3. All interpretation of meaning, like all scientific observation, strives for clarity and verifiable accuracy of insight and comprehension (*Evidenz*). The basis for certainty in understanding can be either rational, which can be further subdivided into logical and mathematical, or it can be of an emotionally empathic or artistically appreciative quality. In the sphere of action things are rationally evident chiefly when we attain a completely clear intellectual grasp of the action-elements in their intended context of meaning. Empathic or appreciative accuracy is attained when, through sympathetic participation, we can adequately grasp the emotional context in which the action took place. The highest degree of rational understanding is attained in cases involving the meanings of logically or mathematically related propositions; their meaning may be immediately and unambiguously intelligible. We have a perfectly clear understanding of what it means when somebody employs the proposition $2 \times 2 = 4$ or the Pythagorean theorem in reasoning or argument, or when someone correctly carries out a logical train of reasoning according to our accepted modes of thinking. In the same way we also understand what a person is doing when he tries to achieve certain ends by choosing appropriate means on the basis of the facts of the situation as experience has accustomed us to interpret them. Such an interpretation of this type of rationally purposeful action possesses, for the understanding of the choice of means, the highest degree of verifiable certainty. With a lower degree of certainty, which is, however, adequate for most purposes of explanation, we are able to understand errors, including confusion of problems of the sort that we ourselves are liable to, or the origin of which we can detect by sympathetic self-analysis.

On the other hand, many ultimate ends or values toward which experience shows that human action may be oriented, often cannot be understood completely, though sometimes we are able to grasp them intellectually. The more radically they differ from our own ultimate values, however, the more difficult it is for us to make them understandable by imaginatively participating in them. Depending upon the circumstances of the particular case we must be content either with a purely intellectual understanding of such values or when even that fails, sometimes we must simply accept them as given data.

Then we can try to understand the action motivated by them on the basis of whatever opportunities for approximate emotional and intellectual interpretation seem to be available at different points in its course. These difficulties apply, for instance, for people not susceptible to the relevant values, to many unusual acts of religious and charitable zeal; also certain kinds of extreme rationalistic fanaticism of the type involved in some forms of the ideology of the "rights of man" are in a similar position for people who radically repudiate such points of view.

The more we ourselves are susceptible to them the more readily can we imaginatively participate in such emotional reactions as anxiety, anger, ambition, envy, jealousy, love, enthusiasm, pride, vengefuless, loyalty, devotion, and appetites of all sorts, and thereby understanding the irrational conduct which grows out of them. Such conduct is "irrational," that is, from the point of view of the rational pursuit of a given end. Even when such emotions are found in a degree of intensity of which the observer himself is completely incapable, he can still have a significant degree of emotional understanding of their meaning and can interpret intellectually their influence on the course of action and the selection of means.

For the purposes of a typological scientific analysis it is convenient to treat all irrational, effectually determined elements of behaviour as factors of deviation from a conceptually pure type of rational action. For example a panic on the stock exchange can be most conveniently analysed by attempting to determine first what the course of action would have been if it had not been influenced by irrational affects; it is then possible to introduce the irrational components as accounting for the observed deviations from this hypothetical course. Similarly, in analysing a political or military campaign it is convenient to determine in the first place what would have been a rational course, given the ends of the participants and adequate knowledge of all the circumstances. Only in this way is it possible to assess the causal significance of irrational factors as accounting for the deviations from this type. The construction of a purely rational course of action in such cases serves the sociologist as a type ("ideal type") which has the merit of clear understandability and lack of ambiguity. By comparison with this it is possible to understand the ways in which actual action is influenced by irrational factors of all sorts, such as affects[5] and errors, in that they account for the deviation from the line of conduct which would be expected on the hypothesis that the action were purely rational.

Only in this respect and for these reasons of methodological convenience, is the method of sociology "rationalistic." It is naturally not legitimate to interpret this procedure as involving a "rationalistic bias" of sociology, but only as a methodological device. It certainly does not involve a belief in the actual predominance of rational elements in human life, for on the question of how far this predominance does or does not exist, nothing whatever has been said. That there is, however, a danger of rationalistic interpretations where they are out of place naturally cannot be denied. All experience unfortunately confirms the existence of this danger.

4. In all the sciences of human action, account must be taken of processes and phenomena which are devoid of subjective meaning,[6] in the role of stimuli, results, favouring or hindering circumstances. To be devoid of meaning is not identical with being lifeless or non-human; every artifact, such as for example a machine, can be understood only in terms of the meaning which its production and use have had or will have for a human action; a meaning which may derive from a relation to exceedingly various purposes. Without reference to this meaning such an object remains wholly unintelligible.[7] That which is intelligible or understandable about it is thus its relation to human action in the role either of means or of end; a relation of which the actor or actors can be said to have been aware and to which their action has been oriented. Only in terms of such categories is it possible to "understand" objects of this kind. On the other hand processes or conditions, whether they are animate or inanimate, human or non-human, are in the present sense devoid of meaning in so far as they cannot be related to an intended purpose. That is to say they are devoid of meaning if they cannot be related to action in the role of means or ends but constitute only the stimulus, the favouring or hindering circumstances.[8] It may be that the incursion of the Dollart at the beginning of the twelfth century[9] had historical significance as a stimulus to the beginning of certain migrations of considerable importance. Human mortality, indeed the organic life cycle generally from the helplessness of infancy to that of old age, is naturally of the very greatest sociological importance through the various ways in which human action has been oriented to these facts. To still another category of facts devoid of meaning belong certain

psychic or psychophysical phenomena such as fatigue, habituation, memory, etc.; also certain typical states of euphoria under some conditions of ascetic mortification; finally, typical variations in the reactions of individuals according to reaction-time, precision, and other modes. But in the last analysis the same principle applies to these as to other phenomena which are devoid of meaning. Both the actor and the sociologist must accept them as data to be taken into account.

It is altogether possible that future research may be able to discover non-understandable uniformities underlying what has appeared to be specifically meaningful action, though little has been accomplished in this direction thus far. Thus, for example, differences in hereditary biological constitution, as of "races," would have to be treated by sociology as given data in the same way as the physiological facts of the need of nutrition or the effect of senescence on action. This would be the case if, and in so far as, we had statistically conclusive proof of their influence on sociologically relevant behaviour. The recognition of the causal significance of such factors would naturally not in the least alter the specific task of sociological analysis or of that of the other sciences of action, which is the interpretation of action in terms of its subjective meaning. The effect would be only to introduce certain non-understandable data of the same order as others which, it has been noted above, are already present, into the complex of subjectively understandable motivation at certain points. Thus it may come to be known that there are typical relations between the frequency of certain types of teleological orientation of action or of the degree of certain kinds of rationality and the cephalic index or skin colour or any other biologically inherited characteristic.

5. Understanding may be of two kinds: the first is the direct observational understanding[10] of the subjective meaning of a given act as such, including verbal utterances. We thus understand by direct observation, in this sense, the meaning of the proposition $2 \times 2 = 4$ when we hear or read it. This is a case of the direct rational understanding of ideas. We also understand an outbreak of anger as manifested by facial expression, exclamations or irrational movements. This is direct observational understanding of irrational emotional reactions. We can understand in a similar observational way the action of a woodcutter or of somebody who reaches for the knob

to shut a door or who aims a gun at an animal. This is rational observational understanding of actions.

Understanding may, however, be of another sort, namely explanatory understanding. Thus we understand in terms of *motive* the meaning an actor attaches to the proposition twice two equals four, when he states it or writes it down, in that we understand what makes him do this at precisely this moment and in these circumstances. Understanding in this sense is attained if we know that he is engaged in balancing a ledger or in making a scientific demonstration, or is engaged in some other task of which this particular act would be an appropriate part. This is rational understanding of motivation, which consists in placing the act in an intelligible and more inclusive context of meaning.[11] Thus we understand the chopping of wood or aiming of a gun in terms of motive in addition to direct observation if we know that the wood chopper is working for a wage or is chopping a supply of firewood for his own use or possibly is doing it for recreation. But he might also be "working off" a fit of rage, an irrational case. Similarly we understand the motive of a person aiming a gun if we know that he has been commanded to shoot as a member of a firing squad, that he is fighting against an enemy, or that he is doing it for revenge. The last is affectually determined and thus in a certain sense irrational. Finally we have a motivational understanding of the outburst of anger if we know that it has been provoked by jealousy, injured pride, or an insult. The last examples are all affectually determined and hence derived from irrational motives. In all the above cases the particular act has been placed in an understandable sequence of motivation, the understanding of which can be treated as an explanation of the actual course of behaviour. Thus for a science which is concerned with the subjective meaning of action, explanation requires a grasp of the complex of meaning in which an actual course of understandable action thus interpreted belongs.[12] In all such cases, even where the processes are largely affectual, the subjective meaning of the action, including that also of the relevant meaning complexes, will be called the "intended" meaning.[13] This involves a departure from ordinary usage, which speaks of intention in this sense only in the case of rationally purposive action.

6. In all these cases understanding involves the interpretive grasp of the meaning present in one of the following contexts: (a) as in the historical approach, the actually intended meaning for concrete

individual action; or (b) as in cases of sociological mass phenomena the average of, or an approximation to, the actually intended meaning; or (c) the meaning appropriate to a scientifically formulated pure type (an ideal type) of a common phenomenon. The concepts and "laws" of pure economic theory are examples of this kind of ideal type. They state what course a given type of human action would take if it were strictly rational, unaffected by errors or emotional factors and if, furthermore, it were completely and unequivocally directed to a single end, the maximization of economic advantage. In reality, action takes exactly this course only in unusual cases, as sometimes on the stock exchange; and even then there is usually only an approximation to the ideal type.[14]

Every interpretation attempts to attain clarity and certainty, but no matter how clear an interpretation as such appears to be from the point of view of meaning, it cannot on this account alone claim to be the causally valid interpretation. On this level it must remain only a peculiarly plausible hypothesis. In the first place the "conscious motives" may well, even to the actor himself, conceal the various "motives" and "repressions" which constitute the real driving force of his action. Thus in such cases even subjectively honest self-analysis has only a relative value. Then it is the task of the sociologist to be aware of this motivational situation and to describe and analyse it, even though it has not actually been concretely part of the conscious "intention" of the actor; possibly not at all, at least not fully. This is a borderline case of the interpretation of meaning. Secondly, processes of action which seem to an observer to be the same or similar may fit into exceedingly various complexes of motive in the case of the actual actor. Then even though the situations appear superficially to be very similar we must actually understand them or interpret them as very different, perhaps, in terms of meaning, directly opposed.[15] Third, the actors in any given situation are often subject to opposing and conflicting impulses, all of which we are able to understand. In a large number of cases we know from experience it is not possible to arrive at even an approximate estimate of the relative strength of conflicting motives and very often we cannot be certain of our interpretation. Only the actual outcome of the conflict gives a solid basis of judgment.

More generally, verification of subjective interpretation by comparison with the concrete course of events is, as in the case of all hypotheses, indispensable. Unfortunately this type of verification is feasible with relative accuracy only in the few very special cases susceptible of psychological experimentation. The approach to a satisfactory degree of accuracy is exceedingly various, even in the limited number of cases of mass phenomena which can be statistically described and unambiguously interpreted. For the rest there remains only the possibility of comparing the largest possible number of historical or contemporary processes which, while otherwise similar, differ in the one decisive point of their relation to the particular motive or factor the role of which is being investigated. This is a fundamental task of comparative sociology. Often, unfortunately, there is available only the dangerous and uncertain procedure of the "imaginary experiment" which consists in thinking away certain elements of a chain of motivation and working out the course of action which would then probably ensue, thus arriving at a causal judgment.[16]

For example, the generalization called Gresham's Law is a rationally clear interpretation of human action under certain conditions and under the assumption that it will follow a purely rational course. How far any actual course of action corresponds to this can be verified only by the available statistical evidence for the actual disappearance of under-valued monetary units from circulation. In this case our information serves to demonstrate a high degree of accuracy. The facts of experience were known before the generalization, which was formulated afterwards; but without this successful interpretation our need for causal understanding would evidently be left unsatisfied. On the other hand, without the demonstration that what can here be assumed to be a theoretically adequate interpretation also is in some degree relevant to an actual course of action, a "law," no matter how fully demonstrated theoretically, would be worthless for the understanding of action in the real world. In this case the correspondence between the theoretical interpretation of motivation and its empirical verification is entirely satisfactory and the cases are numerous enough so that verification can be considered established. But to take another example, Eduard Meyer has advanced an ingenious theory of the causal significance of the battles of Marathon, Salamis, and Platea for the development of the cultural peculiarities of Greek, and hence, more generally, Western civilization.[17] This is derived from a meaningful interpretation of certain symptomatic facts having to do with the attitudes of the Greek oracles and prophets towards the Persians. It can only be directly verified by reference to the examples of the conduct of the Persians in cases where they were victorious, as in Jerusalem, Egypt, and Asia Minor, and even this verification must necessarily remain unsatisfactory in certain respects. The striking rational plausibility of the hypothesis must here necessarily be relied on as a support. In very many cases of historical interpretation which seem highly plausible, however, there is not even a possibility of the order of verification which was feasible in this case. Where this is true the interpretation must necessarily remain a hypothesis.

7. A motive is a complex of subjective meaning which seems to the actor himself or to the observer an adequate ground for the conduct in question. We apply the term "adequacy on the level of meaning" [18] to the subjective interpretation of a coherent course of conduct when and in so far as, according to our habitual modes of thought and feeling, its component parts taken in their mutual relation are recognized to constitute a "typical" complex of meaning. It is more common to say "correct." The interpretation of a sequence of events will on the other hand be called *causally* adequate in so far as, according to established generalizations from experience, there is a probability that it will always actually occur in the same way. An example of adequacy on the level of meaning in this sense is what is, according to our current norms of calculation or thinking, the correct solution of an arithmetical problem. On the other hand, a causally adequate interpretation of the same phenomenon would concern the statistical probability that, according to verified generalizations from experience, there would be a correct or an erroneous solution of the same problem. This also refers to currently accepted norms but includes taking account of typical errors or of typical confusions. Thus causal explanation depends on being able to determine that there is a probability, which in the rare ideal case can be numerically stated, but is always in some sense calculable, that a given observable event (overt or subjective) will be followed or accompanied by another event.

A correct causal interpretation of a concrete course of action is arrived at when the overt action and the motives have both been correctly apprehended and at the same time their relation has become meaningfully comprehensible. A correct causal interpretation of typical action means that the process which is claimed to be typical is shown to be both adequately grasped on the level of meaning and at the same time the interpretation is to some degree causally adequate. If adequacy in respect to meaning is lacking, then no matter how high the degree of uniformity and how precisely its probability can be numerically determined, it is still an incomprehensible statistical probability, whether dealing with overt or subjective processes. On the other hand, even the most perfect adequacy on the level of meaning has causal significance from a sociological point of view only in so far as there is some kind of proof for the existence of a probability[19] that action in fact normally takes the course which has been held to be meaningful. For this there must be some degree of determinable frequency of approximation to an average or a pure type.

Statistical uniformities constitute understandable types of action in the sense of this discussion, and thus constitute "sociological generalizations," only when they can be regarded as manifestations of the understandable subjective meaning of a course of social action. Conversely, formulations of a rational course of subjectively understandable action constitute sociological types of empirical process only when they can be empirically observed with a significant degree of approximation. It is unfortunately by no means the case that the actual likelihood of the occurrence of a given course of overt action is always directly proportional to the clarity of subjective interpretation. There are statistics of processes devoid of meaning such as death rates, phenomena of fatigue, the production rate of machines, the amount of rainfall, in exactly the same sense as there are statistics of meaningful phenomena. But only when the phenomena are meaningful is it convenient to speak of sociological statistics. Examples are such cases as crime rates, occupational distributions, price statistics, and statistics of crop acreage. Naturally there are many cases where both components are involved, as in crop statistics.

NOTES

[1] In this series of definitions Weber employs several important terms which need discussion. In addition to *Verstehen*, which has already been commented upon, there are four important ones: *Deuten, Sinn, Handeln,* and *Verhalten. Deuten* has generally been translated as "interpret." As used by Weber in this context it refers to the interpretation of subjective states of mind and the meanings which can be imputed as intended by an actor. Any other meaning of the word "interpretation" is irrelevant to Weber's discussion. The term *Sinn* has generally been translated as "meaning"; and its variations, particularly the corresponding adjectives, *sinnhaft,*

sinnvoll, sinnfremd, have been dealt with by appropriately modifying the term meaning. The reference here again is always to features of the content of subjective states of mind or of symbolic systems which are ultimately referable to such states of mind.

The terms *Handeln* and *Verhalten* are directly related. *Verhalten* is the broader term referring to any mode of behavior of human individuals, regardless of the frame of reference in terms of which it is analysed. "Behaviour" has seemed to be the most appropriate English equivalent. *Handeln,* on the other hand, refers to the concrete phenomenon of human behavior only in so far as it is capable of "understanding" in Weber's technical sense, in terms of subjective categories. The most appropriate English equivalent has seemed to be "action." This corresponds to the editor's usage in *The Structure of Social Action* and would seem to be fairly well established. "Conduct" is also closely similar and has sometimes been used. *Deuten, Verstehen,* and *Sinn* are thus applicable to human behaviour only in so far as it constitutes action or conduct in this specific sense.—Ed.

2 Weber's text is organized in a somewhat unusual manner. He lays down certain fundamental definitions and then proceeds to comment upon them. The definitions themselves are in the original printed in large type, the subsidiary comments in smaller type. For the purposes of this translation it has not seemed best to make a distinction in type form, but the reader should be aware that the numbered paragraphs which follow a definition or group of them are in the nature of comments, rather than the continuous development of a general line of argument. This fact accounts for what is sometimes a relatively fragmentary character of the development and for the abrupt transition from one subject to another. Weber apparently did not intend this material to be "read" in the ordinary sense, but rather to serve as a reference work for the clarification and systematization of theoretical concepts and their implications. While the comments under most of the definitions are relatively brief, under the definitions of Sociology and of Social Action, Weber wrote what is essentially a methodological essay. This makes sec. 1 out of proportion to the other sections of this and the following chapters. It has, however, seemed best to retain Weber's own plan for the subdivision of the material.—Ed.

3 Weber means by "pure type" what he himself generally called and what has come to be known in the literature about his methodology as the "ideal type." The reader may be referred for general orientation to Weber's own essay (to which he himself refers below), *Die Objektivität sozialwissenschaftlicher Erkenntnis;* to two works of Dr. Alexander von Schelting, "Die logische Theorie der historischen Kulturwissenschaften von Max Weber" (*Archiv fuer Sozialwissenschaft,* vol. xlix), and *Max Webers Wissenschaftslehre;* and to the editor's *Structure of Social Action,* chap. xvi. A somewhat different interpretation is given in Theodore Abel, *Systematic Sociology in Germany,* chap. iv.—Ed.

4 This is an imperfect rendering of the German term *Evidenz,* for which, unfortunately, there is no good English equivalent. It has hence been rendered in a number of different ways, varying with the particular context in which it occurs. The primary meaning refers to the basis on which a scientist or thinker becomes satisfied of the certainty or acceptability of a proposition. As Weber himself points out, there are two primary aspects of this. On the one hand a conclusion can be "seen" to follow from given premises by virtue of logical, mathematical, or possibly other modes of meaningful relation. In this sense one "sees" the solution of an arithmetical problem or the correctness of the proof of a geometrical theorem. The other aspect is concerned with empirical observation. If an act of observation is competently performed, in a similar sense one "sees" the truth of the relevant descriptive proposi-

168   CULTURE AND CONSCIOUSNESS: *The Human Center*

tion. The term *Evidenz* does not refer to the process of observing, but to the quality of its result, by virtue of which the observer feels justified in affirming a given statement. Hence "certainty" has seemed a suitable translation in some contexts, "clarity" in others, "accuracy" in still others. The term "intuition" is not usable because it refers to the process rather than to the result.—Ed.

⁵ A term now much used in psychological literature, especially that of psychoanalysis. It is roughly equivalent to "emotion" but more precise.—Ed.

⁶ The German term is *sinnfremd*. This should not be translated by "meaningless" but interpreted in the technical context of Weber's use of *Verstehen* and *Sinndeutung*. The essential criterion is the impossibility of placing the object in question in a complex of relations on the meaningful level.—Ed.

⁷ *Unverstehbar.*

⁸ Surely this passage states too narrow a conception of the scope of meaningful interpretation. It is certainly not *only* in terms such as those of the rational means-end schema, that it is possible to make action understandable in terms of subjective categories. This probably can actually be called a source of rationalistic bias in Weber's work. In practice he does not adhere at all rigorously to this methodological position. For certain possibilities in this broader field, see the editor's *Structure of Social Action*, chaps. vi and xi.—Ed.

⁹ A gulf of the North Sea which broke through the Netherlands coast, flooding an area.—Ed.

¹⁰ Weber here uses the term *aktuelles Verstehen*, which he contrasts with *erklärendes Verstehen*. The latter he also refers to as *motivationsmaessig*. "Aktuell" in this context has been translated as "observational." It is clear from Weber's discussion that the primary criterion is the possibility of deriving the meaning of an act or symbolic expression from immediate observation without reference to any broader context. In *erklärendes Verstehen*, on the other hand, the particular act must be placed in a broader context of meaning involving facts which cannot be derived from immediate observation of a particular act or expression.—Ed.

¹¹ The German term is *Sinnzusammenhang*. It refers to a plurality of elements which form a coherent whole on the level of meaning. There are several possible modes of meaningful relation between such elements, such as logical consistency, the esthetic harmony of a style, or the appropriateness of means to an end. In any case, however, a *Sinnzusammenhang* must be distinguished from a system of elements which are causally interdependent. There seems to be no single English term or phrase which is always adequate. According to variations in the context, "context of meaning," "complex of meaning," and sometimes "meaningful system" have been employed.—Ed.

¹² On the significance of this type of explanation for causal relationship. See para. 6, pp. 96 ff. below in the present section.

¹³ The German is *gemeinter Sinn*. Weber departs from ordinary usage not only in broadening the meaning of this conception. As he states at the end of the present methodological discussion, he does not restrict the use of this concept to cases where a clear self-conscious awareness of such meaning can be reasonably attributed to every individual actor. Essentially, what Weber is doing is to formulate an operational concept. The question is not whether in a sense obvious to the ordinary person such an intended meaning "really exists," but whether the concept is capable of providing a logical framework within which scientifically important observations can be made. The test of validity of the observations is not whether their object is immediately clear to common sense, but whether the results of these technical

observations can be satisfactorily organized and related to those of others in a systematic body of knowledge.—Ed.

[14] The scientific functions of such construction have been discussed in the author's article in the *Archiv für Sozialwissenschaft*, vol. xix, p. 64 ff.

[15] Simmel, in his *Probleme der Geschichtsphilosophie*, gives a number of examples.

[16] The above passage is an exceedingly compact statement of Weber's theory of the logical conditions of proof of causal relationship. He developed this most fully in his essay *Die Objektivität sozialwissenschaftlicher Erkenntnis*, op. cit. It is also discussed in certain of the other essays which have been collected in the volume, *Gesammelte Aufsätze zur Wissenschaftslehre*. The best and fullest secondary discussion is to be found in Von Schelting's book, *Max Webers Wissenschaftslehre*. There is a briefer discussion in chap. xvi of the editor's *Structure of Social Action*. —Ed.

[17] See Eduard Meyer, *Geschichte des Altertums*, Stuttgart, 1901, vol. iii, pp. 420, 444 ff.

[18] The expression *sinnhafte Adäquanz* is one of the most difficult of Webster's technical terms to translate. In most places the cumbrous phrase "adequacy on the level of meaning" has had to be employed. It should be clear from the progress of the discussion that what Weber refers to is a satisfying level of knowledge for the particular purposes of the subjective state of mind of the actor or actors. He is, however, careful to point out that *causal* adequacy involves in addition to this a satisfactory correspondence between the results of observations from the subjective point of view and from the objective; that is, observations of the overt course of action which can be described without reference to the state of mind of the actor. For a discussion of the methodological problem involved here, see *Structure of Social Action,* chaps. ii and v.—Ed.

[19] This is the first occurrence in Weber's text of the term *Chance* which he uses very frequently. It is here translated by "probability," because he uses it as interchangeable with *Wahrscheinlichkeit*. As the term "probability" is used in a technical mathematical and statistical sense, however, it implies the possibility of numerical statement. In most of the cases where Weber uses *Chance* this is out of the question. It is, however, possible to speak in terms of higher and lower degrees of probability. To avoid confusion with the technical mathematical concept, the term "likelihood" will often be used in the translation. It is by means of this concept that Weber, in a highly ingenious way, has bridged the gap between the interpretation of meaning and the inevitably more complex facts of overt action.—Ed.

Karl Mannheim

The Epistemological Consequences of the Sociology of Knowledge

Another of the thinkers who have offered the social sciences a perspective from which to assess and evaluate their activities, and the
implication of these activities for society, is Karl Mannheim. Mannheim's refusal to see human social behavior as the product of irrational forces led him to stress methods by which one could recognize
and understand the influence of ideology that lay beneath the
methodological arguments of the social sciences.

WE MAINTAINED that it was possible to present the sociology of
knowledge as an empirical theory of the actual relations of knowledge
to the social situation without raising any epistemological problems.
On this assumption, all epistemological problems have been avoided
or put into the background. This reserve on our part is possible, and
this artificial isolation of a purely abstracted set of problems is even
desirable as long as our goal is merely the disinterested analysis of
given concrete relationships, without distortion through theoretical
preconceptions. But once the fundamental relationships between social
situations and corresponding aspects are reliably established, one
cannot but devote oneself to the frank disclosure of the valuations
following from them. Anyone who has a sense for the interconnection
of problems which inevitably arise out of the interpretation of empirical data, and who at the same time is not blinded by the intricacy of specialization in modern learning, which very often pre-
vents a direct attack on problems, must have noticed that the facts

presented under the section of "Particularization" are in their very nature hard to accept as mere facts. They transcend bare fact, and call for further epistemological reflection. On the one hand, we have the mere fact that when, through the sociology of knowledge, a relationship is pointed out between an assertion and a situation, there is contained in the very intent of this procedure the tendency to "particularize" its validity. Phenomenologically, one may take cognizance of this fact without disputing the claim to validity implied in it. But, on the other hand, the further fact that the position of the observer does influence the results of thought, and the fact (intentionally dealt with by us in great detail) that the partial validity of a given perspective is fairly exactly determinable, must sooner or later lead us to raise the question as to the significance of this problem for epistemology.

Our point is not, therefore, that the sociology of knowledge will, by its very nature, supplant epistemological and noological inquiry, but rather that it has made certain discoveries which have more than a mere factual relevance, and which cannot be adequately dealt with until some of the conceptions and prejudices of contemporary epistemology have been revised. In the fact, then, that we always attribute only partial validity to particular assertions, we find that new element which compels us to revise the fundamental presuppositions of present-day epistemology. We are dealing here with a case in which the pure determination of a fact (the fact of the partiality of a perspective which is demonstrable in concrete assertions) may become relevant for determining the validity of a proposition and in which the nature of the genesis of an assertion may become relevant to its truth (*wo eine Genesis Sinngenesis zu sein vermag*). This, to say the least, furnishes an obstacle to the construction of a sphere of validity in which the criteria of truth are independent of origins.

Under the dominant presuppositions of present-day philosophy it will be impossible to utilize this new insight for epistemology, because modern theory of knowledge is based on the supposition that bare fact-finding has no relevance to validity. Under the sanctions of this article of faith, every enrichment of knowledge arising out of concrete research, which—seen from a wider point of view—dares to open up more fundamental considerations, is stigmatized with the phrase "sociologism." Once it is decided and elevated into the realm of the *a priori* that nothing can come out of the world of empirical facts which has relevance for the validity of assertions, we become blind to the observation that this *a priori* itself originally was a premature hypostatization of a factual interrelationship which was derived from a particular type of assertion and was formulated over-hastily into an epistemological axiom. With the peace of mind that comes from the *a priori* premise that epistemology is independent of the "empirical" special sciences, the mind is once and for all closed to the insight which a broadened empiricism might bring. The result is that one fails to see that this theory of self-sufficiency, this gesture of self-preservation, serves no other purpose than that of a bulwark for a certain type of academic epistemology which, in its last stages, is attempting to preserve itself from the collapse which might result from a more developed empiricism. The holders of the older view overlook the fact that they are thereby perpetuating not epistemology as such and preserving it from revision at the hands of the individual sciences, but rather merely one specific kind of epistemology, the uniqueness of which consists only in the fact that it once was at war with an earlier stage of a more narrowly conceived empiricism. It then stabilized the conception of knowledge which was derived from merely one particular segment of reality and represented merely one of the many possible varieties of knowledge.

In order to discover where the sociology of knowledge may lead us, we must once more go into the problem of the alleged primacy of epistemology over the special sciences. Having opened the problem by a critical examination, we shall be in a position to formulate, at least sketchily, a positive presentation of the epistemology already implicit in the very problem of the sociology of knowledge. First we must adduce these arguments which undermine or at least call into question the absolute autonomy and primacy of epistemology as over against the special sciences.

Epistemology and the Special Sciences. There is a twofold relationship between epistemology and the special sciences. The former, according to its constructive claims, is fundamental to all the special sciences, since it supplies the basic justifications for the types of knowledge and the conceptions of truth and correctness which these others rely upon in their concrete methods of procedure, and affects their findings. This, however, does not alter the fact that every theory of knowledge is itself influenced by the form which science takes at the time and from which alone it can obtain its conception of the nature of knowledge. In principle, no doubt, it claims to be the basis of all science but in fact it is determined by the condition of science at any given time. The problem is thus made the more difficult by the fact that the very principles, in the light of which knowledge is to be criticized, are themselves found to be socially and historically conditioned. Hence their application appears to be limited to given historical periods and the particular types of knowledge then prevalent.

Once these interrelationships are clearly recognized, then the belief is no longer tenable that epistemology and noology, because of their justifiable claim to foundational functions, must develop autonomously and independently of the progress of the special sciences, and are not subject to basic modifications by these. Consequently we are forced to recognize that a wholesome development of epistemology and noology is possible only if we conceive of their relationship to the special sciences in the following sense:—

New forms of knowledge, in the last analysis, grow out of the conditions of collective life and do not depend for their emergence upon the prior demonstration by a theory of knowledge that they are possible; they do not therefore need to be first legitimized by an epistemology. The relationship is actually quite the reverse: the development of theories of scientific knowledge takes place in the preoccupation with empirical data and the fortunes of the former vary with those of the latter. The revolutions in methodology and epistemology are always sequels and repercussions of the revolutions in the immediate empirical procedures for getting knowledge. Only through constant recourse to the procedure of the special empirical sciences can the epistemological foundations be made sufficiently flexible and extended so that they will not only sanction the claims of the older forms of knowledge (their original purpose) but will also support the newer forms. This peculiar situation is characteristic of all theoretical, philosophic disciplines. Its structure is more clearly perceivable in the philosophy of law which presumes to be the judge and critic of positive law, but which is actually, in most cases, no more than a *post facto* formulation and justification of the principles of positive law.

In saying this, no denial is made of the importance of epistemology or philosophy as such. The basic inquiries which they undertake are indispensable, and indeed, if one attacked epistemology and philosophy on theoretical grounds, one could not avoid dealing with theoretical principles oneself. Such a theoretical attack would, of course, precisely to the extent that it penetrates into fundamental issues, be in itself a philosophical concern. To every factual form of knowledge belongs a theoretical foundation. This basic function of theory, which is to be understood in a structural sense, must never be misapplied by using its character to give an *a priori* certainty to particular findings. If misused in this manner it would frustrate the progress of science and would lead to the displacement, by *a priori* certainties, of views deriving from empirical observations. The errors and the partiality in the theoretical bases of science must continually be revised in the light of new developments in the immediate scientific activities themselves. The light that is thrown by new factual knowledge upon the theoretical foundation must not be allowed to be obscured by the obstacles to thought which theory may possibly erect. Through the particularizing procedure of the sociology of knowledge, we discover that the older epistemology is a correlate of a particular mode of thought. This is one example of the possibility of extending our field of vision by allowing newly discovered empirical evidence to throw new light upon our theoretical foundations. We are thus implicitly called upon to find an epistemological foundation appropriate to these more varied modes of thought. Moreover we are required to find if possible a theoretical basis under which can be subsumed all the modes of thought which, in the course of history, we have succeeded in establishing. We can now examine how far it is true that the hitherto dominant epistemologies and noologies furnish only one particular foundation for a single type of knowledge.

Robert MacIver

Refuges of the Social Sciences

Robert MacIver's recognition that sociological analysis is as valid as
the philosophical base upon which it rests offers us a way out of some
of the methodological tangles into which sociology—in adherence to
operational principles—has fallen. His suggestion that social events
exhibit a type of causal process to some extent different from that of
external nature, indicates that the method of investigation of social
phenomena must be adapted to the nature of the causation itself.
MacIver's insistence that there is no single "truth" nor monistic method
of science, and that, moreover, our models cannot integrate all the
manifestations within them, suggests that sociology be regarded as a
process toward an unattainable but approachable goal of complete
knowledge.

I

What Can We Know That Is Not Causally Known?

The perplexities of social causation have fostered a tendency to resort
to modes of explanation that avoid or seem to avoid the causal challenge. This tendency has particularly marked attempts to explain the
large-scale phenomena of social change. . . . We shall consider the
most characteristic and the most prevalent of these attempts. But first
we shall raise the preliminary question . . . In what sense, if any, is
it possible to explain things without reference to causation? Is causal
explanation only one of several ways of explaining things? What kind

or degree of knowledge can we attain that dispenses altogether with causality?

Whenever we seek to explain anything we relate it to other things: we assign it to some order of things, we place it in some rank or station or category, we compare it with other things, considering wherein it resembles them and wherein it differs from them. We investigate how it has come to be what it is, relating its present state to its past states. We consider its various aspects, properties, parts, or functions, examining their relation to one another, their interdependence within the unity of the whole. All our investigating is a search for relationships and all our science is the knowledge of systems of relations. The more we know, the more widely and the more fully do we apprehend things as related to others and things as themselves systems of relations. Thus the data of perception are brought into the realms of knowledge.

So our preliminary question becomes: Can we apprehend relations that are not, explicitly or by implication, causal relations? This question goes too deep to be adequately answered here. We are postulating relations between things, not merely between our ideas or mental images. We are assuming a real world, not a phantasmagoria. Suppose, then, we are engaged in the simplest act of knowing, in discerning any kind of resemblances and differences between things, between any things in the universe. We may observe that a cloud is "very like a whale," and that is in some sort knowledge. It would certainly be difficult to claim any causal relationship between a whale and a whale-shaped cloud. We may observe that a particular species of mushroom is shaped like a parasol. No one would suggest on that score a causal connection between mushrooms and parasols. But science is not concerned with resemblances of this kind. It does not classify its phenomena on the basis of such resemblances. If we ask why not, the answer is obvious. Science is interested not in superficial resemblances between things, but in resemblances that reveal like processes of development or continuous structural types, or that can be traced back to a single origin, or that in some way can be utilized to organize the data of science in an articulated scheme of orders and categories. Science is not interested in superficial differences between things, but in differences such as represent variations of a structural type, or distinguish one order or suborder or class of things from another, or raise problems concerning the adequacy, inclusiveness, or exactitude of the systems already constructed. In short, science is interested in how things belong together, and it studies and classifies resemblances and differences from this point of view. Everything from a galaxy to an atom is conceived as system, as system beyond system and system within system. Let us go one step further—let us make explicit the hypothesis that at once vitalizes the scientific pursuit and finds progressive support in all scientific achievement, namely, the hypothesis that *things belong together in systems because it is their nature to do so.* When we have taken this step we have reached the causal significance of the relations the knowledge of which is scientific knowledge.

The position thus reached we shall not endeavor to explore. Our subject is social causation, and we have here a special set of conditions that invest our data with their own kind of causality. They fall within social systems, and social systems are in part directly constructed and in large part the resultant of innumerable smaller constructive activities of individuals and groups. Whatever else these activities are they are means-ends activities. They incorporate aspects of objective, motivation, and design. The relations they create and the relations they sustain are immersed in their own causality. We can superficially describe them, we can superficially classify their phenomena as we might classify together animals and animal-shaped clouds, but we cannot comprehend their nature except in so far as we penetrate the causal nexus between social structure and the social being.

It is thus not unreasonable to conclude that all relations between things, if not themselves relations of causation, at least have somewhere a causal ground. Consider, for example, the difference between correlation and causal relation. Correlation, as we have already pointed out, is not a relation between things at all. The relation between quantitative variables is a mathematical relation, a relation of index numbers that *may* lead us to discover a relation of things. Correlation as such has no dynamic significance, any more than have the resemblances between animals and clouds. We seek out correlations in our search for knowledge of the relations of things. We count the instances of a certain phenomenon or we measure some property of a class of things. Then we count the instances of some other phenomenon or measure another property of the same things or the same property of another class of things. Correlation is simply the correspondence between the fluctuations of our numbers or measurements for the two (or more) groups, taken over a period of time or over an area of their spatial distribution. If the correspondence is close, whether directly or inversely, we want to know why. Does it mean that the correspondent variables are interdependent either on one another or on conditions common to them both? The prospect of an answer to this question alone sustains the scientific quest of correlation. We look for correlations only where we suspect they may be causally significant. We do not suspect a connection between the climate of Jupiter and the fashions of Western civilization. We may suspect a connection between sun-spots and harvests. We certainly suspect a connection between temperature and industrial productivity. Such considerations determine the amount of effort we bestow on the discovery of correlations and the amount of study we devote to them after their discovery.

We are not contending that all knowledge, or even all scientific knowledge, is exclusively the apprehension of causal relations. We can appreciate the unity or coherence of things, even as we appreciate their resemblances and differences, without express reference to the causal implications of unity or coherence. We can have perspectives and reflections and intuitions that contemplate the sheerly existent, the enduring, even the timeless. We can apprehend the contours of things, their configurations and symmetries, their qualities of every kind, without examining the causal conditions on which these properties depend. We can follow the historical sequence of events as a series of vicissitudes happening to men and nations, with only a surmise of the causal links that bind them together. Often, in fact, the causal scheme of things is too complex, too obscure, or too deep for us to fathom, and we have to content ourselves with descriptive recognition, just as we watch the waves of the sea without reckoning the forces that determine their shapes and their motions. But such knowledge is not only very partial, it also contains glimpses of an unexplored causality; at the very least it contains the postulate of causation. It takes things together because it presumes, without knowing how, that they belong together. Science, however, engages itself in the endless task of learning *how* they belong together. And social science takes up a variety of the endless task, which introduces other forms as well of the eternal question: *Why?*

II

Change as Periodicity

No "explanation" of social change has had so continuous and so wide an appeal as that which views it as a form of rhythmic motion, the successive stages or recurrent patterns of which constitute the main theme of human history. This conception has pervaded alike popular reflection and philosophical theory. In its broadest and most ancient form it appeared in the doctrine of the ages of man, looking back to an age of gold that in the fulness of time would return. It animated the theories of the successive rise and fall of civilizations and of the stages through which each passed from birth to death. From the time of Plato to our own days this doctrine has been variously embroidered according to the fancy of poet or philosopher, among the more recent exponents being Nietzsche, Pareto, and Spengler. Historical evidences have been massed to support it, and quite recently statistical techniques have been vigorously employed to confirm it.[1] Social scientists of every kind, economists, political scientists, sociologists, anthropologists, have traced the short-time and long-time oscillations, waves, cycles, and spirals of numerous social and cultural phenomena—business activity, employment, population growth, systems of government, opinions, creeds, fashions, inventions, and so forth. The total picture thus presented is one of an endless procession of cycles and epicycles, constituting the intrinsic rhythm of social change beneath all the commotion of its confused surface manifestations.

Most of these descriptions of social change present it as conforming to one or other of two main rhythmic patterns, which we may distinguish as the wave pattern and the closed curve pattern. There are, of course, other types, such as the continuous upward spiral congenial to views of human progress prevalent in the late eighteenth and in the nineteenth century. But the wave pattern and the closed curve pattern have been dominant throughout the history of thought. Each of them is revealed in various aspects of human experience, and the tendency to rediscover them in the processes of social change comes very easily to us.

The wave pattern is represented by the motions of the breath, by the beating of the heart, by the periodicity of organic processes of every kind, by the alternation of light and darkness, by the recurrent seasons, by the ebb and flow of the tides, and by myriad other phenomena that pulsate or recur with a regularity of succession far greater than that of the sea-waves, from which the pattern takes its name. The search for similar periodicities in the institutions as well as in the fortunes of men and peoples is never entirely unrewarded, for in the unstable balance of human affairs there are ups and downs without end. But this intriguing search is beset by two great temptations. One is the temptation to impose a simple symmetry on the facts, by simplifying or smoothing them, even by selecting them, to fit a repetitive rhythmic pattern. The history of the investigation of the "business cycle," for example, offers many illustrations of the seductiveness of this temptation. The other is the tendency to assume that the discovery of symmetries and periodicities is the discovery of a "principle of order" in the phenomena themselves.[2] The wave-like motion may be intrinsic to the phenomena, as in the pulsations of light, or it may be extrinsic, as are the symmetries we can trace by drawing the contours, in any direction taken at random, of a line of hills. These patterns do not reveal the eruptive forces that created the hills or the erosive forces that moulded them; no more may superficial symmetries in the succession of human affairs reveal the dynamics of social change. It is perhaps not without significance that some of the leading representatives of the undulatory theory of social change have been strong believers in the essential sameness of the fate and fortunes of mankind throughout the ages. It is the doctrine put forward by Machiavelli when he declared that "the world has always been the same and always contained as much good and evil, though variously distributed according to the times."[3] It is the view of Pareto, who thinks of social change as a protean scheme of oscillations, in which now dominant elements become recessive and now recessive elements become again dominant. "And so the pendulum continues swinging back and forth from one extreme to the other, indefinitely."[4] Revolutions come and go, élites are dethroned and others take their place and are dethroned in turn. There are endless variations of the recurring tides, but the tides forever recur. Since there is no direction, no evolution, no genuinely creative or constructive processes, since there is little that is inherently different or essentially new, the problem of causation can be largely ignored. The determinant factors are constant and are given from the first. These constant factors are merely reshuffled and recombined.

The doctrine of the closed curve dispenses much more radically with the specific investigation of causes, since it assumes a generic causal principle of a type that is peculiarly screened from investigation. We think in terms of the closed curve whenever we envisage the history of peoples, races, civilizations, institutional systems, as conforming to the curve of the individual organism, that is, as presenting the successive stages of birth, growth, maturity, decline, and death. From this point of view we do not look upon an unbroken sequence of ups and downs, retreats and advances, recovery after decline, the reassertion in new guise of constant factors. Instead we have the picture of determinate beginnings and endings, of determinate life-histories each self-enclosed, each endowed with its own germinal energy, each having an allotted span and following an allotted course. The contrast between the two patterns may be exhibited graphically as follows:

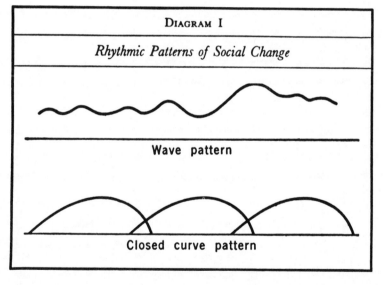

DIAGRAM I

Rhythmic Patterns of Social Change

Wave pattern

Closed curve pattern

The application to social unities of the concept of the closed curve rests on a tempting analogy. All the time things change and pass, in the social sphere as everywhere else. It is easy to think of all this changing and passing as evidence that social unities and organizations are also subject to the fate that befalls the individuals who compose them. There is, of course, no logical ground for the supposition that a unity must follow the course to which its units are predestinated. The trees fall and the forest remains. The generations pass and the nation lives on. The individuals perish and the race endures. Sometimes forests and nations and races also perish, but where can we find clear evidence of a law that prescribes this mortality? No doubt if we make the span of time long enough *the conditions* become at length unfavorable to the continued existence of any form or order of life that previously favorable conditions have sustained. But this is an entirely different consideration from that which ascribes an organic being to these forms and orders of life, such that their life span, inherently predetermined, follows the pattern of the closed organic curve. There are those who, seduced by this analogy, claim that the "expectation of life" of a social epoch or of a civilization is just so many hundred years.[5] The gross liberties of historical dating that must be taken to support such notions are well exemplified by Oswald Spengler, who assigns to each of his great "cultures" a lifetime of fourteen hundred years. So he makes the Egyptian "culture" end about 1800 B.C., and the Indian and the Chinese at the opening of the Christian era! It also suits his purpose to date our present Western culture from about 900 A.D. The identity of each culture, so conceived, is tenuously mystical, and is distinguished by such terms as "Faustian," "Apollonian," "Magian," and so forth. Furthermore, this organicist schema cannot cope with the intermixture of races and nations and cultures, with the endless fusions of the old and the new, with the secessions and the reunions and reformations of groups and cultural elements, which characterize the processes of civilization but are totally inconsistent with the compact unity of a strictly organic structure.

With these and various other difficulties of the closed curve theory we are not here concerned.[6] Our point is that it evades the issue of causation. Since all the stages of a culture, society, or social organization succeed one another, from birth to death, in a predetermined course, the environmental factors are ignored or at best subordinated. The germinal life-structure accounts for the process of development. If a society or a civilization declines, it is because its vital energies are spent, because it has reached the stage of senility, because "societies, like individuals, have a natural self-poisoning function." If it revives, it is only the recovery from a temporary sickness, and the final outcome cannot be stayed. From this point of view the vast transformations of social life responsive to the technological control of environment are merely episodes in the fulfilment of a culture, merely expressions of its stage of expansion. To Spengler, for example, the great city and its modes of activity and of thought represent that period in the life-history of a culture in which its original cohesion and vitality are being dissipated; they are expressions of ageing, relative to each particular culture, with no enduring or cumulative effect on the social history of mankind.[7] For thinkers of this school there is indeed no history of mankind, only the histories of the successive cultures as they rise and flower and fall.[8] Spengler insists that every significant culture scheme reveals the character or "soul" of an organic unity occupying some area of the earth for some fourteen hundred years—unless it untimely dies. Here we have perhaps the extreme example of the dogmatic neglect of causality that is always fostered by the closed curve theory.

III

Explanation by Origins

The doctrines we have just been considering frequently dispense altogether with causal investigation; there are other doctrines that invoke causality but ignore or set aside the crucial issue of social causation—the relation of the phenomena of social change to the complex interplay of various and diverse conditions. The latter tendency we find in many theories that account for social phenomena by appealing to their presumptive origins. Such origins may be conceived of as organic impulses, inherent in the biological or psychological constitution of man, as when a social formation is traced back to some particular instinct, emotion, or native disposition. Incidentally, this mode of explanation may be combined with a periodicity explanation, as in the doctrines of Pareto. Again, the origins may be presented anthropologically, as primary or nuclear situations whence later or more complex institutional systems are derived. The two modes of explanation are not far apart and they easily merge in one another.

The first mode is illustrated by Herbert Spencer's derivation of religion and of religious institutions from the fear of the dead or of ghosts.[9] Sumner hazarded a number of similar guesses, explaining, for example, that ceremonial originates as a form of propitiation.[10] To this author, hunger, love, vanity, and fear were the four main impulses from which, singly or in combination, social institutions took their start. According to Thorstein Veblen vanity and emulation were the source of fashion.[11] One school of anthropologists has attributed the formation of the family to the operation of male jealousy and possessiveness, while another derives it from the maternal need of protection.[12]

Sigmund Freud developed a remarkable variation of this mode. The originating factor is no longer "instinct" but a psychical complex, itself determined by an early type-situation in which the "libido" is canalized, suppressed, or deflected. To one of these complexes, the "Oedipus," in which the nascent sex impulse is blocked by the father and vents itself in anger and hate towards the paternal relationship, he attributed a major role. In one work he went so far as to designate a supposititious primal patricide as the "inexorable criminal act with which so many things began, social organization, moral restriction, and religion." [13] His conclusion was in fact all-embracing. "In closing this study I want to state that the beginnings of religion, ethics, society, and art meet in the Oedipus complex." [14] While in other works these sweeping attributions were somewhat more qualified, they remained characteristic of the Freudian system.

The second mode of appeal to origins takes some simple or primitive form of social relationship, presumptive or evidential, and finds therein the core of the most complex institutions of an advanced civilization. This mode is frequently applied to class systems, political institutions, ecclesiastical institutions, and so forth, usually with some accent of evaluation, favorable or condemnatory. Herbert Spencer claimed that "ceremonial forms are naturally initiated by the relation of conqueror to conquered." [15] Marxist and other writers have maintained that the state began with the domination of one man over others or of one group over another group and that it has taken its essential character from this relationship. The state was originally, said Karl Kautsky, an instrument intended to guard the interests of a dominant group.[16] The state was originally, said Franz Oppenheimer, a social institution imposed by victors on vanquished.[17] That original establishment still *defines* the state. The acceptance by Marxist writers of this definition of the state proved very awkward for them when they came to contemplate a state that *ex hypothesi* embodied another set of principles.

This second mode is often associated with evolutionary theories. For example, various theories of the evolution of religion present some one feature or aspect of religion as primordial or aboriginal, and regard it as playing a decisive role in the development of the whole religious system. Some have held that religion developed out of magic, there being in particular an evolution from the magical spell to the religious prayer. Some have found the primary religious expression in the sacramental meal, others in the propitiatory offering or sacrifice.[18] More broadly, the sociological school of Durkheim, Lévy-Bruhl, and Hubert and Mauss have viewed the evolution of religion as the process in which an early sanction or consecration attached to "collective representations" was elaborated and adapted to changing social situations.

In criticizing the various theories that explain later or more developed institutional systems by appeal to their supposed origins, whether psychological or anthropological, we are not casting doubt on the interest and value of research into the earliest knowable types of social situation or of social behavior. Much illumination has come to us and no doubt much more awaits us in the pursuit of this fascinating subject. But there are important cautions we must observe before we apply this knowledge to the interpretation of historical or contemporary changes and formations. The nexus between an early stage and a later one may not be a simple matter of growth, maturation, inherent development, or readaptation to external change. We cannot assume the organic analogy. The dynamic of social institutions or social systems is not, as it were, internal to them. For these social phenomena are sustained by group attitudes and interests operative so long as the phenomena themselves endure. Whenever they change, the social phenomena, from the simplest relationships to the most complex institutional systems, also undergo change. Furthermore, these group attitudes and interests do not create social institutions in the void but as responsive to environmental conditions of various kinds, themselves always changing and in turn reacting on the psychological factors. Present social institutions therefore depend on the interplay, *in the present*, of these complexly co-operating determinants, and are expressive alike of their continuity and of their change.

From this point of view neither mode of explanation by origins, nor yet any combination of the two, can satisfy us. The anthropological mode cannot carry us over the road from the primitive to the later scheme of institutions. If, for example, there is a transition from the magical spell to the religious prayer—though this itself is a very conjectural claim—we still cannot explain, by examining the earlier form, why the later form arose. If the earliest family was matriarchal that knowledge—itself also dubious—would not enable us to understand why the patriarchal family became dominant in many parts of the earth. The mud hut does not explain the skyscraper, even if there is in some sense an evolution from one to the other. A causal explanation must deal with the contemporaneous conditions, whatever light may be thrown on them from the knowledge of earlier conditions.

The evolutionary approach is beset by other dangers. The seemingly simple often hides the complex. We do not distinguish aspects so well in the smaller or more primitive pattern. We are apt to assume that they are absent when they are merely inconspicuous or undeveloped. The difference, for example, between the magical and the religious principle is more easily discerned at more advanced stages of culture. At the less advanced the magical element may predominate but it by no means follows that the religious is entirely absent. At the less advanced stage of religious institutions the sacramental meal or the propitiatory sacrifice may be the most obvious rite but it may be pervaded by a penumbra of attitudes that later manifest themselves in other rites. The discovery of origins is often elusive. The beginnings of many things cannot be dated. We cannot strictly say that they begin at a certain stage of culture or of civilization. They emerge rather than begin. This is what evolution properly means. If so, it may be vain to look for a *specific* origin or original form. If a thing evolves it cannot be dated. We can date events or laws or constitutions, the collapse of power systems, and so forth. Within limits we can date specific fashions, modes, styles, customs, and the rise of power systems. But we cannot date custom itself or ceremony or the family or the state. And we cannot, without arbitrary discrimination, derive such undatable and permanent phenomena from any one of their manifestations, however early or primitive these may be.[19]

Similar arguments may be directed against the resort to psychological origins. We shall have occasion at a later stage to show the hazard and the insufficiency of causal explanations that rely solely on subjective factors.[20] If this is so where we are dealing with situations immediately presented to us it holds still more forcibly when we are adventuring into "the dark backward and abysm of time." The naïve assurance of our adventurers is undisturbed by the conflict of their various claims. What they take for simple may still be very complex— as well as very unexplored. Motives like "fear" and "vanity" are not simple homogeneous impulses, even when entertained by children or by savages. Institutions that abide through time are not the sheer embodiment of some one attitude or emotion that we can single out from the personality of the individuals who maintain them. Institutions are group responses to group conditions. The responses and the conditions are alike complex and complexly related. When I run it is I, not merely my legs, that run. When a man prays, it is he, not merely his fear, that prays. And if prayer becomes the habit of one man or the custom of many men, there must have been various considerations that prompted the formation of the habit or the custom. There is a congeniality of the group and the institution that is overlooked in these simplifying guesses about origins, but even if they were correct they would not suffice to explain the maintenance, the present existence, of the institutional scheme of behavior.

IV

The Key Cause

Of all the devices by which men have evaded the full problem of social causation the most prevalent by far is that which designates some one factor or complex of factors as peculiarly, exclusively, or dominantly determinant. We delight to simplify our problems, we delight to establish order by assigning priority, and we delight to have in our hands a key that will open any door. The whole history of social theory can be cited in evidence. Successive schools of thought have been distinguished one from another mainly by their discovery of a different key cause.[21] Every possible factor has been invested with that role. Sometimes the factor in question is merely prepotent over others, sometimes it is supreme and exclusive. Sometimes its dynamic range is limited to one order of phenomena, sometimes its range is universal over human affairs.

The sovereign factor may be specific or general, simple or complex, concrete or abstract, external to humanity or working in its blood or its brain. Some have found it in the sheerly environmental: to H. T.

Buckle and to E. Huntington civilizations rise and fall in accord with conditions of climate and soil, while some economic theorists, such as W. S. Jevons and H. L. Moore, have maintained that sun-spot cycles or weather cycles dominate the fluctuations of prices and initiate corresponding variations in the whole scheme of business activity.[22] Others have found the key in some inborn quality of men or groups of men, in differentiated heredity, stock, race: sometimes it is the exclusive heredity of intra-communal families or groups, a theme expounded from the time of Plato to the present day; sometimes it is the inclusive heredity of peoples or races, also an ancient doctrine that received fresh stimulus from nineteenth century developments, and in the commotions of the twentieth has been elevated by at least one state into the first article of a political creed. In this version, first explicitly elaborated in the modern world by Gobineau and then Germanized by Houston Stewart Chamberlain, the dynamic factor became not race but superior race, so that its final and might-bearing prophet could announce: "Everything that we today admire on this earth—science and art, technique and inventions—is only the creative product of a few peoples and perhaps originally of *one* race." [23]

Apart from these polarities of limitless imputation there have been numerous attempts to attach the role of key cause to particular principles, activities, or conjunctures. The most famous of these attempts is doubtless the "economic interpretation of history" according to the special formula announced by Karl Marx and Friedrich Engels. It is the doctrine that the mode of economic production or the primary relations of the economic order determine the general character of the whole social structure, and that as this foundation changes so do all the expressions of human life, its cultural styles, philosophies, and faiths.[24] For others the changing scheme of productive activity, viewed technologically rather than economically, has been the artificer of the various processes of cultural change—a tendency encouraged by Thorstein Veblen when he derived the institutional order from the habit-forming lores and skills of the work-a-day life.[25] Others, as we have already seen, have made some imperious urge, some instinct or some complex, the master inspiration of human activities. Some have found the key to social change in science, some in religion, some in dynamic reason, the dialectic of Hegel. Some have followed the ancient line of Heraclitus, discovering again that strife, war, conflict of any sort, was "the father of things." [26] A modern historian has found in the "challenge of hard conditions" the driving force in the rise of civilizations.[27] Some writers explain all social and cultural phenomena as the expression of a few human desires or wishes, of psychical factors however named. An opposing school transfers the onus from factors of individual consciousness to those of "collective consciousness." Another opposing school adjures the resort to consciousness altogether, and maintains that all phenomena, social or other, are alike what it designates as "physical."

This summary list could be extended indefinitely, but it is large enough for our present purpose. We do not propose to examine the grounds of these endlessly conflicting imputations. All of them omit or "reduce" or devaluate some aspects or elements of the presented totality within which the causal nexus obtains. Sometimes this is done on metaphysical grounds, as by the physicalists who would translate into physical terms the data of consciousness and are apt to dismiss from scientific discourse the language of "motives and goals." But metaphysics of this sort does not help us to discover why a man quarrels with his wife or why a war occurs. Whatever the causal role of purposes and valuations may be they cannot be dismissed as nonexistent. Sometimes the exponents of key causes rely on correlations and concomitances between the chosen factor and the various conditions alleged to be determined by it. This is the type of evidence offered, for example, by such environmentalists as Huntington, when they show that a particular range of climate is associated with a high level of civilization. But they do not reflect on the fact that a high level of civilization is correlated with other things than climate. Even were Huntington's correlations much more firmly established than they are, we would still ask the question: Why dwell so exclusively on one only of the favoring circumstances when many others are clearly involved? Are we to say that, because all the life we know exists between the temperature ranges of minus 50 degrees F. and plus 150 degrees F., the main determinant of organic life is therefore temperature? The tendency to ignore alternative correlations is peculiarly characteristic of many advocates of key causes. But there are many others who do not offer us even a decent show of evidence. The racialists make grandiose claims and practically never cite, unless to dispute them, any facts or considerations that run counter to their theories. The economic determinists present a dogma and not a reasoned conclusion. In all the voluminous writings of Karl Marx there is nowhere any attempt to test the doctrine of the "materialistic interpretation of history." Constantly we are bidden to view events and situations in the light of the doctrine. We are told, for example, that "the ideas of freedom of thought and of religion express only the dominance of free competition within the sphere of knowledge." [28] The analogy is ingenious, if left as such. The "only" turns it into a dogma. It forbids us to view a many-angled situation from any angle but one.

Sometimes the advocates of key causes make concessions, but in such a way as to assign an inferior causal status to all other factors. They admit that there are "conditions" without which the key cause would not function. Or they admit that, besides the key cause, other causes operate as "secondary factors." The latter is the line of defence adopted by the Marxists. They do not deny that political and cultural factors have some efficacy, but it is the efficacy of the created "reacting back" on the creator.[29] The economic or "material" factor is still fundamental, primary. But obviously, if various factors are interactive, their relationship can in any particular instance be discovered only by rigorous investigation and it may be entirely different in different instances. The hypothesis that it is always the same, that it is always the relation of a dominant factor to subsidiary ones, is not ranked by the Marxists as a hypothesis but always as an *a priori* truth. The evidences that apparently are in conflict with it are not examined but are given a coloration congenial to the doctrine. We turn on what the economic historian G. Schmoller called a "dry light," and then what seemed a struggle for religious liberty becomes a scramble for colonies or a protest against taxation or a class uprising. The most precarious of all imputations, the imputation of motives, is resorted to with complete assurance, although the least reflection tells us that in everyday affairs motives are often obscure and mixed and hard to disentangle. But this is a subject that will meet us again.

To criticize at any length the numerous expositions of key causes would take space and time we can better bestow on the central problem they alike evade. In every problem of social causation we are confronted with a variety of factors or determinants. How are we to deal with them, how are they bound together in the social nexus? The problem is presented to us on two levels. Those who postulate key causes present it—and claim to solve it—in abstraction from particular situations or conjunctures. They assert the *universal* priority of one factor over others, as though it had some inherent efficacy, some predetermined status before which, on all occasions, the other factors make obeisance. Whatever factor they exalt to this status— whether it be religion or political power or reason or the sex drive or education or geography or technology or economic relationship— the same unwarranted principle animates the doctrine. The factor is detached from the conjuncture in which alone it has dynamic virtue and is erected into thing-hood as an independent and integral cause. On this level the only answer is the logical exposure of the dogma that falsely claims to be science.[30] Then we can descend to the other level, the level of particular situations. Here we are confronted with the variety of aspects that define a situation, the variety of conditions that contain it. If we call these aspects and conditions "factors," let us remember that in the causal process they are always interwoven and that we cannot isolate them severally within that process in order to study the causal efficacy of each. Since they are always interwoven, how can we claim that some one thread, no matter which, in the growing, changing pattern controls the further weaving? Even to speak of the "factor" as interwoven is to assert of each a degree of independence that simplifies and mechanizes their causal interdependence. Viewed apart from its relation to the rest every factor of the socio-psychological complex, whether named "economic" or "political" or "religious" or "sexual" or whatever else, becomes unreal or at least undynamic. What we strive towards, as conscious beings, is some state of conscious being, and none of these categories refers to that state in its whole-ness, but only to some mode of attaining it or at most to some aspect of it. We abstract our categories from the wholeness of experience. We do so either for purposes of intellectual analysis, for the under-standing (and therewith the misunderstanding) of situations; or for purposes of practical control, for the direction of our energies through the development of techniques and organizations. Thus these cate-gories, our "factors," are modes of reference to experience but are not to be regarded as separable components that somehow make it up.

NOTES

[1] P. Sorokin, *Social and Cultural Dynamics* (New York, 1937), Vol. III.

[2] Thus, for example, A. L. Kroeber postulates a "principle of order in civilization" on the strength of certain periodicities in dress fashions, *American Anthropologist* (July–September, 1919), Vol. 21, pp. 235–263.

[3] *Discorsi*, Book II.

[4] *The Mind and Society* (New York, 1935), edited by A. Livingston, Vol. IV, § 2340.

[5] For example, Oswald Spengler, *Decline of the West* (New York, 1926), translated by Atkinson; W. M. Flinders Petrie, *The Revolutions of Civilizations*, London, 1911.

[6] The writer has dealt with them in other works, particularly *Community* (New York, 1928), Book III, Chap. II; *The Modern State* (Oxford, 1926), Chap. X; *Society: Its Structure and Changes* (New York, 1931), Chap. XXV.

[7] Spengler, *op. cit.*, Vol. II, Chap. 4.

[8] Spengler, *op. cit.* Vol. I, Chap. 1.

[9] *Principles of Sociology* (American edition, New York, 1900), Vol. III, p. 21.

[10] W. G. Sumner and A. G. Keller, *The Science of Society* (New Haven, 1927), Vol. II, p. 279.

[11] *The Theory of the Leisure Class,* (New York, 1922), Chaps. I, IV.

[12] For the former claim see E. Westermarck, *Short History of Marriage* (London, 1926), Chap. VIII; for the latter, R. Briffault, *The Mothers* (New York, 1927), 1, Chaps. III–VI and *passim*.

[13] *Totem and Taboo* (New York, 1932), p. 237.

[14] *Ibid,* p. 260.

[15] *Political Institutions* (New York, 1882), p. 310.

[16] *The Class Struggle* (Chicago, 1910), Chap. IV.

[17] *The State* (New York, 1926), Introduction and Chap. I.

[18] *Cf.* W. Robertson Smith, *Religion of the Semites* (Third Edition, New York, 1927); E. Durkheim, *Elementary Forms of the Religious Life* (London, 1915), translated by Swain.

[19] The more scholarly studies of "origins" fully accept these principles. We may cite, as examples, R. H. Lowie, *The Origin of the State* (New York, 1927); G. Landtman, *The Origin of the Inequality of the Social Classes* (Chicago, 1938); Paul Radin, *Primitive Religion* (New York, 1937); S. H. Hooke, *The Origins of Early Semitic Ritual* (London, 1938).

[20] Chapter Seven. We leave for examination in that chapter the particular difficulties of the Freudian variety of the appeal to origins.

[21] The critical survey by P. Sorokin, *Contemporary Sociological Theories* (New York, 1928), affords particularly good corroboration of this point.

[22] H. T. Buckle, *Introduction to the History of England*, recent edition (New York, 1925); E. Huntington, *Civilization and Climate* (New Haven, 1924) and *World Power and Evolution* (New Haven, 1919); W. S. Jevons, *Investigations in Currency and Finance* (London, 1909); H. L. Moore, *Economic Cycles: Their Law and Causes* (New York, 1914).

[23] A. de Gobineau, *The Inequality of Human Races* (New York, 1914), translated by Collins; H. S. Chamberlain, *Foundations of the Nineteenth Century* (London, 1911), translated by Lees. The quotation is from Adolf Hitler, *Mein Kampf* (New York, 1930), unabridged translation, Vol. I, Chap. XI, italics as in original.

[24] Karl Marx, *Critique of Political Economy* (New York, 1904), translated by Stone, Chap. I; Marx and Engels, *Selected Correspondence* (New York, 1934); F. Engels, *Socialism, Utopian and Scientific* (Chicago, 1908).

[25] *The Instinct of Workmanship* (New York, 1914), Chap. I; *The Theory of the*

Leisure Class, First Edition (New York, 1899); *Imperial Germany and the Industrial Revolution* (New York, 1915).

[26] For a list of modern philosophers and sociologists who have expounded this doctrine see P. Sorokin, *op. cit.,* Chap. VI.

[27] Arnold J. Toynbee, *A Study of History* (London, 1937).

[28] *Communist Manifesto.*

[29] This interpretation is made in various letters of Engels in the Marx-Engels correspondence. See, for example, the letter of Engels to Schmidt, 1890.

[30] A good example of such logical exposure is Max Weber's critique of R. Stammler's work, *Wirtschaft und Recht nach der materialistischen Geschichtsauffassung,* in *Archiv für Sozialwissenschaft und Sozialpolitik* (1907), Vol. 24, pp. 94–151.

Fritz J. Machlup

Are the Social Sciences Really Inferior?

Fritz Machlup analyzes the differences between social and natural sciences to suggest that the social sciences are, in fact, different from the natural sciences. He believes that it is more useful to understand the nature of the fundamental differences between them and to construct methodologies suitable to the differences, than to attempt continually to judge social science in terms of natural science and thereby attempt to force the social world into a mold set by physicists dealing with very different phenomena.

IF WE ASK WHETHER the "social sciences" are "really inferior," let us first make sure that we understand each part of the question.

"Inferior" to what? Of course to the natural sciences. "Inferior" in what respect? It will be our main task to examine all the "respects," all the scores on which such inferiority has been alleged. I shall enumerate them presently.

The adverb *"really"* which qualifies the adjective "inferior" refers to allegations made by some scientists, scholars, and laymen. But it refers also to the "inferiority complex" which I have noted among many social scientists. A few years ago I wrote an essay entitled "The Inferiority Complex of the Social Sciences." [1] In that essay I said that "an inferiority complex may or may not be justified by some 'objective' standards," and I went on to discuss the consequences which "the *feeling* of inferiority"—conscious or subconscious—has for the behavior of the social scientists who are suffering from it. I did not then discuss whether the complex has an objective basis, that is, whether the social sciences are "really" inferior. This is our question to-day.

The subject noun would call for a long disquisition. What is meant by *"social sciences,"* what is included, what is not included? Are they the same as what others have referred to as the "moral sciences," the "Geisteswissenschaften," the "cultural sciences," the "behavioral sciences"? Is Geography, or the part of it that is called "Human Geography," a social science? Is History a social science—or perhaps even *the* social science *par excellence,* as some philosophers have contended? We shall not spend time on this business of defining and classifying. A few remarks may later be necessary in connection with some points of methodology, but by and large we shall not bother here with a definition of "social sciences" and with drawing boundary lines around them.

The Grounds of Comparison

The social sciences and the natural sciences are compared and contrasted on many scores, and the discussions are often quite unsystematic. If we try to review them systematically, we shall encounter a good deal of overlap and unavoidable duplication. None the less, it will help if we enumerate in advance some of the grounds of comparison most often mentioned, grounds on which the social sciences are judged to come out "second best":

1. Invariability of observations
2. Objectivity of observations and explanations
3. Verifiability of hypotheses
4. Exactness of findings
5. Measurability of phenomena
6. Constancy of numerical relationships
7. Predictability of future events
8. Distance from every-day experience
9. Standards of admission and requirements

We shall examine all these comparisons.

Invariability of Observations

The idea is that you cannot have much of a science unless things recur, unless phenomena repeat themselves. In nature we find many factors and conditions "invariant." Do we in society? Are not conditions in society changing all the time, and so fast that most events are unique, each quite different from anything that has happened before? Or can one rely on the saying that "history repeats itself" with sufficient invariance to permit generalizations about social events?

There is a great deal of truth, and important truth, in this comparison. Some philosophers were so impressed with the invariance of nature and the variability of social phenomena that they used this difference as the criterion in the definitions of natural and cultural sciences. Following Windelband's distinction between generalizing ("nomothetic") and individualizing ("ideographic") propositions, the German philosopher Heinrich Rickert distinguished between the generalizing sciences of nature and the individualizing sciences of cultural phenomena; and by individualizing sciences he meant historical sciences.[2] In order to be right, he redefined both "nature" and "history" by stating that reality is "nature" if we deal with it in terms of the *general* but becomes "history" if we deal with it in terms of the *unique*. To him, geology was largely history, and economics, most similar to physics, was a natural science. This implies a rejection of the contention that all fields which are normally called social sciences suffer from a lack of invariance; indeed, economics is here considered so much a matter of immutable laws of nature that it is handed over to the natural sciences.

This is not satisfactory, nor does it dispose of the main issue that natural phenomena provide *more* invariance than social phenomena. The main difference lies probably in the number of factors that must be taken into account in explanations and predictions of natural and social events. Only a small number of reproducible facts will normally be involved in a physical explanation or prediction. A much larger number of facts, some of them probably unique historical events, will be found relevant in an explanation or prediction of economic or other social events. This is true, and methodological devices will not do away with the difference. But it is, of course, only a difference in degree.

The physicist Robert Oppenheimer once raised the question whether, if the universe is a *unique* phenomenon, we may assume that *universal* or *general* propositions can be formulated about it. Economists of the Historical School insisted on treating each "stage" or phase of economic society as a completely unique one, not permitting the formulation of universal propositions. Yet, in the physical world, phenomena are not quite so homogeneous as many have liked to think; and in the social world, phenomena are not quite so heterogeneous as many have been afraid they are. (If they were, we could not even have generalized concepts of social events and words naming them.) In any case, where reality seems to show a bewildering number of variations, we construct an ideal world of abstract models in which we create enough homogeneity to permit us to apply reason and deduce the implied consequences of assumed constellations. This artificial homogenization of types of phenomena is carried out in natural and social sciences alike.

There is thus no difference in invariance in the sequences of events in nature and in society as long as we theorize about them—because in the abstract models homogeneity is assumed. There is only a difference of degree in the variability of phenomena of nature and society if we talk about the real world—as long as heterogeneity is not reduced by means of deliberate "controls." There is a third world, between the abstract world of theory and the real unmanipulated world, namely, the artificial world of the experimental laboratory. In this world there is less variability than in the real world and more than in the model world. But this third world does not exist in most of the social sciences (nor in all natural sciences). We shall see later that the mistake is often made of comparing the artificial laboratory world of manipulated nature with the real world of unmanipulated society.

We conclude on this point of comparative invariance, that there is indeed a difference between natural and social sciences, and that the difference—apart from the possibility of laboratory experiments—lies chiefly in the number of relevant factors, and hence of possible combinations, to be taken into account for explaining or predicting events occurring in the real world.

Objectivity of Observations and Explanations

The idea behind a comparison between the "objectivity" of observations and explorations in the natural and social sciences may be conveyed by an imaginary quotation: "Science must be objective and not affected by value judgments; but the social sciences are inherently concerned with values and, hence, they lack the disinterested objectivity of science." True? Frightfully muddled. The trouble is that the problem of "subjective value," which is at the very root of the social sciences, is quite delicate and has in fact confused many, including some fine scholars.

To remove confusion one must separate the different meanings of "value" and the different ways in which they relate to the social sciences, particularly economics. I have distinguished eleven different kinds of value-reference in economics, but have enough sense to spare you this exhibition of my pedagogic dissecting zeal. But we cannot dispense entirely with the problem and overlook the danger of confusion. Thus, I offer you a bargain and shall reduce my distinctions from eleven to four. I am asking you to keep apart the following four meanings in which value judgment may come into our present discussion: (a) The analyst's judgment may be biased for one reason or another, perhaps because his views of the social "Good" or his personal pecuniary interests in the practical use of his findings interfere with the proper scientific detachment. (b) Some normative issues may be connected with the problem under investigation, perhaps ethical judgments which may color some of the investigator's incidental pronouncements—*obiter dicta*—without however causing a bias in his reported findings of his research. (c) The interest in solving the problems under investigation is surely affected by values since, after all, the investigator selects his problems because he believes that their solution would be of value. (d) The investigator in the social sciences has to explain his observations as results of human actions which can be interpreted only with reference to motives and purposes of the actors, that is, to values entertained by them.

With regard to the first of these possibilities, some authorities have held that the social sciences may more easily succumb to temptation and may show obvious biases. The philosopher Morris Cohen, for example, spoke of "the subjective difficulty of maintaining scientific detachment in the study of human affairs. Few human beings can calmly and with equal fairness consider both sides of a question such as socialism, free love, or birth-control." [3] This is quite true, but one should not forget similar difficulties in the natural sciences. Remember the difficulties which, in deference to religious values, biologists had in discussions of evolution and, going further back, the troubles of astronomers in discussions of the heliocentric theory and of geologists in discussions of the age of the earth. Let us also recall that only

25 years ago, German mathematicians and physicists rejected "Jewish" theorems and theories, including physical relativity, under the pressure of nationalistic values, and only ten years ago Russian biologists stuck to a mutation theory which was evidently affected by political values. I do not know whether one cannot detect in our own period here in the United States an association between political views and scientific answers to the question of the genetic dangers from fallout and from other nuclear testing.

Apart from political bias, there have been cases of real cheating in science. Think of physical anthropology and its faked Piltdown Man. That the possibility of deception is not entirely beyond the pale of experimental scientists can be gathered from a splendid piece of fiction, a recent novel, *The Affair*, by C. P. Snow, the well-known Cambridge don.

Having said all this about the possibility of bias existing in the presentation of evidence and findings in the natural sciences, we should hasten to admit that not a few economists, especially when concerned with current problems and the interpretation of recent history, are given to "lying with statistics." It is hardly a coincidence if labor economists choose one base year and business economists choose another base year when they compare wage increases and price increases; or if for their computations of growth rates expert witnesses for different political parties choose different statistical series and different base years. This does not indicate that the social sciences are in this respect "superior" or "inferior" to the natural sciences. Think of physicists, chemists, medical scientists, psychiatrists, etc., appearing as expert witnesses in court litigation to testify in support of their clients' cases. In these instances the scientists are in the role of analyzing concrete individual events, of interpreting recent history. If there is a difference at all between the natural and social sciences in this respect, it may be that economists these days have more opportunities to present biased findings than their colleagues in the physical sciences. But even this may not be so. I may underestimate the opportunities of scientists and engineers to submit expert testimonies with paid-for bias.

The second way in which value judgments may affect the investigator does not involve any bias in his findings or his reports on his findings. But ethical judgments may be so closely connected with his problems that he may feel impelled to make evaluative pronouncements on the normative issues in question. For example, scientists may have strong views about vivisection, sterilization, abortion, hydrogen bombs, biological warfare, etc., and may express these views in connection with their scientific work. Likewise, social scientists may have strong views about the right to privacy, free enterprise, free markets, equality of income, old-age pensions, socialized medicine, segregation, education, etc., and they may express these views in connection with the results of their research. Let us repeat that this need not imply that their findings are biased. There is no difference on this score between the natural and the social sciences. The research and its results may be closely connected with values of all sorts, and value judgments may be expressed, and yet the objectivity of the research and of the reports on the findings need not be impaired.

The third way value judgments affect research is in the selection of the project, in the choice of the subject for investigation. This is unavoidable and the only question is what kinds of value and whose values are paramount. If research is financed by foundations or by the government, the values may be those which the chief investigator believes are held by the agencies or committees that pass on the allocation of funds. If the research is not aided by outside funds, the project may be chosen on the basis of what the investigator believes to be "social values," that is, he chooses a project that may yield solutions to problems supposed to be important for society. Society wants to know how to cure cancer, how to prevent hay fever, how to eliminate mosquitoes, how to get rid of crab grass and weeds, how to restrain juvenile delinquency, how to reduce illegitimacy and other accidents, how to increase employment, to raise real wages, to aid farmers, to avoid price inflation, and so on, and so forth. These examples suggest that the value component in the project selection is the same in the natural and in the social sciences. There are instances, thank God, in which the investigator selects his project out of sheer intellectual curiosity and does not give "two hoots" about the social importance of his findings. Still, to satisfy curiosity is a value too, and indeed a very potent one. We must not fail to mention the case of the graduate student who lacks imagination as well as intellectual curiosity and undertakes a project just because it is the only one he can think of, though neither he nor anybody else finds it interesting, let alone important. We may accept this case as the exception to the rule. Such exceptions probably are equally rare in the natural and the social sciences.

Now we come to the one real difference, the fourth of our value-references. Social phenomena are defined as results of human action, and all human action is defined as motivated action. Hence, social phenomena are explained only if they are attributed to definite types of action which are "understood" in terms of the values motivating those who decide and act. This concern with values—not values which the investigator entertains but values he understands to be effective in guiding the actions which bring about the events he studies—is the crucial difference between the social sciences and the natural sciences. To explain the motion of molecules, the fusion or fission of atoms, the paths of celestial bodies, the growth or mutation of organic matter, etc., the scientist will not ask why the molecules want to move about, why atoms decide to merge or to split, why Venus has chosen her particular orbit, why certain cells are anxious to divide. The social scientist, however, is not doing his job unless he explains changes in the circulation of money by going back to the decisions of the spenders and hoarders, explains company mergers by the goals that may have persuaded managements and boards of corporate bodies to take such actions, explains the location of industries by calculations of such things as transportation costs and wage differentials, and economic growth by propensities to save, to invest, to innovate, to procreate or prevent procreation, and so on. My social-science examples were all from economics, but I might just as well have taken examples from sociology, cultural anthropology, political science, etc., to show that explanation in the social sciences regularly requires the interpretation of phenomena in terms of idealized motivations of the idealized persons whose idealized actions bring forth the phenomena under investigation.

An example may further elucidate the difference between the explanatory principles in non-human nature and human society. A rock does not say to us: "I am a beast," [4] nor does it say: "I came here because I did not like it up there near the glaciers, where I used to live; here I like it fine, especially this nice view of the valley." We do not inquire into value judgments of rocks. But we must not fail to take account of valuations of humans; social phenomena must be explained as the results of motivated human actions.

The greatest authorities on the methodology of the social sciences have referred to this fundamental postulate as the requirement of "subjective interpretation," and all such interpretation of "subjective meanings" implies references to values motivating actions. This has of course nothing to do with value judgments impairing the "scientific objectivity" of the investigators or affecting them in any way that would make their findings suspect. Whether the postulate of subjective interpretation which *differentiates* the social sciences from the natural sciences should be held to make them either "inferior" or "superior" is a matter of taste.

Verifiability of Hypotheses

It is said that verification is not easy to come by in the social sciences, while it is the chief business of the investigator in the natural sciences. This is true, though many do not fully understand what is involved and, consequently, are apt to exaggerate the difference.

One should distinguish between what a British philosopher has recently called "high-level hypotheses" and "low-level generalizations." [5] The former are postulated and can never be *directly* verified; a single high-level hypothesis cannot even be *indirectly* verified, because from one hypothesis standing alone nothing follows. Only a *whole system* of hypotheses can be tested by deducing from some set of general postulates and some set of specific assumptions the logical consequences, and comparing these with records of observations regarded as the approximate empirical counterparts of the specific assumptions and specific consequences.[6] This holds for both the natural and the social sciences. (There is no need for *direct* tests of the fundamental postulates in physics—such as the laws of conservation of energy, of angular momentum, of motion—or of the fundamental postulates in economics—such as the laws of maximizing utility and profits.)

While entire theoretical systems and the low-level generalizations derived from them are tested in the natural sciences, there exist at any one time many unverified hypotheses. This holds especially with regard to theories of creation and evolution in such fields as biology, geology, and cosmogony; for example (if my reading is correct), of the theory of the expanding universe, the dust-cloud hypothesis of the formation of stars and planets, of the low-temperature or high-temperature theories of the formation of the earth, of the various (conflicting) theories of granitization, etc. In other words, where the natural sciences deal with non-reproducible occurrences and with sequences for which controlled experiments cannot be devised, they have to work with hypotheses which remain untested for a long time, perhaps forever.

In the social sciences, low-level generalizations about recurring events are being tested all the time. Unfortunately, often several conflicting hypotheses are consistent with the observed facts and there are no crucial experiments to eliminate some of the hypotheses. But every one of us could name dozens of propositions that have been discomfirmed, and this means that the verification process has done what it is supposed to do. The impossibility of controlled experiments and the relatively large number of relevant variables are the chief obstacles to more efficient verification in the social sciences. This is not an inefficiency on the part of our investigators, but it lies in the nature of things.

Exactness of Findings

Those who claim that the social sciences are "less exact" than the natural sciences often have a very incomplete knowledge of either of them, and a rather hazy idea of the meaning of "exactness." Some mean by exactness measurability. This we shall discuss under a separate heading. Others mean accuracy and success in predicting future events, which is something different. Others mean reducibility to mathematical language. The meaning of exactness best founded in intellectual history is the possibility of constructing a theoretical system of idealized models containing abstract constructs of variables and of relations between variables, from which most or all propositions concerning particular connections can be deduced. Such systems do not exist in several of the natural sciences—for example, in several areas of biology—while they do exist in at least one of the social sciences: economics.

We cannot foretell the development of any discipline. We cannot say now whether there will soon or ever be a "unified theory" of political science, or whether the piecemeal generalizations which sociology has yielded thus far can be integrated into one comprehensive theoretical system. In any case, the quality of "exactness," if this is what is meant by it, cannot be attributed to all the natural sciences nor denied to all the social sciences.

Measurability of Phenomena

If the availability of numerical data were in and of itself an advantage in scientific investigation, economics would be on the top of all sciences. Economics is the only field in which the raw data of experience are already in numerical form. In other fields the analyst must first quantify and measure before he can obtain data in numerical form. The physicist must weigh and count and must invent and build instruments from which numbers can be read, numbers standing for certain relations pertaining to essentially non-numerical observations. Information which first appears only in some such form as "relatively" large, heavy, hot, fast, is later transformed into numerical data by means of measuring devices such as rods, scales, thermometers, speedometers. The economist can begin with numbers. What he observes are prices and sums of moneys. He can start out with numerical data given to him without the use of measuring devices.

The compilation of masses of data calls for resources which only large organizations, frequently only the government, can muster. This, in my opinion, is unfortunate because it implies that the availability of numerical data is associated with the extent of government intervention in economic affairs, and there is therefore an inverse relation between economic information and individual freedom.

Numbers, moreover, are not all that is needed. To be useful, the numbers must fit the concepts used in theoretical propositions or in comprehensive theoretical systems. This is rarely the case with regard to the raw data of economics, and thus the economic analyst still has the problem of obtaining comparable figures by transforming his raw data into adjusted and corrected ones, acceptable as the operational counterparts of the abstract constructs in his theoretical models. His success in this respect has been commendable, but very far short of what is needed; it cannot compare with the success of the physicist in developing measurement techniques yielding numerical data that can serve as operational counterparts of constructs in the models of theoretical physics.

Physics, however, does not stand for all natural sciences, nor economics for all social sciences. There are several fields, in both natural and social sciences, where quantification of relevant factors has not been achieved and may never be achieved. If Lord Kelvin's phrase, "Science is Measurement," were taken seriously, science might miss some of the most important problems. There is no way of judging whether non-quantifiable factors are more prevalent in nature or in society. The common reference to the "hard" facts of nature and the "soft" facts with which the student of society has to deal seems to imply a judgment about measurability. "Hard" things can be firmly gripped and measured, "soft" things cannot. There may be something to this. The facts of nature are perceived with our "senses," the facts of society are interpreted in terms of the "sense" they make in a motivational analysis. However, this contrast is not quite to the point, because the "sensory" experience of the natural scientist refers to the *data,* while the "sense" interpretation by the social scientist of the ideal-typical inner experience of the members of society refers to basic *postulates* and intervening variables.

The conclusion, that we cannot be sure about the prevalence of non-quantifiable factors in natural and social sciences, still holds.

Constancy of Numerical Relationships

On this score there can be no doubt that some of the natural sciences have got something which none of the social sciences has got: "constants," unchanging numbers expressing unchanging relationships between measurable quantities.

The discipline with the largest number of constants is, of course, physics. Examples are the velocity of light ($c = 2.99776 \times 10^{10}$ cm/sec), Planck's constant for the smallest increment of spin or angular momentum ($h = 6.624 \times 10^{-27}$ erg sec), the gravitation constant ($G = 6.6 \times 10^{-8}$ dyne cm^2 gram^{-2}), the Coulomb constant ($e = 4.8025 \times 10^{-10}$ units), proton mass ($M = 1.672 \times 10^{-24}$ gram), the ratio of proton mass to electron mass ($M/m = 1836.13$), the fine-structure constant ($\alpha^{-1} = 137.0371$). Some of these constants are postulated (conventional), others (the last two) are empirical, but this makes no difference for our purposes. Max Planck contended, the postulated "universal constants" were not just "invented for reasons of practical convenience, but have forced themselves upon us irresistibly because of the agreement between the results of all relevant measurements." [7]

I know of no numerical constant in any of the social sciences. In economics we have been computing certain ratios which, however, are found to vary relatively widely with time and place. The annual income-velocity of circulation of money, the marginal propensities to consume, to save, to import, the elasticities of demand for various goods, the savings ratios, capital-output ratios, growth rates—none of these has remained constant over time or is the same for different countries. They all have varied, some by several hundred per cent of the lowest value. Of course, one has found "limits" of these variations, but what does this mean in comparison with the virtually immutable physical constants? When it was noticed that the ratio between labor income and national income in some countries has varied by "only" ten per cent over some twenty years, some economists were so perplexed that they spoke of the "constancy" of the relative shares. (They hardly realized that the 10 per cent variation in that ratio was the same as about a 25 per cent variation in the ratio between labor income and non-labor income.) That the income velocity of circulation of money has rarely risen above 3 or fallen below 1 is surely interesting, but this is anything but a "constant." That the marginal propensity to consume cannot in the long run be above 1 is rather obvious, but in the short run it may vary between .7 and 1.2 or even more. That saving ratios (to national income) have never been above 15 per cent in any country regardless of the economic system (communistic or capitalistic, regulated or essentially free) is a very important fact; but saving ratios have been known to be next to zero, or even negative, and the variations from time to time and country to country are very large indeed.

Sociologists and actuaries have reported some "relatively stable" ratios—accident rates, birth rates, crime rates, etc.—but the "stability" is only relative to the extreme variability of other numerical ratios. Indeed, most of these ratios are subject to "human engineering," to governmental policies designed to change them, and hence they are not even thought of as constants.

The verdict is confirmed: while there are important numerical constants in the natural sciences, there are none in the social sciences.

Predictability of Future Events

Before we try to compare the success which natural and social sciences have had in correctly predicting future events, a few important distinctions should be made. We must distinguish hypothetical or conditional predictions from unconditional predictions or forecasts. And among the former we must distinguish those where all the stated conditions can be controlled, those where all the stated conditions can be either controlled or unambiguously ascertained before the event, and finally those where some of the stated conditions can neither be controlled nor ascertained early enough (if at all). A conditional prediction of the third kind is such an "iffy" statement that it may be of no use unless one can know with confidence that it would be highly improbable for these problematic conditions (uncontrollable and not ascertainable before the event) to interfere with the prediction. A different kind of distinction concerns the numerical definiteness of the prediction: one may predict that a certain magnitude (a) will change, (b) will increase, (c) will increase by at least so-and-so much, (d) will increase within definite limits, or (e) will increase by a definite amount. Similarly, the prediction may be more or less definite with respect to the time within which it is supposed to come true. A prediction without any time specification is worthless.

Some people are inclined to believe that the natural sciences can beat the social sciences on any count, in unconditional predictions as well as in conditional predictions fully specified as to definite conditions, exact degree and time of fulfilment. But what they have in mind are the laboratory experiments of the natural sciences, in which predictions have proved so eminently successful; and then they look at the poor record social scientists have had in predicting future events in the social world which they observe but cannot control. This comparison is unfair and unreasonable. The artificial laboratory world in which the experimenter tries to control all conditions as best as he can is different from the real world of nature. If a comparison is made, it must be between predictions of events in the real natural world and in the real social world.

Even for the real world, we should distinguish between predictions of events which we try to bring about by design and predictions of events in which we have no part at all. The teams of physicists and engineers who have been designing and developing machines and apparatuses are not very successful in predicting their performance when the design is still new. The record of predictions of the paths of moon shots and space missiles has been rather spotty. The so-called "bugs" that have to be worked out in any any new contraption are nothing but predictions gone wrong. After a while predictions become more reliable. The same is true, however, with predictions concerning the performance of organized social institutions. For example, if I take an envelope, put a certain address on it and a certain postage stamp, and deposit it in a certain box on the street, I can predict that after three or four days it will be delivered at a certain house thousands of miles away. This prediction and any number of similar predictions will prove correct with a remarkably high frequency. And you don't have to be a social scientist to make such successful predictions about an organized social machinery, just as you don't have to be a natural scientist to predict the result of your pushing the electric-light switch or of similar manipulations of a well-tried mechanical or electrical apparatus.

There are more misses and fewer hits with regard to predictions of completely unmanipulated and unorganized reality. Meteorologists have a hard time forecasting the weather for the next 24 hours or two or three days. There are too many variables involved and it is too difficult to obtain complete information about some of them. Economists are only slightly better in forecasting employment and income, exports and tax revenues for the next six months or for a year or two. Economists, moreover, have better excuses for their failures because of the unpredictable "interferences" by governmental agencies or power groups which may even be influenced by the forecasts of the economists and may operate to defeat their predictions. On the other hand, some of the predictions may be self-fulfilling in that people, learning of the predictions, act in ways which bring about the predicted events. One might say that economists ought to be able to include the "psychological" effects of their communications among the variables of their models and take full account of these influences. There are, however, too many variables, personal and political, involved to make it possible to allow for all effects which anticipations, and anticipations of anticipations, may have upon the end results. To give an example of a simple self-defeating prediction from another social science: traffic experts regularly forecast the number of automobile accidents and fatalities that are going to occur over holiday weekends, and at the same time they hope that their forecasts will influence drivers to be more careful and thus to turn the forecasts into exaggerated fears.

We must not be too sanguine about the success of social scientists in making either unconditional forecasts or conditional predictions. Let us admit that we are not good in the business of prophecy and let us be modest in our claims about our ability to predict. After all, it is not our stupidity which hampers us, but chiefly our lack of information, and when one has to make do with bad guesses in lieu of information the success cannot be great. But there is a significant difference between the natural sciences and the social sciences in this respect: Experts in the natural sciences usually do not try to do what they know they cannot do; and nobody expects them to do it. They would never undertake to predict the number of fatalities in a train wreck that might happen under certain conditions during the next year. They do not even predict next year's explosions and epidemics, floods and mountain slides, earthquakes and water pollution. Social scientists, for some strange reason, are expected to foretell the future and they feel badly if they fail.

Distance from Every-Day Experience

Science is, almost by definition, what the layman cannot understand. Science is knowledge accessible only to superior minds with great effort. What everybody can know cannot be science.

A layman could not undertake to read and grasp a professional article in physics or chemistry or biophysics. He would hardly be able to pronounce many of the words and he might not have the faintest idea of what the article was all about. Needless to say, it would be out of the question for a layman to pose as an expert in a natural science. On the other hand, a layman might read articles in descriptive economics, sociology, anthropology, social psychology. Although in all these fields technical jargon is used which he could not really understand, he might *think* he knows the sense of the words and grasps the meanings of the sentences; he might even be inclined to poke fun at some of the stuff. He believes he is—from his own experience and from his reading of newspapers and popular magazines—familiar with the subject matter of social sciences. In consequence, he has little respect for the analyses which the social scientists present.

The fact that social scientists use less Latin and Greek words and less mathematics than their colleagues in the natural science departments and, instead, use everyday words in special, and often quite technical, meanings may have something to do with the attitude of the layman. The sentences of the sociologist, for example, make little sense if the borrowed words are understood in their non-technical, every-day meaning. But if the layman is told of the special meanings that have been bestowed upon his words, he gets angry or condescendingly amused.

But we must not exaggerate this business of language and professional jargon because the problem really lies deeper. The natural sciences talk about nuclei, isotopes, galaxies, benzoids, drosophilas, chromosomes, dodecahedrons, Pleistocene fossils, and the layman marvels that anyone really cares. The social sciences, however,—and the layman usualy finds this out—talk about—him. While he never identifies himself with a positron, a pneumococcus, a coenzyme, or a digital computer, he does identify himself with many of the ideal types presented by the social scientist, and he finds that the likeness is poor and the analysis "consequently" wrong.

The fact that the social sciences deal with man in his relations with fellow man brings them so close to man's own every-day experience that he cannot see the analysis of this experience as something above and beyond him. Hence he is suspicious of the analysts and disappointed in what he supposes to be a portrait of him.

Standards of Admission and Requirements

High-school physics is taken chiefly by the students with the highest I.Q.'s. At college the students majoring in physics, and again at graduate school the students of physics, are reported to have on the average higher I.Q.'s than those in other fields. This gives physics and physicists a special prestige in schools and universities, and this prestige carrries over to all natural sciences and puts them somehow above the social sciences. This is rather odd, since the average quality of students in different departments depends chiefly on departmental policies, which may vary from institution to institution. The preeminence of physics is rather general because of the requirement of calculus. In those universities in which the economics department requires calculus, the students of economics rank as high as the students of physics in intelligence, achievement, and prestige.

The lumping of all natural sciences for comparisons of student quality and admission standards is particularly unreasonable in view of the fact that at many colleges some of the natural science departments, such as biology and geology, attract a rather poor average quality of student. (This is not so in biology at universities with many applicants for a pre-medical curriculum.) The lumping of all social sciences in this respect is equally wrong, since the differences in admission standards and graduation requirements among departments, say between economics, history, and sociology, may be very great. Many sociology departments have been notorious for their role as refuge for mentally underprivileged undergraduates. Given the propensity to overgeneralize, it is no wonder then that the social sciences are being regarded as the poor relations of the natural sciences and as disciplines for which students who cannot qualify for *the* sciences are still good enough.

Since I am addressing economists, and since economics departments, at least at some of the better colleges and universities, are maintaining standards as high as physics and mathematics departments, it would be unfair to level exhortations at my present audience. But perhaps we should try to convince our colleagues in all social science departments of the disservice they are doing to their fields and to the social sciences at large by admitting and keeping inferior students as majors. Even if some of us think that one can study social sciences without knowing higher mathematics, we should insist on making calculus and mathematical statistics absolute requirements—as a device for keeping away the weakest students.

Despite my protest against improper generalizations, I must admit that averages may be indicative of something or other, and that the average I.Q. of the students in the natural science departments is higher than that of the students in the social science department.[8] No field can be better than the men who work in it. On this score, therefore, the natural sciences would be superior to the social sciences.

The Score Card

We may now summarize the tallies on the nine scores.

1. With respect to the invariability or recurrence of observations, we found that the greater number of variables—of relevant factors— in the social sciences makes for more variation, for less recurrence of exactly the same sequences of events.

2. With respect to the objectivity of observations and explanations, we distinguished several ways in which references to values and value judgments enter scientific activity. Whereas the social sciences have a requirement of "subjective interpretation of value-motivated ac-

tions" which does not exist in the natural sciences, this does not affect the proper "scientific objectivity" of the social scientist.

3. With respect to the verifiability of hypotheses, we found that the impossibility of controlled experiments combined with the larger number of relevant variables does make verification in the social sciences more difficult than in most of the natural sciences.

4. With respect to the exactness of the findings, we decided to mean by it the existence of a theoretical system from which most propositions concerning particular connections can be deduced. Exactness in this sense exists in physics and in economics, but much less so in other natural and other social sciences.

5. With respect to the measurability of phenomena, we saw an important difference between the availability of an ample supply of numerical data and the availability of such numerical data as can be used as good counterparts of the constructs in theoretical models. On this score, physics is clearly ahead of all other disciplines. It is doubtful that this can be said about the natural sciences in general relative to the social sciences in general.

6. With respect to the constancy of numerical relationships, we entertained no doubt concerning the existence of constants, postulated or empirical, in physics and in other natural sciences, whereas no numerical constants can be found in the study of society.

7. With respect to the predictability of future events, we ruled out comparisons between the laboratory world of some of the natural sciences and the unmanipulated real world studied by the social sciences. Comparing only the comparable, the real worlds—and excepting the special case of astronomy—we found no essential differences in the predictability of natural and social phenomena.

8. With respect to the distance of scientific from every-day experience, we saw that in linguistic expression as well as in their main concerns the social sciences are so much closer to pre-scientific language and thought that they do not command the respect that is accorded to the natural sciences.

9. With respect to the standards of admission and requirements, we found that they are on the average lower in the social than in the natural sciences.

The last of these scores relates to the current practice of colleges and universities, not to the character of the disciplines. The point before the last, though connected with the character of the social sciences, relates only to the popular appreciation of these disciplines; it does not aid in answering the question whether the social sciences are "really" inferior. Thus the last two scores will not be considered relevant to our question. This leaves seven scores to consider.

On four of the seven no real differences could be established. But on the other three scores, on "Invariance," "Verifiability," and "Numerical Constants," we found the social sciences to be inferior to the natural sciences.

The Implications of Inferiority

What does it mean if one thing is called "inferior" to another with regard to a particular "quality"? If this "quality" is something that is highly valued in any object, and if the absence of this "quality" is seriously missed regardless of other qualities present, then, but only then, does the noted "inferiority" have any evaluative implications. In order to show that "inferiority" sometimes means very little, I shall present here several statements about differences in particular qualities.

> "Champagne is inferior to rubbing alcohol in alcoholic content."
> "Beef steak is inferior to strawberry jello in sweetness."
> "A violin is inferior to a violoncello in physical weight."
> "Chamber music is inferior to band music in loudness."
> "Hamlet is inferior to Joe Palooka in appeal to children."
> "Sandpaper is inferior to velvet in smoothness."
> "Psychiatry is inferior to surgery in ability to effect quick cures."
> "Biology is inferior to physics in internal consistency."

It all depends on what you want. Each member in a pair of things is inferior to the other in some respect. In some instances it may be precisely this inferiority that makes the thing desirable. (Sandpaper is wanted *because* of its inferior smoothness.) In other instances the inferiority in a particular respect may be a matter of indifference. (The violin's inferiority in physical weight neither adds to nor detracts from its relative value.) Again in other instances the particular inferiority may be regrettable, but nothing can be done about it and the thing in question may be wanted none the less. (We need psychiatry, however much we regret that in general it cannot effect quick cures; and we need biology, no matter how little internal consistency has been attained in its theoretical systems.)

We have stated that the social sciences are inferior to the natural sciences in some respects, for example, in verifiability. This is regrettable. If propositions cannot be readily tested, this calls for more judgment, more patience, more ingenuity. But does it mean much else?

The Crucial Question: "So What?"

What is the pragmatic meaning of the statement in question? If I learn, for example, that drug E is inferior to drug P as a cure for hay fever, this means that, if I want such a cure, I shall not buy drug E. If I am told Mr. A is inferior to Mr. B as an automobile mechanic, I shall avoid using Mr. A when my car needs repair. If I find textbook K inferior to textbook S in accuracy, organization, as well as exposition, I shall not adopt textbook K. In every one of these examples, the statement that one thing is inferior to another makes pragmatic sense. The point is that all these pairs are *alternatives* between which a choice is to be made.

Are the natural sciences and the social sciences alternatives between which we have to choose? If they were, a claim that the social sciences are "inferior" could have the following meanings:

1. We should not study the social sciences.

2. We should not spend money on teaching and research in the social sciences.

3. We should not permit gifted persons to study social sciences and should steer them toward superior pursuits.

4. We should not respect scholars who so imprudently chose to be social scientists.

If one realizes that none of these things could possibly be meant, that every one of these meanings would be preposterous, and that the social sciences and the natural sciences can by no means be regarded as alternatives but, instead, that both are needed and neither can be dispensed with, he can give the inferiority statement perhaps one other meaning:

5. We should do something to improve the social sciences and remedy their defects.

This last interpretation would make sense if the differences which are presented as grounds for the supposed inferiority were "defects" that can be remedied. But they are not. That there are more variety and change in social phenomena; that, because of the large number of relevant variables and the impossibility of controlled experiments, hypotheses in the social sciences cannot be easily verified; and that no numerical constants can be detected in the social world—these are not defects to be remedied but fundamental properties to be grasped, accepted, and taken into account. Because of the properties research and analysis in the social sciences hold greater complexities and difficulties. If you wish, you may take this to be a greater challenge, rather than a deterrent. To be sure, difficulty and complexity alone are not sufficient reasons for studying certain problems. But the problems presented by the social world are certainly not unimportant. If they are also difficult to tackle, they ought to attract ample resources and the best minds. Today they are getting neither. The social sciences are "really inferior" regarding the place they are accorded by society and the priorities with which financial and human resources are allocated. This inferiority is curable.

NOTES

[1] Published in *On Freedom and Free Enterprises*: *Essays in Honor of Ludwig von Mises,* ed. Mary Sennholz, pp. 161–172.

[2] H. Rickert, *Die Grenzen der naturwissenschaftlichen Begriffsbildung.*

[3] M. Cohen, *Reason and Nature,* p. 348.

[4] H. Kelsen, *Allgemeine Staatslebre,* p. 129. Quoted with illuminating comments in A. Schutz, *Der sinnhafte Aufbau der sozalen Welt.*

[5] R. B. Braithwaite, *Scientific Explanation: A Study of the Function of Theory, Probability and Law in Science.*

[6] F. Machlup, "The Problem of Verification in Economics," *Southern Economic Journal,* XXII, 1955, 1–21.

[7] M. Planck, *Scientific Autobiography and Other Papers,* p. 173.

[8] The average I.Q. of students receiving bachelor's degrees was, according to a 1954 study, 121 in the biological sciences, and 122 in economics, 127 in the physical sciences, and 119 in business. See D. Wolfe, *America's Resources of Specialized Talent: The Report of the Commission on Human Resources and Advanced Training,* pp. 319–322.

Contemporary Perspectives
in the Social Sciences

George Lundberg

The Postulates of Science and Their Implications for Sociology

George Lundberg's insistence on a purely operational approach in the social sciences and on the maintenance of objectivity is to a great extent a sophisticated version of the mechanistic and dualistic notions of nineteenth-century social science. But Lundberg's view is, unlike that of his predecessors, based upon awareness of the implications of use of objective methods.

The Nonethical Nature of Science [1]

It should be clear . . . that it is the primary function of all science to formulate the sequences that are observable in *any* phenomena in order to be able to predict their recurrence. . . . It is desirable to point out, as another corollary of the position stated above, that questions of ethics or of what "ought to be" must not in science be confused with what observations indicate. Nor must sociological problems be confused with "social" problems in the sense of adjustments deemed desirable by anyone in any time, place, or circumstance. The prevention of crime is a social problem. The relationship between criminality and population density or any other social condition is a sociological problem. Sociological and all other scientific questions have to do with the formulation of verifiable relationships. Social questions have to do with other and more general readjustments of social conditions with reference to any goals toward which man may aspire.

The fact that there is a relationship between these fields is no reason for confusing them. It is entirely permissible for society to maintain educational institutions and courses to transmit to the young a knowledge of past and current social events from the viewpoint of the dominant ethical and social system that prevails or which is idealized at any given time. Orientation courses, courses in reform, ethics, idealism, religion, current events, and social work are doubtless a useful and necessary part of the educational program of contemporary society. If it is found administratively convenient or otherwise advisable to give this instruction in departments of sociology and by "sociologists" that is again a practical question of educational administration. To confuse such subject matter with scientific problems, however, is mere confusion and cannot lead to the solution of scientific problems. If we give little attention to traditional "social" problems in the present work it is not because we are not personally interested in these problems as all members of human society are likely to be, but because we do not wish to confuse them with certain *other* problems with which we wish to concern ourselves.

. . . The approach to societal phenomena here proposed provides a place for all societal data whatsoever including those conventionally designated as ethical, idealistic, spiritual, or esthetic. It does not follow that we must adopt the conventional categories in terms of which these phenomena are treated in other systems. Only *the behavior designated by these conventional categories* is entitled to recognition. Much confusion results from overlooking the fact that no theory legitimately can be required to adopt the *categories* of another theory. Take, for example, the constant demand upon thoroughgoing social scientists as to how they propose within their frame of reference to deal with "spiritual" data—what about "values," "ideals," "ethics," the good, the true, and the beautiful? Frightened by the prestige of the source from which these inquiries frequently come, the sociologist, himself often a bit worried over his own heterodoxy, makes ludicrous attempts to provide within a scientific framework place for *categories* which have no place in that framework any more than scientific categories have a place in a theological framework. It is not necessary for a priest to give an account of the cellular structure of the Holy Ghost. The only answer which a scientist needs to give to the question as to how "spiritual" data are to be handled within the scientific framework is to point out that all the *observable behavior* covered by this category is readily and fully provided for in the scientific framework. The *category itself* clearly does not have to be, and should not be, incorporated, any more than the categories of science can or need be incorporated into theology.

The root of this difficulty lies, of course, in the naïve conceit of man which induces him to believe that any word which he may invent inevitably has a necessary counterpart in nature or in supernatural regions. A slight sophistication in the nature and functions of language would render obsolete the major controversies of the day in sociological theory, as hundreds of similar time-honored discussions of other philosophical subjects have been rendered obsolete by the advancement of science.

Our principal concern . . . has been to emphasize that the apparent difference between the data of the "physical" and the social sciences springs chiefly from a failure to recognize that the immediate data of *all* sciences are human responses to whatever arouses those responses. Much of scientific development depends, as we shall see, upon the type of symbols we develop to represent the phenomena to which we respond. We need only suggest in this connection what would be the state of any of our sciences if arabic numerals, the zero, and the calculus had never been invented. With these symbols and the rules governing their use, any fourth-grade child can solve problems—relevant, important problems—which staggered the most brilliant intellect of ancient Greece. Clearly it makes a difference with what symbolic equipment we approach our scientific tasks. It would be strange indeed if this lesson from the other sciences should be entirely inapplicable to the study of sociological problems.

This point has been emphasized not so much to minimize the uniqueness and intricacy of societal phenomena as to suggest the type of approach to which these difficulties are most likely to yield. It is not necessary to argue that societal and "physical" data are the "same," or "similar." No phenomena in the universe are identical, and to admit that societal phenomena are "different" from "physical" is a highly irrelevant concession in the present context unless we further specify *in what respect* we allege they are different. *All* phenomena are different in some respects. *All* of them are similar in one highly vital respect, namely, in that they are all known, if at all, through sense experience conceptualized and organized into the patterns determined by the nature of the human organism as conditioned by all its environments. This is the only similarity relevant to the present discussion because we are concerned at present only with the means by which valid knowledge of *any* phenomena is achieved. Are the means by which we know societal phenomena fundamentally different from the means by which we know physical phenomena? If they are not, then it is as irrelevant for our present purpose to enumerate "differences" between "physical" and societal phenomena as it would be to claim that the differences between ants, spiders, and grasshoppers preclude a science of biology. Indeed, all discussion of similarities and differences of phenomena without specifying explicitly or through the context with respect to what aspect of the phenomena we are concerned may be said to be quite meaningless. Such discussion is not uncommon in sociological treatises on differences between societal and "physical" phenomena.

Much has been said in this connection about the ability of "physical" scientists to bring their "subject-matters" (i.e., the referents of their symbolized responses) into the laboratory and otherwise manipulate them. This possibility varies considerably with different sciences. The solar system has never been brought into any laboratory. Astronomical laboratories do contain very ingenious symbolic and mechanical representations of the astronomical aspects of that system and remarkable instruments for observing it. These every science must unquestionably develop. Beyond this, the question of laboratory conditions becomes one of convenience and technical and mechanical ingenuity. Already it is possible to observe illuminating sociological situations in the laboratory through sound and motion pictures not to mention the extensive sociological experiments involving laboratory observations of children and college students.

In short, most of us have been brought up in a world in which we are taught that the physical sciences deal with metals, fluids, gases, and such "matter" which we like to describe with such reassuring sounds as "tangible," "visible," "actual," "real." The phenomena of the social sciences, on the other hand, we have been taught to consider "intangible," and "invisible" entities described by words like customs, mores, competition, sovereignty, justice, etc., etc. Yet these words if they mean anything at all, certainly refer to *behavior—events* impinging on our senses. The aspects of the universe with which chemists and physicists deal, and which folk-language designates by such broad categories as metals, fluids, and gases refer just as certainly to *other* behavior events. Yet such is the tendency for us to project upon nature the structure of our language that we develop a superstitious reverence for the categories which . . . are merely constructs which man somewhere, sometime, found a convenient framework within which to assort his experiences.[2]

To those who still find that these traditional frameworks serve their purposes, the present essay has nothing to offer. There are doubtless also those who still find the pre-Copernican astronomy, pre-Newtonian physics, and pre-Darwinian biology quite adequate to their needs. But they will perhaps find themselves increasingly disturbed by the intrusions and by-products of the scientific quest as represented by our technological age. Frequently the findings of that quest will, as Veblen said, "go beyond the breaking-point of their jungle-fed spiritual sensibilities." At such times they will "furtively or by an overt breach of consistency . . . seek comfort in marvelous articles of savage-born lore." [3] Take, for example, the following honest confession of a distinguished president of Columbia University in 1873. President Barnard had himself specialized in the natural sciences, served as president of the American Association for the Advancement of Science, and was noted for his liberal views. With reference to the doctrine of evolution he said:

> Much as I love truth in the abstract I love my sense of immortality still more; and if the final outcome of all the boasted discoveries of modern science is to disclose to men that they are more evanescent than the shadow of the swallow's wing upon the lake . . . if this, after all is the best that science can give me, give me then, I pray, no more science. I will live on in my simple ignorance, as my fathers did before me; and when I shall at length be sent to my final repose, let me . . . lie down to pleasant, even though they may be deceitful dreams.[4]

To those who find themselves in this unhappy predicament I can only say with Bentley:

> I can deeply sympathize with anyone who objects to being tossed into such a floating cosmology. Much as I have stressed its substantiality, I can hardly expect everyone to feel it. The firm land of "matter" or even of "sense" or "self" is pleasanter, if only it stands firm. To anyone whose tasks can be performed on such ground, I have not the slightest thought of bringing disturbance. But for many of us tasks are pressing, in the course of which our firmest

spots of conventional departure themselves dissolve in function. When they have so dissolved, and when we are so involved, there is no hope of finding refuge in some chance island of "fact" which may appear. The continents go, and the islands. The pang may be like that felt by a confirmed landsman at his first venture on the ocean, but the ocean in time becomes familiar and secure. Or, if I may change the figure, the fledgling will vastly prefer his firm nest to falling with untried wings. But the parent sciences are pushing; the nest, even, is disintegrating; and there is air for flight, even though it is not so vividly felt and seen as the sticks and straws of the nest.[5]

NOTES

[1] I have dealt elsewhere in some detail with this subject. See especially, "Science, Scientists, and Values," *Social Forces*, XXX, 1932, 373–379. Also, see *Can Science Save Us?* 2nd ed., pp. 30–41.

[2] It is unfortunately not possible here to give an adequate account of the full extent to which linguistic and semantic difficulties at present handicap the social sciences. The reader is urged to supplement the present chapter by readings from the following sources. The first two sources are popular and elementary treatises. S. Chase, *The Tyranny of Words;* T. W. Arnold, *The Folklore of Capitalism;* P. W. Bridgman, *The Logic of Modern Physics;* C. K. Ogden and I. A. Richards, *The Meaning of Meaning;* A. Korzybski, *Science and Sanity;* J. F. Markey, *The Symbolic Process and Its Integration in Children.* By far the best brief source is C. W. Morris, "Foundations of the Theory of Signs," in *International Encyclopedia of Unified Science,* I, Univ. of Chicago Press, 1938. Consider, for example, the following extracts:

No contradiction arises in saying that every sign has a designatum but not every sign refers to an actual existent. Where what is referred to actually exists as referred to, the object of reference is a *denotatum*. It thus becomes clear that, while every sign has a designatum, not every sign has a denotatum. A designatum is not a thing, but a kind of object or class of objects—and a class may have many members, or one member, or no members. The denotata are the members of the class. This distinction makes explicable the fact that one may reach in the icebox for an apple that is not there and make preparations for living on an island that may never have existed or has long since disappeared beneath the sea. [P. 5]

By "actual existent" Morris here apparently means those stimuli-phenomena which evoke universal or at least very general confirmatory responses in all or large numbers of men. The explanation of the behavior of reaching for the apple which "is there" and the apple which "is not there" lies in the description of the sequence or combination of events leading up to the reaching. This set of events will be different in the two cases, but subject to description within the same framework. Morris continues:

The interpreter of a sign is an organism; the interpretant is the habit of the organism to respond, because of the sign vehicle, to absent objects which are relevant to a present problematic situation as if they were present. In virtue of semiosis an organism takes account of relevant properties of absent objects, or unobserved properties of objects which are present, and in this lies the general instrumental significance of ideas. Given the sign vehicle as an object of response, the organism expects a situation of such and such a kind and, on the basis of this expectation, can partially prepare itself in advance for what may develop. The response to things through the intermediacy of signs is thus biologically a continuation of the same process in which the distance senses have taken precedence over the contact senses in the control of conduct in higher animal forms, such animals through sight, hearing, and smell are already responding to distant parts of the environment through certain properties. This process of taking account of a constantly more remote environment is simply continued in the complex processes of semiosis made possible by language, the object taken account of no longer needing to be perceptually present. [Pp. 31–32]

... If, following the lead of the pragmatist, mental phenomena be equated with sign responses, consciousness with reference by signs, and rational (or "free") behavior with the control of conduct in terms of foreseen consequences made available by signs, then psychology and the social sciences may recognize what is distinctive in their tasks and at the same time see their place within a unified science. Indeed, it does not seem fantastic to believe that the concept of sign may prove as fundamental to the sciences of man as the concept of cell for the biological sciences. [P. 42]

3 T. Veblen, *The Place of Science in Modern Civilization*, pp. 26, 27.

4 Quoted by S. Ratner, "Evolution and the Rise of the Scientific Spirit in America," *Philosophy of Science*, III, 1936, 115. For a good summary of the present scientific status of "materialism" see W. Seifriz, "A Materialistic Interpretation of Life," *Philosophy of Science*, VI, 1939, 266–284.

5 A. F. Bentley, *Behavior, Knowledge, Fact*, p. 183.

Julian Steward

The Concept and Method of Cultural Ecology

Like Leslie White, Julian Steward has attempted to renew anthropology's interest in evolutionary problems. His ecological approach provides an answer to some of the objections to unilinear evolutionary theories which could not encompass within their stages the bewildering variety of human social forms. Instead of seeing human development in terms of some overall scheme, Steward sees it as the result of specific adaptation. Each society must adapt to a particular environment but adaptations may differ because each society brings with it certain cultural techniques or traits. Evolution or change *can* derive out of contact between two groups in different environments, out of migration of a group from one environment to another, and out of the adaptive process itself which, by developing methods of dealing with the environment, in effect alters that environment and creates both new needs and new adaptations. Steward's attempt to replace the inadequate unilinear theories of evolution with this multilinear view is based to some degree on an analogy between cultures and animal species. Though many objections can be made to aspects of Steward's ecological approach—to its emphasis on material and technological factors and disinterest in ideological and psychological aspects of evolution—by and large, Steward's concern with evolutionary adaptive processes has helped refocus attention on some of the problems that resulted from anthropology's adherence to purely functional and superorganic explanations of cultural change.

226

Cultural Ecology

Cultural ecology differs from human and social ecology in seeking to explain the origin of particular cultural features and patterns which characterize different areas rather than to derive general principles applicable to any cultural-environmental situation. It differs from the relativistic and neo-evolutionist conceptions of culture history in that it introduces the local environment as the extracultural factor in the fruitless assumption that culture comes from culture. Thus, cultural ecology presents both a problem and a method. The problem is to ascertain whether the adjustments of human societies to their environments require particular modes of behavior or whether they permit latitude for a certain range of possible behavior patterns. Phrased in this way, the problem also distinguishes cultural ecology from "environmental determinism" and its related theory "economic determinism" which are generally understood to contain their conclusions within the problem.

The problem of cultural ecology must be further qualified, however, through use of a supplementary conception of culture. According to the holistic view, all aspects of culture are functionally interdependent upon one another. The degree and kind of interdependency, however, are not the same with all features. Elsewhere, I have offered the concept of *cultural core*—the constellation of features which are most closely related to subsistence activities and economic arrangements. The core includes such social, political, and religious patterns as are empirically determined to be closely connected with these arrangements. Innumerable other features may have great potential variability because they are less strongly tied to the core. These latter, or secondary features, are determined to a greater extent by purely cultural-historical factors—by random innovations or by diffusion—and they give the appearance of outward distinctiveness to cultures with similar cores. Cultural ecology pays primary attention to those features which empirical analysis shows to be most closely involved in the utilization of environment in culturally prescribed ways.

The expression "culturally prescribed ways" must be taken with caution, for its anthropological usage is frequently "loaded." The normative concept, which views culture as a system of mutually reinforcing practices backed by a set of attitudes and values, seems to regard all human behavior as so completely determined by culture that environmental adaptations have no effect. It considers that the entire pattern of technology, land use, land tenure, and social features derive entirely from culture. Classical illustrations of the primacy of cultural attitudes over common sense are that the Chinese do not drink milk nor the Eskimo eat seals in summer.

Cultures do, of course, tend to perpetuate themselves, and change may be slow for such reasons as those cited. But over the millennia cultures in different environments have changed tremendously, and these changes are basically traceable to new adaptations required by changing technology and productive arrangements. Despite occasional cultural barriers, the useful arts have spread extremely widely, and the instances in which they have not been accepted because of pre-existing cultural patterns are insignificant. In pre-agricultural times, which comprised perhaps 99 per cent of cultural history, technical devices for hunting, gathering, and fishing seem to have diffused largely to the limits of their usefulness. Clubs, spears, traps, bows, fire, containers, nets, and many other cultural features spread across many areas, and some of them throughout the world. Later, domesticated plants and animals also spread very rapidly within their environmental limits, being stopped only by formidable ocean barriers.

Whether or not new technologies are valuable is, however, a function of the society's cultural level as well as of environmental potentials. All pre-agricultural societies found hunting and gathering techniques useful. Within the geographical limits of herding and farming, these techniques were adopted. More advanced techniques, such as metallurgy, were acceptable only if certain pre-conditions, such as stable population, leisure time, and internal specialization were present. These conditions could develop only from the cultural ecological adaptations of an agricultural society.

The concept of cultural ecology, however, is less concerned with the origin and diffusion of technologies than with the fact that they may be used differently and entail different social arrangements in each environment. The environment is not only permissive or prohibitive with respect to these technologies, but special local features may require social adaptations which have far-reaching consequences. Thus, societies equipped with bows, spears, surrounds, chutes, brush-burning, deadfalls, pitfalls, and other hunting devices may differ among themselves because of the nature of the terrain and fauna. If the principal games exists in large herds, such as herds of bison or caribou, there is advantage in co-operative hunting, and considerable numbers of peoples may remain together throughout the year. If, however, the game is nonmigratory, occurring in small and scattered groups, it is better hunted by small groups of men who know their territory well. In each case, the cultural repertory of hunting devices may be about the same, but in the first case the society will consist of multifamily or multilineage groups, as among the Athabaskans and Algonkians of Canada and probably the pre-horse Plains bison hunters, and in the second case it will probably consist of localized patrilineal lineages or bands, as among the Bushmen, Congo Negritoes, Australians, Tasmanians, Fuegians, and others. These latter groups consisting of patrilineal bands are similar, as a matter of fact, not because their total environments are similar—the Bushmen, Australians, and southern Californians live in deserts, the Negritoes in rain forests, and the Fuegians in a cold, rainy area—but because the nature of the game and therefore of their subsistence problem is the same in each case.

Other societies having about the same technological equipment may exhibit other social patterns because the environments differ to the extent that the cultural adaptations must be different. For example, the Eskimo use bows, spears, traps, containers and other widespread technological devices, but, owing to the limited occurrence of fish and sea mammals, their population is so sparse and co-operative hunting is so relatively unrewarding that they are usually dispersed in family groups. For a different but equally compelling reason the Nevada Shoshoni were also fragmented into family groups. In the latter case, the scarcity of game and the predominance of seeds as the subsistence basis greatly restricted economic co-operation and required dispersal of the society into fairly independent family groups.

In the examples of the primitive hunting, gathering, and fishing societies, it is easy to show that if the local environment is to be exploited by means of the culturally-derived techniques, there are limitations upon the size and social composition of the groups involved. When agricultural techniques are introduced, man is partially freed from the exigencies of hunting and gathering, and it becomes possible for considerable aggregates of people to live together. Larger aggregates, made possible by increased population and settled communities, provide a higher level of sociocultural integration, the nature of which is determined by the local type of sociocultural integration.

The adaptative processes we have described are properly designated ecological. But attention is directed not simply to the human community as part of the total web of life but to such cultural features as are affected by the adaptations. This in turn requires that primary attention be paid only to relevant environmental features rather than to the web of life for its own sake. Only those features to which the local culture ascribes importance need be considered.

The Method of Cultural Ecology

Although the concept of environmental adaptation underlies all cultural ecology, the procedures must take into account the complexity and level of the culture. It makes a great deal of difference whether a community consists of hunters and gatherers who subsist independently by their own efforts or whether it is an outpost of a wealthy nation, which exploits local mineral wealth and is sustained by railroads, ships, or airplanes. In advanced societies, the nature of the culture core will be determined by a complex technology and by productive arrangements which themselves have a long cultural history.

Three fundamental procedures of cultural ecology are as follows:

First, the interrelationship of exploitative or productive technology and environment must be analyzed. This technology includes a considerable part of what is often called "material culture," but all features may not be of equal importance. In primitive societies, subsistence devices are basic: weapons and instruments for hunting and fishing; containers for gathering and storing food; transportational devices used on land and water; sources of water and fuel; and, in some environments, means of counteracting excessive cold (clothing and housing) or heat. In more developed societies, agriculture and herding techniques and manufacturing of crucial implements must be considered. In an industrial world, capital and credit arrangements, trade systems and the like are crucial. Socially-derived needs—special tastes in foods, more ample housing and clothing, and a great variety of appurtenances to living—become increasingly important in the productive arrangement as culture develops; and yet these originally were probably more often effects of basic adaptations than causes.

Relevant environmental features depend upon the culture. The simpler cultures are more directly conditioned by the environment than advanced ones. In general, climate, topography, soils, hydrography, vegetational cover, and fauna are crucial, but some features may be more important than others. The spacing of water holes in the desert may be vital to a nomadic seed-gathering people, the habits of game will affect the way hunting is done, and the kinds and seasons of fish runs will determine the habits of riverine and coastal tribes.

Second, the behavior patterns involved in the exploitation of a particular area by means of a particular technology must be analyzed. Some subsistence patterns impose very narrow limits on the general mode of life of the people, while others allow considerable latitude. The gathering of wild vegetable products is usually done by women who work alone or in small groups. Nothing is gained by co-operation and in fact women come into competition with one another. Seed-gatherers, therefore, tend to fragment into small groups unless their resources are very abundant. Hunting, on the other hand, may be either an individual or a collective project, and the nature of hunting societies is determined by culturally prescribed devices for collective hunting as well as by the species. When surrounds, grass-firing, corrals, chutes, and other co-operative methods are employed, the take per man may be much greater than what a lone hunter could bag. Similarly, if circumstances permit, fishing may be done by groups of men using dams, weirs, traps, and nets as well as by individuals.

The use of these more complex and frequently co-operative techniques, however, depends not only upon cultural history—i.e., invention and diffusion—which makes the methods available but upon the environment and its flora and fauna. Deer cannot be hunted advantageously by surrounds, whereas antelope and bison may best be hunted in this way. Slash-and-burn farming in tropical rain forests requires comparatively little co-operation in that a few men clear the land after which their wives plant and cultivate the crops. Dry farming may or may not be co-operative; and irrigation farming may run the gamut of enterprises of ever-increasing size based on collective construction of waterworks.

The exploitative patterns not only depend upon the habits concerned in the direct production of food and of goods but upon facilities for transporting the people to the source of supply or the goods to the people. Watercraft have been a major factor in permitting the growth of settlements beyond what would have been possible for a foot people.

Among all nomads, the horse has had an almost revolutionary effect in promoting the growth of large bands.

The third procedure is to ascertain the extent to which the behavior patterns entailed in exploiting the environment affect other aspects of culture. Although technology and environment prescribe that certain things must be done in certain ways if they are to be done at all, the extent to which these activities are functionally tied to other aspects of culture is a purely empirical problem. I have shown elsewhere that the occurrence of patrilineal bands among certain hunting peoples and of fragmented families among the Western Shoshoni is closely determined by their subsistence activities, whereas the Carrier Indians are known to have changed from a composite hunting band to a society based upon moieties and inherited statuses without any change in the nature of subsistence. In the irrigation areas of early civilizations the sequence of sociopolitical forms or cultural cores seems to have been very similar despite variation in many outward details or secondary features of these cultures. If it can be established that the productive arrangements permit great latitude in the sociocultural type, then historical influences may explain the particular type found. The problem is the same in considering modern industrial civilizations. The question is whether industrialization allows such latitude that political democracy, communism, state socialism, and perhaps other forms are equally possible, so that strong historical influences, such as diffused ideology—e.g., propaganda—may supplant one type with another, or whether each type represents an adaptation which is specific to the area.

The third procedure requires a genuinely holistic approach, for if such factors as demography, settlement pattern, kinship structures, land tenure, land use, and other key cultural features are considered separately, their interrelationships to one another and to the environment cannot be grasped. Land use by means of a given technology permits a certain population density. The clustering of this population will depend partly upon where resources occur and upon transportational devices. The composition of these clusters will be a function of their size, of the nature of subsistence activities, and of cultural-historical factors. The ownership of land or resources will reflect subsistence activities on the one hand and the composition of the group on the other. Warfare may be related to the complex of factors just mentioned. In some cases, it may arise out of competition for resources and have a national character. Even when fought for individual honors or religious purposes, it may serve to nucleate settlements in a way that must be related to subsistence activities.

The Methodological Place of Cultural Ecology

Cultural ecology has been described as a methodological tool for ascertaining how the adaptation of a culture to its environment may entail certain changes. In a larger sense, the problem is to determine whether similar adjustments occur in similar environments. Since in any given environment, culture may develop through a succession of very unlike periods, it is sometimes pointed out that environment, the constant, obviously has no relationship to cultural type. This difficulty disappears, however, if the level of sociocultural integration represented by each period is taken into account. Cultural types therefore, must be conceived as constellations of core features which arise out of environmental adaptations and which represent similar levels of integration.

Cultural diffusion, of course, always operates, but in view of the seeming importance of ecological adaptations its role in explaining culture has been greatly overestimated. The extent to which the large variety of world cultures can be systematized in categories of types and explained through cross-cultural regularities of developmental process is purely an empirical matter. Hunches arising out of comparative studies suggest that there are many regularities which can be formulated in terms of similar levels and similar adaptations.

Omar K. Moore and
Alan R. Anderson

Puzzles, Games and Social Interaction

Game theory is only one of a number of mathematical models that social scientists are using to help answer some of their questions. Although its value is restricted to those situations in which a society can be viewed as one player and nature as the opponent, games theory has offered a model that accurately predicts the moves a society must make to maximize its survival. Game theory tends to support the intuitive notion of anthropologists who have always insisted that the seemingly irrational behavior of primitive peoples is in fact not irrational at all but highly functional and adaptive.

THEORIES OF GAMES OF chance ("probability theory") and theories of games of strategy (after von Neumann) . . . grew directly out of the study of *autotelic* activities—that is, activities undertaken by human beings solely because of their intrinsic interest. Engaging in social games, playing with puzzles or aesthetic objects, simply being sociable, are examples of activities we call *autotelic,* i.e., activities which are, or should be, undertaken solely because they are enjoyable.

The close connection between game theory and probability theory on the one hand, and social games on the other, is not open to question. It is simply a fact of history that for both theories, the first models to be considered were ordinary social games. But one may wish to raise doubts about the claim that social games and the like are *autotelic* (especially if one belongs to one of the more austere schools of social psychology according to which it is not possible for

234

anyone ever to do *anything* just for fun). To such critics we make the following minor concession (perhaps putting the matter in a way which will satisfy even the most puritanical) : even if no one ever does enjoy anything, the rules of our society make it clear that people are under an *obligation* to enjoy *some* things, at least. There are severely sanctioned rules, for example, to the effect that one should take part in sports only because one wants to play. We are all supposed to give short shrift to grand-standers, cheaters, and people who "let the side down" or otherwise exhibit "bad form." And the rules governing autotelic activity, which have the effect of *keeping* the activity auto-telic, are remarkably pervasive. We may not do business at a party; we may not go to the opera in order to be seen there by the right people; we may not join the country club simply to meet the right people. Rather: we must go to the party because we enjoy being sociable; we must go to the opera because we love music; we must join the country club because we like golf. People break these rules, of course; but it seems clear that there *are* such rules to be broken, and also that *some* behavior is autotelic in the required sense (i.e., that *sometimes* these rules are consciously complied with).

Now the striking fact that both these mathematical theories, probability theory and game theory, have models not only in the autotelic activities which led to their development, but also in the successful conduct of the more serious matters of survival and welfare, suggests the possibility that in acting autotelically we are "modeling" our own more serious behavior. This idea seems to be at the bottom of "formal sociology," in the sense of Simmel,[1] who talks, for example, about sociability as the "play form" of sociation: at a party we engage playfully in competition, cooperation, deceit, love, hostility, and the thousand and one other forms that social behavior may take—but we *play* at it, for no stakes.

[These considerations can be summed up] as follows: It might prove fruitful to look at autotelic cultural products (puzzles, games of chance, games of strategy, plays, novels, and the like) as *models* in the folk-culture, or *folk-models,* of the serious concerns of survival and human welfare—models with the help of which we come to understand and "be at home with" our natural and social environments. So put the thesis risks banality; what gives the thesis such teeth as it has, is the fact that social games and certain serious (say) economic problems are models of the same theory (regardless of the actual behavior of players, buyers, and sellers), and so may be said to have a *formal* similarity sufficient to lend some credibility to our contention. . . .

It is characteristic of social interaction that I cannot maximize my own utility without "taking into account" (in some vague sense which we understand only darkly) what *you* are up to. I must have some theories or intuitions about how you are likely to behave, how you will respond to my actions, and the like. Worse than that, I must be aware that you are very likely doing the same thing in regard to me, and I have to take *that* possibility into account as well. But of course you may know that I am aware of this possibility, and you adjust your behavior accordingly. And so it goes—we are both involved in a tortuous labyrinth of relations, and though we act in this way quite easily and freely, it is better than even money that neither of us could even *begin* to give an explicit account of how we do it. (It is the complexity of this kind of behavior, together with our inability to explain it, which lends plausibility to the suggestion that we *learn* to behave in this way by playing games of strategy. This is *exactly* the kind of behavior hide-and-seek (say) requires—but in hide-and-seek, failure to win is relatively inexpensive.)

The interactional models provided by games of strategy may be contrasted with the noninteractional models found in puzzles. It is of course true that we *can* regard puzzles as one-player games—but it still seems clear that puzzles do not share the interactional features of games of strategy. Once the conditions of a puzzle are set, they do not change on us suddenly with a view to thwarting our efforts at a solution; indeed this is exactly how we distinguish between "puzzles" and "games": no social interaction takes place between the puzzle and the solver.

Now if we are correct in our estimate of the importance of such folk-models as puzzles and games of strategy for the process which sociologists call "socialization," we should expect that their influence would be pervasive, and that their presence in the backs of our minds might, in subtle ways, not only intervene in much of our thinking, but even constitute the warp and woof of many of our thought patterns. Acting on this assumption, at any rate, we shall now try to develop some plausible considerations concerning the relations between these folk-models and scientific inquiry.

We observe first that both natural and behavioral sciences are, among other things, social enterprises, undertaken in a societal context, and that they both presuppose social selves (in the sense of Mead),[2] capable of social *interaction.* Now our own informal observations lead us to believe that the principal problems faced by (and produced by) infants, at least as they begin to learn speech, are interactional in character: the problems faced have to do with certain social rules, as laid down, enforced by, or exemplified by, other human beings. There are many examples: talking in accord with linguistic conventions, eating, toilet-training, playing together peaceably, respecting seniors, etc. All of these activities are rule-ridden,[3] and it seems plausible to suggest therefore that social games should be prior, both temporally and in order of importance, to puzzles, in the socialization process. Even noninteractional folk-models, say puzzles, presuppose social interaction, in the sense that they require a social context, and an ability to understand the restraints put on those artificial problems we call "puzzles."

Indeed we find some support for the notion that interactional models have a deep hold on us from the prevalence of animistic thinking in so-called "primitive" societies. In fact it is hard to eradicate even in "civilized" societies; many research scientists half-believe Finagle's Laws (which presuppose that inanimate objects are out to get us).

In social interaction we recognize that our opposite number is potentially friendly, potentially hostile, potentially indifferent, to us and our concerns. It would moreover seem quite natural, especially in a state of ignorance, to endow nature with these same attributes. This is in fact a sound conservative strategy and one we have all followed from time to time. A person finding an inert bat on his doorstep does well to treat it as if it were alive until he is pretty certain that it is not. If we know little of nature generally, it might do trivial harm, and considerable good, if we treat nature as if it *might,* suddenly, turn on us.[4]

Now it seems to us to require a vertiginous act of abstraction to *remove* the interactional elements from our view of nature. "Dehumanizing" an anthropomorphic nature ought to require a sizable wrench, as experience with civilizing primitive peoples indicates. It is therefore not altogether surprising that it took millennia of human history before the natural sciences developed, especially if it is conceded that physics demands an abandonment of animism. It is central to the classical Newtonian view of natural phenomena that they be regarded as isolated systems, which run entirely by themselves, and are not influenced at all by *us*. Nature is, in short, assimilated to a puzzle.[5] *People* (as opposed to *bodies*) have been eradicated from the picture as ruthlessly and as completely as may be, and we are left with a mindless mechanism which dominated, and still dominates, the attitude of many working natural scientists. No one of course can maintain that as a heuristic principle, mechanism has been unsuccessful in the natural sciences—our astonishing theoretical and technological progress would seem to indicate that this is *precisely* the right view to take, as regards physics.

In view of the success of the puzzle model in the natural sciences, it is not at all surprising that those interested in the behavioral sciences should have tried equally to remove *people* from their considerations. The principal thesis of behaviorism, at least in its early and crude forms, was that a human organism is a black box, subject to certain inputs and outputs, which should be studied like any other physical system. Social and psychological processes were to be regarded as isolated phenomena of a mechanistic sort, to be studied in complete abstraction from the social, interactional context in which they occur. Such an attitude is at least strongly suggested by the preoccupation in the first half of this century with rote-learning experiments and psycho-physical measurements, and more recently by attempts to simulate various kinds of problem-solving on computers. . . .

Consider the following problem. Suppose you were to find yourself on a lifeless moon, with no possibility of returning to, or communicating with, the earth. Suppose also that you were in a frame of mind to do something bad. What would you do?

In informal conversation, this question has elicited a wide variety of initial responses, but after a little thought the answer generally settles on the following point: the only way to do something bad in those circumstances is somehow to break some *rule*. It may be moot whether there are any rules to break in the quasi-solipsistic universe we are considering; the examples we have heard (spitting, say, or offending God, or oneself, by committing suicide) have a farfetched ring to them. But note that even this kind of outrageous rule-breaking is doing something *against* someone or something: the idea of rule-breaking in which no one (or nothing) gets hurt in any way seems, or seems almost, self-contradictory. . . .

We have, in this essay, been trying (from time to time) to appear to be sane arguers, and also (from time to time) to say what we believe, even without the kind of evidence we would like to have. Here we come on one of the latter points. The "conclusion" seems to us inescapable that *self-consciously acting in accordance with a rule* (or formulating such rule) is one of the fundamental aspects of social interaction, and any experimental studies which neglect this point simply have nothing to do with that topic. Indeed this is implicit in our earlier claims that social games of strategy are *models* of social interaction; obedience to game rules must be self-conscious. The whole point is, as Hume [6] says in comparing games with other social interaction:

> In societies for play, there are laws required for the conduct of the game; and these laws are different in each game. The foundation, I own, of such societies is frivolous; and the laws are, in a great measure, though not altogether, capricious and arbitrary. . . . The comparison, therefore, in these respects, is very imperfect. We may only learn from it the necessity of rules, wherever men have any intercourse with each other. . . . It is impossible for men so much as to murder each other without statutes, and maxims. . . .

. . . In puzzle-solving, a person [has] to think of himself in his own capacity as an *agent,* and from that perspective to try to make things come out right. We [might also say] that he [has] to think of what the realization of the goal might mean to *him,* that is, he [has] to have some *value* in mind which would (or could) help him to assess the outcome of his activity.[7] We would now like to suggest that one of the "points" of games of chance, as opposed to puzzles, is that games of chance make clearer and more apparent the relation of agents to patients (adopting classical philosophical terminology). A "patient" is one to whom something is done: a recipient of an action. And we contend that in playing games of chance, we are setting afoot certain events of which the outcome to *us* is not known (though we do place a *value* on the outcome). In the same way that puzzles, as we have argued earlier, are models of problem-solving, so games of chance are models of situations in which the outcomes to the patient are not predictable.

Upshot: it is necessary for human beings, if they use both puzzles and games of chance, to be able to adopt at least two perspectives: that of *agent,* who might act, or set chains of events going, and that of *patient,* on whom actions initiated by themselves or others might impinge.

We therefore posit at least two systems of perspectives for human beings: (1) a system of *goals,* which are related to possibilities for action, and (2) a system of *values,* which are related to the possible outcomes of action for the actor. Each human being must be able to take both of these perspectives: goal-directed (or *actor*), and value-directed (or *patient*). These might coincide; we assume in some rat experiments that the goal is the food, and the value is eating it, so that rats eat the goal, with a result of value to the rat. But the existence of puzzles and games of chance may be an indication that human beings are a little more subtle, since one thinks of them as *reaching,* rather than eating, their goals.

So we are at least even with rats.

But so far as we know, rats have neither games of strategy, nor music, nor art, in any very significant sense. Since we have found both games of strategy and aesthetic objects on earth, we now pause to consider the differences between men and rats.

It is true that there are some psychological (we would prefer to say "philosophical") positions according to which there are no important differences between men and rats. Such we consider naïve behaviorism to be (you give them some inputs; they give you some outputs). But we can tell men and rats apart very easily, and not *simply* because they do not look alike. There are, from the point of view we now wish to explain, more important differences. Being human requires not only goal-sensitivity, together with goal-directedness, but also some other abilities. So we move on to consider . . . games of strategy.

We note first that nothing we have said so far is incompatible with a solipsistic stance. Even the silliest solipsist sees that *he* exists as an agent, and that things happen to *him* as a patient, even though he supposes that all the rest of us are figments of his imagination. But in the case of games of strategy, this attitude will not do. One *can* adopt it for games of strategy, but von Neumann's theory [8] would indicate that one then would not be in the best position to win.

To play games of strategy seems to require that, in addition to the agent and patient perspectives, we must be able to "see ourselves as ithers see us" (Burns [9]). That is, we must recognize that ladies, unlike lice, are analyzing us much as we are analyzing them. For lack of better terminology we entitle this third perspective the *reciprocal perspective.*

Implicit in the idea that I recognize, or take account of, the fact that there are other human beings who *also* have agent and patient perspectives, is the notion that they are looking at me as I am looking at them. I must be able to evaluate my own behavior, not only from my own agent-patient point of view, but also from the agent-patient points of view (as well as I can understand them) of others. When I act, I have to see (a) what possibilities are open for myself as agent, (b) what the consequences are likely to be for me as patient, and (c) what the consequences are likely to be for the other fellow as patient, and how he is likely to react to the situation as agent—and all this in the knowledge that he probably is doing the same thing to me. In this sense each of us is "represented" as a personality in each. We cannot get along socially without taking each other into account as *social* human beings.

At the very least it seems obvious that games of strategy give us opportunities for endless practice in viewing our actions from all three of these points of view, always recognizing the existence of other beings like ourselves. What the reciprocal perspective allows us to do is to reciprocate. In a play of the game of chess, for example, we reciprocate in just the sense that we take each other's actions into account, and guide our own behavior by considering not only what our Knight can do, but what his Queen can do, and what the outcome of the game will be.

It is hard to see how human beings could handle games of strategy, as we find them on earth, without being able to take account of the agent-patient perspectives of *others*. Some such ability would seem necessary for games of strategy. We might sometimes confuse the various "parts" of the personalities involved, or we may sometimes ignore a part of someone else—usually to our peril: if we do not sufficiently take into account another's role as agent or patient, we might lose a knight which is pinned to the King. But unless we could keep these various perspectives "in perspective," it would seem difficult to understand how we could play at all. . . .

But . . . do not animals also interact in the sense that they guide their own behavior in part by the behavior of their colleagues? Consider the following example of George Herbert Mead's: [10]

> The act of each dog becomes the stimulus to the other dog for his response. There is then a relationship between these two; and as the act is responded to by the other dog, it, in turn, undergoes change. The very fact that the dog is ready to attack another be-

comes a stimulus to the other dog to change his own position or his own attitude. He has not sooner done this than the change of attitude in the second dog in turn causes the first dog to change his attitude. We have here a conversation of gestures. They are not, however, gestures in the sense that they are significant. We do not assume that the dog says to himself, "If the animal comes from this direction he is going to spring at my throat and I will turn in such a way." What does take place is an actual change in his own position due to the direction of the approach of the other dog.

Now it may be debatable whether or not a dog, in approaching a bone, actually *takes the role of* another dog doing the same. (We, along with Mead, think it does not, in any significant sense, but the matter hardly seems worth arguing, in view of the vagueness of the issues.) But one thing seems perfectly clear: one cannot imagine a dog saying, or even thinking, "Tut, tut, tut; that is not in accordance with the rules." We can of course imagine a dog being *surprised* by some unexpected event which "breaks rules" with which the dog is familiar; but the surprise is rather more like the surprise we feel at a sudden and unexpected earthquake, than the surprise we feel when a close friend suddenly slips a knife between our ribs. The former is a physical sort of surprise, and we are all partially prepared for those. But the latter are social surprises, and are available to dogs only in the same metaphorical sense that household pets are "people."

We have referred to the earthquake surprise as "physical," and the being-knifed-by-a-friend surprise as "social," and though we are not very clear as to what this distinction involves, we will still try to give an account of it.

It does not make much sense to say that the earth "is not supposed to" (in the sense of "ought not") quake. We can all see that it would be nicer if the earth did not quake, or if volcanoes did not erupt; things like this hurt people. But if one were to say "volcanoes ought not erupt," in any sense which involved adherence to rules on the part of volcanoes, it would be hard to attach any sense to the utterance. It would be odd if, after the burial of Pompeii, someone were to shake a finger at Mt. Vesuvius and say in a severe voice, "Sceleste, sceleste, Vesuvi!"

It *would* be appropriate, however, to treat our treacherous exfriend in this way. *All of us* can see what "Et tu, Brute," means, once the story and the Latin are explained. What it means is simply that friends are not supposed to do that kind of thing to one another. Which is to say that the notion of "friendship" involves conducting oneself according to certain *rules*. (We do not specify these for reasons which ought to be obvious: the problem is too difficult.)

Whatever feelings the treachery of our *own* friend in these circumstances might engender, it seems perfectly clear that all of us can see how Caesar might have felt—not about the wound, that is, but the treachery. And note that this understanding really has nothing to do with Caesar, Brutus, or ourselves (ourselves viewed as agents, patients, or from the reciprocal perspective of anyone we know). We could substitute "Caesar" for "Brutus," and "Brutus" for "Caesar" throughout the whole play, without losing anything except such historical accuracy as the play has. We seem to be able to look at the matter, thinking not so much about Caesar or Brutus, or ourselves as individuals, but rather of the *role* of a friend, and the obligations it lays on anyone whatever, including ourselves. We are by such considerations led to postulate the existence of a fourth (and, we are happy to say, final) social human perspective, namely, that of an umpire—a detached standpoint from which we decide whether rules have or have not been broken.

It is important to see that the umpire's perspective can be applied to our own behavior as well as to that of others. When so applied, it goes under the name "conscience." When our conscience bothers us, it is, we claim, because we are able to look at our own actions, not only from the point of view of ourselves as agents, or patients, or from the reciprocal point of view of other individuals, but also from the point of view of a third party, who was really not there—namely, from the perspective of the umpire,[11] who is watching to see that the play goes fairly. . . .

. . . We are inclined to guess that all the elements required for games of strategy are present when we contemplate or enjoy aesthetic objects, but again that the emphasis is different. When we watch a performance of Sheridan's *The Rivals,* two principal things seem to be involved: (1) our perspectives as patient to spectacle, from which we feel enjoyment, or illumination, or any of the emotions appropriate to appreciation (or lack of it) of a play; and (2) our perspectives as referees, or umpires; i.e., as critics, who understand in an impersonal way the rules for enacting *The Rivals,* the rules for competent acting, and who can tell whether or not the affair is coming off properly—with the appropriate emotions of consternation, fright, or delight.

It seems clear, at any rate, that our perspectives as agents are involved in aesthetic responses in a very minimal way, unless we happen to be the performers, or we are on a showboat, where hissing the villain is good form. And it seems equally clear that the reciprocal perspective—looking at ourselves from the point of view of another person—is involved at best vicariously. But the way in which the performance is carried on (that is, the extent to which performers follow the rules, where rules are looked at from a referee's point of view), seems to be of much more importance in encounters with aesthetic objects.

NOTES

¹ Simmel, G., *The Sociology of Georg Simmel,* Glencoe, Ill.: Free Press, 1950.

² Mead, G. H., *Mind, Self, and Society,* Chicago: University [of Chicago] Press, 1934.

³ The importance of the concept *following a rule,* especially a linguistic rule, has probably been recognized more clearly by Wittgenstein [in *Philosophical Investigations,* New York: The Macmillian Co., 1953] than by anyone else in the history of philosophy, sociology, or psychology.

⁴ We note that this fiction of a hostile, animistic nature lies behind Wald's treatment [in *Statistical Decision Functions,* New York: John Wiley & Sons, 1950] of confidence levels in the behavioral sciences. For a similar idea see Moore [O. K., "Devination—a New Perspective," *American Anthropologist,* February 1957, pp. 69–74].

⁵ It might be objected that a conception of natural processes devoid of social interaction was known to several early Greek cosmologists, for example Democritus, and that consequently we are on shaky ground historically. In reply we explain that we do not mean to hold the position in such a sharp form. It must at least be conceded that Homer and Hesiod had a view of nature which was pervaded by social interaction—and all we wish to claim is that the latter kind of view is likely to come first. Even so, the classical views which pervaded western attempts at science up until the scientific Renaissance were those of Aristotle which, if not involving social interaction explicitly, at least embodied many anthropomorphic norms. Planets moved in circular orbits *because* (as Aristotle and his colleagues seemed to feel) circular motion was the *most perfect* form of nonrectilinear motion. And an early critic of Galileo's claim to have found an eighth planet cited in opposition the facts that there were seven deadly sins, seven cardinal virtues, seven days of the week, seven apertures in the head—*it stands to reason* that there are seven planets.

⁶ Hume, D., *Enquiries Concerning the Human Understanding and Concerning the Principles of Morals* (Selby-Bigge, 2nd edition), Oxford: Clarendon, 1951, p. 210.

[7] This point is hardly new. Santayana. . . says: "Reason is as old as man and as prevalent as human nature; for we should not recognize an animal to be human unless his instincts were to some degree conscious of their *ends* and rendered his ideas in that measure relevant to conduct." (Italics ours.) [*The Life of Reason: Reason in Common Sense*, 2d ed., New York: Scribner, 1932, p. 4–Ed.]

[8] Neumann, J. von, "Zur Theorie der Gesellschaftsspiele," *Mathematische Annalen*, C (1928), 295–320.

[9] Burns, R., "To a louse," in *Poems chiefly in the Scottish dialect*. Kilmarnock, 1786.

[10] Mead, *op. cit.*, pp. 42–43.–Ed.

[11] The term "umpire" is of some interest. It derives from old French, *nomper*, from *non* not, and *per* peer or equal. I.e., the umpire's role is that of a third party and not that of a fellow interactor. (*Umpire*, without initial *n-*, arose through the incorrect division of *a numpire* as *an umpire*.)

Konrad Lorenz

Morals and Weapons

In stating that man evolved from an animal, we must recognize that evolution does not imply that he is, therefore, nothing other than an animal. Conversely, in attempting to separate man from the animal world, whether through assertion of the dominance of the superorganic, or through religious notions of special creation—which are, perhaps, the unconscious base of much superorganic thinking—we must recognize that this dualistic, neo-Platonic form of thought does not provide an adequate model of human life as it is. We are extraordinarily reluctant to relinquish our notions of special creation—and as a result, our social sciences have largely ignored the study of animal social behavior as largely irrelevant to human social arrangements. Development of the science of ethology has indicated that animal behavior is, indeed, very relevant. From studies made by Konrad Lorenz and others we are obtaining valuable hypotheses about animal and human aggression, about how such aggression may have evolved, and about its adaptive and cohesive—as well as its disruptive—functions in group social development.

> *They that have power to hurt and will do none,*
> *That do not do the thing they most do show. . . .*
>
> SHAKESPEARE, *Sonnets*

IT IS EARLY ONE Sunday morning at the beginning of March, when Easter is already in the air, and we are taking a walk in the Vienna forest whose wooded slopes of tall beeches can be equalled in beauty by few and surpassed by none. We approach a forest glade. The tall smooth trunks of the beeches soon give place to the Hornbeam which are clothed from top to bottom with pale green foliage. We now tread slowly and more carefully. Before we break through the last bushes and out of cover on to the free expanse of the meadow, we do what all wild animals and all good naturalists, wild boars, leopards, hunters and zoologists would do under similar circumstances: we reconnoitre, seeking, before we leave our cover, to gain from it the advantage which it can offer alike to hunter and hunted, namely, to see without being seen.

Here, too, this age-old strategy proves beneficial. We do actually see someone who is not yet aware of our presence, as the wind is blowing away from him in our direction: in the middle of the clearing sits a large fat hare. He is sitting with his back to us, making a big V with his ears, and is watching intently something on the opposite edge of the meadow. From this point, a second and equally large hare emerges and with slow, dignified hops, makes his way towards the first one. There follows a measured encounter, not unlike the meeting of two strange dogs. The cautious mutual taking stock soon develops into sparring. The two hares chase each other round, head to tail, in minute circles. This giddy rotating continues for quite a long time. Then suddenly, their pent-up energies burst forth into a battle royal. It is just like the outbreak of war, and happens at the very moment when the long mutual threatening of the hostile parties has forced one to the conclusion that neither dares to make a definite move. Facing each other, the hares rear up on their hind legs and, straining to their full height, drum furiously at each other with their fore pads. Now they clash in flying leaps and, at last, to the accompaniment of squeals and grunts, they discharge a volley of lightning kicks, so rapidly that only a slow motion camera could help us to discern the mechanism of these hostilities. Now, for the time being, they have had enough, and they recommence their circling, this time much faster than before; then follows a fresh, more embittered bout. So engrossed are the two champions, that there is nothing to prevent myself and my little daughter from tiptoeing nearer, although that venture cannot be accomplished in silence. Any normal and sensible hare would have heard us long ago, but this is March and March Hares are mad! The whole boxing match looks so comical that my little daughter, in spite of her iron upbringing in the matter of silence when watching animals, cannot restrain a chuckle. That is too much even for March Hares—two flashes in two different directions and the meadow is empty, while over the battlefield floats a fistful of fluff, light as a thistledown.

It is not only funny, it is almost touching, this duel of the unarmed, this raging fury of the meek in heart. But are these creatures really so meek? Have they really got softer hearts than those of the fierce beasts of prey? If in a zoo, you ever watched two lions, wolves or eagles in conflict, then, in all probability, you did not feel like laughing. And yet, these sovereigns come off no worse than the harmless hares. Most people have the habit of judging carnivorous and herbivorous animals by quite inapplicable moral criteria. Even in fairy-tales, animals are portrayed as being a community comparable to that of mankind, as though all species of animals were beings of one and the same family, as human beings are. For this reason, the average person tends to regard the animal that kills animals in the same light as he would the man that kills his own kind. He does not judge the fox that kills a hare by the same standard as the hunter who shoots one for precisely the same reason, but with that severe censure that he would apply to the gamekeeper who makes a practice of shooting farmers and frying them for supper! The "wicked" beast of prey is branded as a murderer, although the fox's hunting is quite as legitimate and a great deal more necessary to his existence than is that of the gamekeeper, yet nobody regards the latter's "bag" as his prey, and only one author, whose own standards were indicted by the severest moral criticism, has dared to dub the fox-hunter "the unspeakable in pursuit of the uneatable"! In their dealing with members of their own species, the beasts and birds of prey are far more restrained than many of the "harmless" vegetarians.

Still more harmless than a battle of hares appears the fight between turtle- or ring-doves. The gentle pecking of the frail bill, the light flick of the fragile wing seems, to the uninitiated, more like a caress than an attack. Some time ago I decided to breed a cross between the African blond ring-dove, and our own indigenous somewhat frailer turtle-dove, and, with this object, I put a tame, home-reared male turtle-dove and a female ring-dove together in a roomy cage. I did not take their original scrapping seriously. How could these paragons of love and virtue dream of harming one another? I left them in their cage and went to Vienna. When I returned, the next day, a horrible sight met my eyes. The turtle-dove lay on the floor of the cage; the top of his head and neck, as also the whole length of his back, were not only plucked bare of feathers, but so flayed as to form a single wound dripping with blood. In the middle of this gory surface, like an eagle on his prey, stood the second harbinger of peace. Wearing that dreamy facial expression that so appeals to our sentimental observer, this charming lady pecked mercilessly with her silver bill in the wounds of her prostrated mate. When the latter gathered his last resources in a final effort to escape, she set on him again, struck him to the floor with a light clap of her wing and continued with her slow pitiless work of destruction. Without my interference she would undoubtedly have finished him off, in spite of the fact that she was already so tired that she could hardly keep her eyes open. Only in two other instances have I seen similar horrible lacerations inflicted on their own kind by vertebrates: once, as an observer of the embittered fights of cichlid fishes who sometimes actually skin each other, and again as a field surgeon, in the late war, where the highest of all vertebrates perpetrated mass mutilations on members of his own species. But to return to our "harmless" vegetarians. The battle of the hares which we witnessed in the forest clearing would have ended in quite as horrible a carnage as that of the doves, had it taken place in the confines of a cage where the vanquished could not flee the victor.

If this is the extent of the injuries meted out to their own kind by our gentle doves and hares, how much greater must be the havoc wrought amongst themselves by those beasts to whom nature has relegated the strongest weapons with which to kill their prey? One would certainly think so, were it not that a good naturalist should always check by observation even the most obvious-seeming inferences before he accepts them as truth. Let us examine that symbol of cruelty and voraciousness, the wolf. How do these creatures conduct themselves in their dealings with members of their own species? At Whipsnade, the zoological country paradise, there lives a pack of timber wolves. From the fence of a pine-wood of enviable dimensions we can watch their daily round in an environment not so very far removed from conditions of real freedom. To begin with, we wonder why the antics of the many woolly, fat-pawed whelps have not led them to destruction long ago. The efforts of one ungainly little chap to break into a gallop have landed him in a very different situation from that which he intended. He stumbles and bumps heavily into a wicked-looking old sinner. Strangely enough, the latter does not seem to notice it, he does not even growl. But now we hear the rumble of battle sounds! They are low, but more ominous than those of a dog-fight. We were watching the whelps and have therefore only become aware of this adult fight now that it is already in full swing.

An enormous old timber wolf and a rather weaker, obviously younger one are the opposing champions and they are moving in circles round each other, exhibiting admirable "footwork." At the same time, the bared fangs flash in such a rapid exchange of snaps that the eye can scarcely follow them. So far, nothing has really happened. The jaws of one wolf close on the gleaming white teeth of the other who is on the alert and wards off the attack. Only the lips have received one or two minor injuries. The younger wolf is gradually being forced backwards. It dawns upon us that the older one is purposely manoeuvring him towards the fence. We wait with breathless anticipation what will happen when he "goes to the wall." Now he strikes the wire netting, stumbles . . . and the old one is upon him. And now the incredible happens, just the opposite of what you would expect. The furious whirling of the grey bodies has come to a sudden standstill. Shoulder to shoulder they stand, pressed against each other in a stiff and strained attitude, both heads now facing in the same direction. Both wolves are growling angrily, the elder in a deep bass, the younger in higher tones, suggestive of the fear that underlies his threat. But notice carefully the position of the two opponents; the older wolf has his muzzle close, very close against the neck of the younger, and the latter holds away his head, offering unprotected to his enemy the bend of his neck, the most vulnerable part of his whole body! Less than an inch from the tensed neck-muscles, where the jugular vein lies immediately beneath the skin, gleam the fangs of his antagonist from beneath the wickedly retracted lips. Whereas, during the thick of the fight, both wolves were intent on keeping only their teeth, the one invulnerable part of the body, in opposition to each other, it now appears that the discomfited fighter proffers intentionaly that part of his anatomy to which a bite must assuredly prove fatal. Appearances are notoriously deceptive, but in his case, surprisingly, they are not!

This same scene can be watched any time wherever street-mongrels are to be found. I cited wolves as my first example because they illustrate my point more impressively than the all-too familiar domestic dog. Two adult male dogs meet in the street. Stiff-legged, with tails erect and hair on end, they pace towards each other. The nearer they approach, the stiffer, higher and more ruffled they appear, their advance becomes slower and slower. Unlike fighting cocks they do not make their encounter head to head, front against front, but make as though to pass each other, only stopping when they stand at last flank to flank, head to tail, in close juxtaposition. Then a strict ceremonial demands that each should sniff the hind regions of the other. Should one of the dogs be overcome with fear at this juncture, down goes his tail between his legs and he jumps with a quick, flexible twist, wheeling at a angle of 180 degrees, thus modestly retracting his former offer to be smelt. Should the two dogs remain in an attitude of self-display, carrying their tails as rigid as standards, then the sniffing process may be of a long protracted nature. All may be solved amicably and there is still the chance that first one tail and then the other may begin to wag with small but rapidly increasing beats and then this nerve-racking situation may develop into nothing worse than a cheerful canine romp. Failing this solution the situation becomes more and more tense, noses begin to wrinkle and to turn up with a vile, brutal expression, lips begin to curl, exposing the fangs on the side nearer the opponent. Then the animals scratch the earth angrily with their hind feet, deep growls rise from their chests, and, in the next moment, they fall upon each other with loud piercing yells.

But to return to our wolves, whom we left in a situation of acute tension. This was not a piece of inartistic narrative on my part, since the strained situation may continue for a great length of time which is minutes to the observer, but very probably seems hours to the losing wolf. Every second you expect violence and await with bated breath the moment when the winner's teeth will rip the jugular vein of the loser. But your fears are groundless, for it will not happen. In this particular situation, the victor will definitely not close on his less fortunate rival. You can see that he would like to, but he just cannot. A dog or wolf that offers his neck to its adversary in this way will never be bitten serious. The other growls and grumbles, snaps with his teeth in the empty air and even carries out, without delivering so much as a bite, the movement of shaking something to death in the empty air. However, this strange inhibition from biting persists only so long as the defeated dog or wolf maintains his attitude of humility. Since the fight is stopped so suddenly by this action, the victor frequently finds himself straddling his vanquished foe in anything but a comfortable position. So to remain, with his muzzle applied to the neck of the "under-dog" soon becomes tedious for the champion, and, seeing that he cannot bite anyway, he soon withdraws. Upon this, the underdog may hastily attempt to put distance between himself and his superior. But he is not usually successful in this, for, as soon as he abandons his rigid attitude of submission, the other again falls upon him like a thunderbolt and the victim must again freeze into his former posture. It seems as if the victor is only waiting for the moment when the other will relinquish his submissive attitude, thereby enabling him to give vent to his urgent desire to bite. But, luckily for the "underdog," the top-dog at the close of the fight is overcome by the pressing need to leave his trademark on the battle-field, to designate it as his personal property—in other words, he must lift his leg against the nearest upright object. This right-of-possession ceremony is usually taken advantage of by the under-dog to make himself scarce.

By this commonplace observation, we are here, as so often, made conscious of a problem which is actual in our daily life and which confronts us on all sides in the most various forms. Social inhibitions of this kind are not rare, but so frequent that we take them for granted and do not stop to think about them. An old German proverb says that one crow will not peck out the eye of another and for once the proverb is right. A tame crow or raven will no more think of pecking at your eye than he will at that of one of his own kind. Often when Roah, my tame raven, was sitting on my arm, I purposely put my face so near to his bill that my open eye came close to its wickedly curved point. Then Roah did something positively touching. With a nervous, worried movement he withdrew his beak from my eye, just as a father who is shaving will hold back his razor blade from the inquisitive fingers of his tiny daughter. Only in one particular connection did Roah ever approach my eye with his bill during this facial grooming. Many of the higher, social birds and mammals, above all monkeys, will groom the skin of a fellow-member of their species in those parts of his body to which he himself cannot obtain access. In birds, it is particularly the head and the region of the eyes which are dependent on the attentions of a fellow. In my description of the jackdaw, I have already spoken of the gestures with which these birds invite one another to preen their head fathers. When, with half-shut eyes, I held my head sideways towards Roah, just as corvine birds do to each other, he understood this movement in spite of the fact that I have no head feathers to ruffle, and at once began to groom me. While doing so, he never pinched my skin, for the epidermis of birds is delicate and would not stand such rough treatment. With wonderful precision, he submitted every attainable hair to a dry-cleaning process by drawing it separately through his bill. He worked with the same intensive concentration that distinguishes the "lousing" monkey and the operating surgeon. This is not meant as a joke: the social grooming of monkeys, and particularly of anthropoid apes, has not the object of catching vermin—these animals usually have none—and is not limited to the cleaning of the skin, but serves also more remarkable operations, for instance the dexterous removal of thorns and even the squeezing-out of small carbuncles.

The manipulations of the dangerous-looking corvine beak round the open eye of a man naturally appear ominous and, of course, I was always receiving warnings from onlookers at this procedure. "You never know—a raven is a raven—" and similar woods of wisdom. I used to respond with the paradoxical observation that the warner was for me potentially more dangerous than the raven. It has often happened that people have been shot dead by madmen who have masked their conditions with the cunning and pretence typical of such cases. There was always a posisbility, though admittedly a very small one, that our kind adviser might be afflicted with such a disease. But a sudden and unpredictable loss of the eye-pecking inhibition in a healthy, mature raven is more unlikely by far than an attack by a well-meaning friend.

Why has the dog the inhibition against biting his fellow's neck?

Why has the raven an inhibition against pecking the eye of his friend? Why has the ring-dove no such "insurance" against murder? A really comprehensive answer to these questions is almost impossible. It would certainly involve a *historical* explanation of the process by which these inhibitions have been developed in the course of evolution. There is no doubt that they have arisen side by side with the development of the dangerous weapons of the beast of prey. However, it is perfectly obvious why these inhibitions are necessary to all weapon-bearing animals. Should the raven peck, without compunction, at the eye of his nest-mate, his wife or his young, in the same way as he pecks at any other moving and glittering object, there would, by now, be no more ravens in the world. Should a dog or wolf unrestrainedly and unaccountably bite the neck of his pack-mates and actually execute the movement of shaking them to death, then his species also would certainly be exterminated within a short space of time.

The ring-dove does not require such an inhibition since it can only inflict injury to a much lesser degree, while its ability to flee is so well developed that it suffices to protect the bird even against enemies equipped with vastly better weapons. Only under the unnatural conditions of close confinement which deprive the losing dove of the possibility of flight does it become apparent that the ring-dove has no inhibitions which prevent it from injuring or even torturing its own kind. Many other "harmless" herbivores prove themselves just as unscrupulous when they are kept in narrow captivity. One of the most disgusting, ruthless and blood-thirsty murderers is an animal which is generally considered as being second only to the dove in the proverbial gentleness of its nature, namely the roe-deer. The roe-buck is about the most malevolent beast I know and is possessed, into the bargain, of a weapon, its antlers, which it shows mighty little restraint in putting into use. The species can "afford" this lack of control since the fleeing capacity even of the weakest doe is enough to deliver it from the strongest buck. Only in very large paddocks can the roe-buck be kept with females of his own kind. In smaller enclosures, sooner or later he will drive his fellows, females and young ones included, into a corner and gore them to death. The only "insurance against murder" which the roe-deer possesses, is based on the fact that the onslaught of the attacking buck proceeds relatively slowly. He does not rush with lowered head at his adversary as, for example, a ram would do, but he approaches quite slowly, cautiously feeling with his antlers for those of his opponent. Only when the antlers are interlocked and the buck feels firm resistance does he thrust with deadly earnest. According to the statistics given by W. T. Hornaday, the former director of the New York Zoo, tame deer cause yearly more serious accidents than captive lions and tigers, chiefly because an uninitiated person does not recognize the slow approach of the buck as an earnest attack, even when the animal's antlers have come dangerously near. Suddenly there follows, thrust upon thrust, the amazingly strong stabbing movement of the sharp weapon, and you will be lucky if you have time enough to get a good grip on the aggressor's antlers. Now there follows a wrestling-match in which the sweat pours and the hands drip blood, and in which even a very strong man can hardly obtain mastery over the roe-buck unless he succeeds in getting to the side of the beast and bending his neck backwards. Of course, one is ashamed to call for help—until one has the point of an antler in one's body! So take my advice and if a charming, tame roe-buck comes playfully towards you, with a char-acteristic prancing step and flourishing his antlers gracefully, hit him, with your walking stick, a stone or the bare first, as hard as you can, on the side of his nose, before he can apply his antlers to your person.

And now, honestly judged: who is really a "good" animal, my friend Roah to whose social inhibitions I could trust the light of my eyes, or the gentle ring-dove that in hours of hard work nearly succeeded in torturing its mate to death? Who is a "wicked" animal, the roe-buck who will slit the bellies even of females and young of his own kind if they are unable to escape him, or the wolf who cannot bite his hated enemy if the latter appeals to his mercy?

Now let us turn our mind to another question. Wherein consists the essence of all the gestures of submission by which a bird or animal of a social species can appeal to the inhibitions of its superior? We have just seen, in the wolf, that the defeated animal actually facilitates his own destruction by offering to the victor those very parts of his body which he was most anxious to shield as long as the battle was raging. All submissive attitudes with which we are so far familiar, in social animals, are based on the same principle: The supplicant always offers to his adversary the most vulnerable part of his body, or, to be more exact, that part *against which every killing attack is inevitably directed!* In most birds, this area is the base of the skull. If one jackdaw wants to show submission to another, he squats back on his hocks, turns away his head, at the same time drawing in his bill to make the nape of his neck bulge, and, leaning towards his superior, seems to invite him to peck at the fatal spot. Seagulls and herons present to their superior the top of their head, stretching their neck forward horizontally, low over the ground, also a position which makes the supplicant particularly defenceless.

With many gallinaceous birds, the fights of the males commonly end by one of the combatants being thrown to the ground, held down and then scalped as in the manner described in the ring-dove. Only one species shows mercy in this case, namely the turkey: and this one only does so in response to a specific submissive gesture which serves to forestall the intent of the attack. If a turkey-cock has had more than his share of the wild and grotesque wrestling-match in which these birds indulge, he lays himself with outstretched neck upon the ground. Whereupon the victor behaves exactly as a wolf or dog in the same situation, that is to say, he evidently *wants* to peck and kick at the prostrated enemy, but simply cannot: he would if he could but he can't! So, still in threatening attitude, he walks round and round his prostrated rival, making tentative passes at him, but leaving him untouched.

This reaction—though certainly propitious for the turkey species—can cause a tragedy if a turkey comes to blows with a peacock, a thing which not infrequently happens in captivity, since these species are closely enough related to "appreciate" respectively their mutual manifestations of virility. In spite of greater strength and weight the turkey nearly always loses the match, for the peacock flies better and has a different fighting technique. While the red-brown American is muscling himself up for the wrestling-match, the blue East-Indian has already flown above him and struck at him with sharply pointed spurs. The turkey justifiably considers this infringement of his fighting code as unfair and, although he is still in possession of his full strength, he throws in the sponge and lays himself down in the above depicted manner now. And a ghastly thing happens: the peacock does not "understand" this submissive gesture of the turkey, that is to say, it elicits no inhibition of his fighting drives. He pecks and kicks further at the helpless turkey, who, if nobody comes to his rescue, is doomed, for the more pecks and blows he receives, the more certainly are his escape reactions blocked by the psycho-physiological mechanism of the submissive attitude. It does not and cannot occur to him to jump up and run away.

The fact that many birds have developed special "signal organs" for eliciting this type of social inhibition, shows convincingly the blind instinctive nature and the great evolutionary age of these submissive gestures. The young of the water-rail, for example, have a bare red patch at the back of their head which, as they present it meaningly to an older and stronger fellow, takes on a deep red colour. Whether, in higher animals and man, social inhibitions of this kind are equally mechanical, need not for the moment enter into our consideration. Whatever may be the reasons that prevent the dominant individual from injuring the submissive one, whether he is prevented from doing so by a simple and purely mechanical reflex process or by a highly philosophical moral standard, is immaterial to the practical issue. The essential behaviour of the submissive as well as of the dominant partner remains the same: the humbled creature suddenly seems to lose his objections to being injured and removes all obstacles from the path of the killer, and it would seem that the very removal of these outer obstacles raises an insurmountable inner obstruction in the central nervous system of the aggressor.

And what is a human appeal for mercy after all? Is it so very different from what we have just described? The Homeric warrior who wishes to yield and plead mercy, discards helmet and shield, falls on his knees and inclines his head, a set of actions which should make it easier for the enemy to kill, but, in reality, hinders him from doing so. As Shakespeare makes Nestor say of Hector:

Thou hast hung thy advanced sword i' the air,
Not letting it decline on the declined.

Even to-day, we have retained many symbols of such submissive attitudes in a number of our gestures of courtesy: bowing, removal of the hat, and presenting arms in military ceremonial. If we are to believe the ancient epics, an appeal to mercy does not seem to have raised an "inner obstruction" which was entirely insurmountable. Homer's heroes were certainly not as soft-hearted as the wolves of Whipsnade! In any case, the poet cites numerous instances where the supplicant was slaughtered with or without compunction. The Norse heroic sagas bring us many examples of similar failures of the submissive gesture and it was not till the era of knight-errantry that it was no longer considered "sporting" to kill a man who begged for mercy. The Christian knight is the first who, for reasons of traditional and religious morals, is as chivalrous as is the wolf from the depth of his natural impulses and inhibitions. What a strange paradox!

Of course, the innate, instinctive, fixed inhibitions that prevent an animal from using his weapons indiscriminately against his own kind are only a functional analogy, at the most a slight foreshadowing, a genealogical predecessor of the social morals of man. The worker in comparative ethology does well to be very careful in applying moral criteria to animal behaviour. But here, I must myself own to harbouring sentimental feelings: I think it a truly magnificent thing that one wolf finds himself unable to bite the proffered neck of the other, but still more so that the other relies upon him for this amazing restraint. Mankind can learn a lesson from this, from the animal that Dante calls *"la bestia senza pace."* I at least have extracted from it a new and deeper understanding of a wonderful and often misunderstood saying from the Gospel which hitherto had only awakened in me feelings of strong opposition: "And unto him that smiteth thee on the one cheek offer also the other." (St. Luke VI, 26). A wolf has enlightened me: not so that your enemy may strike you again do you turn the other cheek towards him, but to make him unable to do it.

When, in the course of its evolution, a species of animals develops a weapon which may destroy a fellow-member at one blow, then, in order to survive, it must develop, along with the weapon, a social inhibition to prevent a usage which could endanger the existence of the species. Among the predatory animals, there are only a few which lead so solitary a life that they can, in general, forego such restraint. They come together only at the mating season when the sexual impulse outweighs all others, including that of aggression. Such unsociable hermits are the polar bear and the jaguar and, owing to the absence of these social inhibitions, animals of these species, when kept together in zoos, hold a sorry record for murdering their own kind. The system of special inherited impules and inhibitions, together with the weapons with which a social species is provided by nature, form a complex which is carefully computed and self-regulating. All living beings have received their weapons through the same process of evolution that moulded their impulses and inhibitions; for the structural plan of the body and the system of behaviour of a species are parts of the same whole.

> If such be Nature's holy plan,
> Have I not reason to lament
> What man has made of man?

Wordsworth is right: there is only one being in possession of weapons which do not grow on his body and of whose working plan, therefore, the instincts of his species know nothing and in the usage of which he has no correspondingly adequate inhibition. That being is man. With unarrested growth his weapons increase in monstrousness, multiplying horribly within a few decades. But innate impulses and inhibitions, like bodily structures, need time for their development, time on a scale in which geologists and astronomers are accustomed to calculate, and not historians. We did not receive our weapons from nature. We made them ourselves, of our own free will. Which is going to be easier for us in the future, the production of the weapons or the engendering of the feeling of responsibility that should go along with them, the inhibitions without which our race must perish by virtue of its own creations? We must build up these inhibitions purposefully for we cannot rely upon our instincts. Fourteen years ago, in November 1935, I concluded an article on "Morals and Weapons of Animals" which appeared in a Viennese journal, with the words, "The day will come when two warring factions will be faced with the possibility of each wiping the other out completely. The day may come when the whole of mankind is divided into two such opposing camps. Shall we then behave like doves or like wolves? The fate of mankind will be settled by the answer to this question." We may well be apprehensive.

Frank B. Livingstone

Anthropological Implications of Sickle Cell Gene Distribution in West Africa

The association of the sickle cell gene with a deadly form of anemia puzzled biologists for many years. The gene seemed nonadaptive—yet its prevalence in certain human populations suggested that it did, indeed, serve some adaptive function. The puzzle was solved when biologists learned that the gene, in its heterozygous form, offers some protection against malaria. This information proved of great interest to anthropologists who have been able, by plotting the distribution of the gene, to obtain knowledge that corroborates some linguistic evidence of cultural connections. Anthropologists have always been interested in blood and blood types. Today they have expanded their interest to include many other aspects of medicine. Use of an anthropological approach has had practical results for medicine as well, because it provides an excellent tool for revealing the cultural sources of disease. Discovery of the role of the sickle cell gene in adaptation has not only justified anthropology's inclusion of human biology as part of its discipline, it has served to reassert the interactive nature of biology and culture.

DURING THE PAST FIFTEEN years, data on the frequency of the sickle cell gene have accumulated to such an extent that its world distribution can now be outlined in considerable detail. Frequencies of more than 20 percent of the sickle cell trait have been found in populations across a broad belt of tropical Africa from the Gambia to Mozambique. Similar high frequencies have been found in Greece, South Turkey, and India. At first it appeared that there were isolated "pockets" of high frequencies in India and Greece, but more recently the sickle cell gene has been found to be widely distributed in both countries (Choremis and Zannos 1956; Sukumaran, Sanghvi, and Vyas 1956). Moreover, between these countries where high frequencies are found, there are intermediate frequencies, in Sicily, Algeria, Tunisia, Yemen, Palestine, and Kuwait. Thus, the sickle cell gene is found in a large and rather continuous region of the Old World and in populations which have recently emigrated from this region, while it is almost completely absent from an even larger region of the Old World which stretches from Northern Europe to Australia.

When the broad outlines of the distribution of the sickle cell gene first began to emerge, several investigators attempted to explain various aspects of this distribution by migration and mixture. Lehmann and Raper (1949) attempted to show that the differences in the frequency of the sickle cell gene among the Bantu tribes of Uganda were due to varying degrees of Hamitic admixture; Brain (1953) and Lehmann (1954) postulated migrations from Asia to account for the distribution of the sickle cell gene in Africa; and Singer (1953), using an age-area type of argument, postulated that the sickle cell gene arose by mutation near Mt. Ruwenzori and diffused from there. However, it was recognized early in the development of the sickle cell problem that regardless of the extent to which migration and mixture explained the distribution pattern of the sickle cell gene, its high frequencies in various widely scattered areas raised some additional and striking problems in human population genetics.

Since persons who are homozygous for the sickle cell gene very rarely reproduce, there is a constant loss of sickle cell genes in each generation. In order for the gene to attain frequencies of .1 to .2, which are equivalent to about 20 to 40 percent of the sickle cell trait, there must be some mechanism which is compensating for this loss. In other words, there must be some factor which is tending to increase the number of sickle cell genes in the population. Neel (1951) first pointed out that there are two outstanding possibilities; either the sickle cell gene is arising frequently by mutation, or the heterozygote for the sickle cell gene possesses a selective advantage over the normal homozygote which offsets the selective disadvantage of the sickle cell homozygote (balanced polymorphism). Since the evidence (Vandepitte et al. 1955) indicated that the mutation rate was not sufficient to maintain the high frequencies, selection in favor of individuals with the sickle cell trait seemed to be implicated as the factor which was maintaining them.

When Allison (1954a; 1954b; 1954c) advanced the hypothesis that the heterozygote for the sickle cell gene possessed a relative immunity to falciparum malaria, he marshalled the first clear evidence for the mechanism by which selection maintained the observed high frequencies. In addition to experiments on sicklers and nonsicklers which seemed to show that the sicklers could cope more easily with a malarial infection, Allison (1954b) also showed that the tribal frequencies of the sickle cell gene in Uganda and other parts of East Africa could be explained as well by his malaria hypothesis as by varying degrees of Hamitic admixture. Thus, Allison's work showed that selection must be taken into consideration in any attempt to explain the distribution of the sickle cell gene.

.   .   .

Man, Malaria, and Mosquito in West Africa

In West Africa the relationship between man, malaria, and mosquito is very highly evolved, due largely to the habits of the major vector of malaria, *Anopheles gambiae*. This mosquito is attracted to human habitations and usually rests in the thatched roofs of an African village. It bites man regularly, and breeds in a variety of places. Wilson (1949) has estimated that 75 percent of the malaria in Africa is due to *A. gambiae*. Its breeding places are so diverse that, when attempting to delimit them, entomologists usually state where it cannot breed. *A. gambiae* cannot breed in (1) very shaded water, (2) water with a strong current, (3) brackish water, (4) very alkaline or polluted water (Holstein 1952).

If we now consider the types of water which would be found in the tropical rain forest, it can be seen that there would be few places for *A. gambiae* to breed in unbroken tropical rain forest. The high emergent shade trees and the trees of the middle "story" of the forest so effectively shade the ground that there would be few, if any, areas that were unshaded. In addition, the layer of humus on the forest floor is very absorbent, so there would be few stagnant pools. It is only when man cuts down the forest that breeding places for *A. gambiae* become almost infinite (De Meillon 1949). First, with continued cutting of the forest, the soil loses all of its humus and becomes laterized. At this stage it is practically impervious to water; puddles are constantly renewed by the frequent tropical rains and so persist indefinitely. Second, man's refuse and his villages provide more abundant breeding places for the mosquito. Third, the swamps become open and hence possible breeding places.

In a hunting population, which does not destroy the forest, malaria would thus not develop this complex relation with man. Malaria could still be present, but not the holoendemic malaria which characterizes most of Africa today. Hunters do not build the type of permanent habitation in which *A. gambiae* lives, and since a hunting population moves frequently the mosquito could not keep up with the human population, so to speak. Also, in the epidemiology of any disease there is a critical size for the population below which the disease cannot persist. Since hunting populations are small, they would be closer to this critical size and perhaps even below it.

The Pygmies provide an example of such a hunting population, but unfortunately no malaria surveys of hunting Pygmies are available. Schwetz, Baumann, Peel and Droeshant (1933) did examine three groups of Pygmies for malaria and found that they had less than the surrounding Negroes, but these Pygmies were building houses and farming, and so cannot be considered a hunting population. Putnam (1948), who lived with the hunting Pygmies for 20 years, states that they do not suffer from malaria. His account also shows that the Pygmies do not cut down the forest and do not build their rude huts in a clearing but in the middle of the forest. These customs would appear to be the reasons for the absence of malaria among them.

If this complex relationship between parasite, host, and vector which is characteristic of holoendemic melaria could not have developed in hunting populations, then the selective advantage of the sickle cell gene would not be present in these populations. If, as has been postulated, the Feloop and other peoples in Portuguese Guinea and the Kru peoples of Eastern Liberia and the Western Ivory Coast were the last remnants of hunting populations which once were spread through the tropical forest, then the absence of the selective advantage of the sickle cell gene in these populations would have prevented it from becoming established, even if there had been some gene flow from neighboring Sudanic peoples. Although considerable areas of tropical rain forest are shown on any vegetation map of West Africa, these are greatly broken up by agricultural settlements and fields. Nevertheless, the last northern remnants of the forest are located in Portuguese Guinea near one area of low sickling frequencies, and the other area in Eastern Liberia is in the center of the largest remaining block of tropical rain forest.

The frequencies of the sickle cell trait among the Pygmies also support this theory, although the comments of several authorities might seem to contradict it. Regarding the Pygmies and Pygmoids, Hiernaux (1955:463) states; "They generally show a lower frequency of sicklemia than the surrounding populations, as shown in Table 2. In all cases but one, the frequency is lower in the Pygmoids. The most striking difference is between the Bondjo and Babinga, who are true Pygmies." Since most Pygmy groups have formed symbiotic relationships with their Negro neighbors, the frequencies among them can easily be explained by mixture, which is known to be occurring (Putnam 1948).

There is other evidence that *A. gambiae* has spread rather recently through the West African tropical rain forest. In the area around the Firestone Plantation in Liberia, shortly after the forest had been cut down, Barber, Rice and Brown (1932) found that *A. gambiae* accounted for 46 percent of the mosquito population found in the native huts, while *A. funestus* accounted for 51 percent, and *A. nili* for 3 percent. However, at the present time in this same area, *A. gambiae* accounts for almost 100 percent of the mosquito population (Max J. Miller, personal communication). Barber, Rice, and Brown (1932) found holoendemic malaria, which is not present today; however, this change is due to malaria control and not to changes in the mosquito population. These figures thus indicate a significant increase in *A. gambiae* when the forest is cut down. Even more significant are Barber, Rice, and Brown's comments on the effects of reforestation on the mosquito population. They state (1932:629):

> We felt that it would be interesting to know what would be the condition of things when the rubber trees had grown and the unplanted ravines and swamps had become "rejunglized." We surveyed Mt. Barclay Plantation where the stream borders have grown up with brush or long grass. After a long search in the streams we found only two or three larvae, *A. mauritianius* and *A. obscurus*. In a pool near a village *A. costalis* was plentiful.

It can thus be seen that *A. gambiae* (the authors call the species *A. costalis*) was not present in natural water but only near a village. The authors also discuss "rejuglization" as a means of malaria control, but state that it would not be feasible due to the breeding places which would persist around the villages. In the absence of these villages, which are not built by hunting populations, and in the presence of unbroken tropical forest, the intensity of malaria would be much less. This seems to have been the situation in West Africa prior to the spread of slash and burn agriculture. Therefore, the spread of this agriculture is responsible for the spread of the selective advantage of the sickle cell gene, and hence for the spread of the gene itself.

Sickle Cells, Disease, and Human Evolution

The preceding explanation of the distribution of the sickle cell gene and its relation to the culture history of West Africa has broad implications for the role of disease in human evolution. In considering the epidemiology of the sickle cell gene, Neel (1957:167) suggested that either the mutation which resulted in the sickle cell gene was very rare or else the spread of the gene was at present favored by special circumstances of relatively recent origin. The detailed arguments of this paper would seem to show that there are indeed special circumstances of recent origin, while at the same time not excluding the possibility that the mutation is quite rare. The special circumstances are considered to be the conditions necessary to maintain holoendemic malaria due to *Plasmodium falciparum*. This parasite is in fact regarded as evolutionally the most recent species of malaria to parasitize man (Boyd 1949). If, as has been proposed, a mobile hunting population in the tropical rain forest could not develop holoendemic malaria, then this high endemicity would perhaps be even later than the adaptation of the parasite to man as its host. Since the agricultural revolution occurred only about 7000 years ago and spread much later to Africa, it appears that the development of the environmental conditions which are responsible for the spread of the sickle cell gene are relatively recent, as Neel postulated they should be.

The agicultural revolution has always been considered an important event in man's cultural evolution, but it also seems to have been an important event in man's biological evolution. Prior to this revolution, the size of the human population was controlled to a large extent by the size of its food supply, and man's ecological niche was comparable to that of the large carnivores, or more closely perhaps to that of a large omnivore such as the bear. With the advent of the agricultural revolution, the food supply was no longer the major factor controlling the size of human populations. Man broke out of his ecological confinement and there was a tremendous increase in the size of the human population, an increase which was limited only by the available land. Haldane (1949, 1956) has stated that disease became the major factor controlling the size of human populations at this time, and his statement seems to be supported in one case by the spread of holoendemic malaria.

Two results of the agricultural revolution seem to account for this change in the role of disease in human evolution: (1) the great changes in the environment, and (2) the huge increase in the human population. Both of these seem to be involved in the development of holoendemic malaria. First, when man disrupts the vegetation of any area, he severely disrupts the fauna and often causes the extinction of many mammals, particularly the larger ones. When this happens, there are many known instances of the parasites of these animals adapting to man as the new host (Heisch 1956). It is thus possible that the parasitization of many by *P. falciparum* is due to man's blundering on the scene and causing the extinction of the original host. Second, concomitant with the huge increase in the human population, this population became more sedentary and man also became the most widespread large animal. Thus, he became the most available blood meal for mosquitoes and the most available host for parasites. This change resulted in the adaptation of several species of the Anopheline mosquito to human habilation, this population became more sedentary and man also be host. Under these conditions, holoendemic malaria and probably many other direases developed and became important factors determining human evolution. It should be noted, however, that through domestication man has created large populations of other animals and these have influenced the epidemiology of several human diseases including malaria (for malaria examples, see Hackett 1949; Draper and Smith 1957). The sickle cell gene thus seems to be an evolutionary response to this changed disease environment. Hence, this gene is the first known genetic response to a very important event in man's evolution when disease became a major factor determining the direction of that evolution.

REFERENCES

Allison, A. C. (1954a) "Protection afforded by sickle-cell trait against subtertian malarial infection." *British Medical Journal* I:290–294.

—— (1954b) "The distribution of the sickle-cell trait in East Africa and elsewhere, and its apparent relationship to the incidence of subtertian maleria." *Transactions of the Royal Society of Tropical Medicine and Hygiene* 48:312–318.

—— (1954c) "Notes on sickle-cell polymorphism." *Annals of Human Genetics* 19:39–57.

Barber, M. A., J. B. Rice, and J. Y. Brown (1932) "Malaria studies on the Firestone Rubber Plantation in Liberia, West Africa." *American Journal of Hygiene* 15:601–633.

Boyd, M. F. (1949) "Historical review." In: *Malariology: a comprehensive survey of all aspects of this group of diseases from a global standpoint*, M. F. Boyd, ed. Vol. I:3–25. Philadelphia, W. B. Saunders.

Brain, P. (1953) "The sickle-cell trait: a possible mode of introduction into Africa." *Man* 53:154.

Choremis, C., and L. Zannos (1957) "Microdrepanocytic disease in Greece." *Blood* 12:454–460.

De Meillon, B. (1949) "Anophelines of the Ethiopian Region." In: *Malariology: a comprehensive survey of all aspects of this group of diseases from the global standpoint*, M. F. Boyd, ed. Vol. I:443–482. Philadelphia, W. B. Saunders.

Draper, C. C., and A. Smith (1957) "Malaria in the Pare area of N.E. Tanganyika." *Transactions of the Royal Society of Tropical Medicine and Hygiene* 51:137–151.

Hackett, L. W. (1949) "Conspectus of malaria incidence in Northern Europe, the Mediterranean Region, and the Near East." In: *Malariology: a comprehensive survey of all aspects of this group of diseases from the global standpoint*, M. F. Boyd, ed. Vol. 2:788–799. Philadelphia, W. B. Saunders.

Haldane, J. B. S. (1949) "Disease and evolution." Supplement to *La Ricerca Scientifica* 19:3–10.

—— (1956) "The argument from animals to men, an examination of its validity for anthropology." *Journal of the Royal Anthropological Institute* 86:1–14.

Heisch, R. B. (1956) "Zoonoses as a study in ecology." *British Medical Journal* I: 669–673.

Hiernaux, J. (1955) "Physical anthropology and the frequency of genes with a selective value: the sickle cell gene." *American Journal of Physical Anthropology* 13:455–472.

Holstein, M. H. (1952) Biologie d'*Anopheles gambiae;* Recherche en Afrique-Occidentale Française. World Health Organization, Geneva.

Lehmann, H. (1954) "Distribution of the sickle-cell gene: a new light on the origin of the East Africans." *Eugenics Review* 46:1–23.

Lehmann, H., and A. B. Raper (1949) "Distribution of the sickle-cell trait in Uganda and its ethnological significance." *Nature* 164:494.

Miller, M. N.D. Personal communication.

Neel, J. V. (1951) "The population genetics of two inherited blood dyscrasias in man." *Cold Spring Harbor Symposiums on Quantitative Biology* 15:141–158.

——— (1957) "Human hemoglobin types, their epidemiologic implications." *New England Journal of Medicine* 256:161–171.

Putnam, P. (1948) "The Pygmies of the Ituri Forest." In *A Reader in General Anthropology,* C. S. Coon, ed. New York, Henry Holt.

Schwetz, J. H. Baumann, Peel and Droeshant (1933) "Etude comparative de la malaria chez les pygmées et les indigenes de la forêt de l'Ituri (Congo Belge)." *Bulletin de la Societé de Pathologie Exotique* 26:639–651.

Singer, R. (1953) "The sickle cell trait in Africa." *American Anthropologist* 55:634–648.

Sukumaran, P. K., L. D. Sanghvi, and G. N. Vyas (1956) "Sickle-cell trait in some tribes at Western India." *Current Science* 25:290–291.

Vandepitte, J. M., W. W. Zuelzer, J. V. Neel, and J. Colaert (1955) "Evidence concerning the inadequacy of mutation as an explanation of the frequency of the sickle-cell gene in the Belgian Congo." *Blood* 10:341–350.

Wilson, D. B. (1949) "Malaria incidence in Central and South Africa." In *Malariotogy: a comprehensive survey of all aspects of this group of diseases from a global standpoint,* M. F. Boyd, ed. Vol. 2:800–809. Philadelphia, W. B. Saunders.

Talcott Parsons

Social Structure and the Development of Personality: Freud's Contribution to the Integration of Psychology and Sociology

Talcott Parsons' theory of social interaction cannot be understood without some reference to much that had gone before. Throughout their history, the social sciences have vacillated between viewpoints that saw man as the object of forces that happened without his awareness and without any intention on the part of the participants, and viewpoints that insisted upon the ability of human beings to intentionally remake their worlds. Both the discoveries of Sigmund Freud and the shock of World War II weakened human belief in man's rationality, and both sociology and anthropology tended to go to the other extreme and discount altogether the effect of human rationality upon social behavior. Vilfredo Pareto's appeal to a postwar generation rests upon his belief in the ascendancy of nonrational systems over rational ones. For Talcott Parsons, however, the problem was to integrate and understand the effect of rational thought upon social systems. His theory of "action," which stresses man's ability to affect his environment according to rational belief, is based upon sound psychology that recognizes both the social and the unconscious basis of personality structure.

I EMPHASIZE THIS CONTINUITY FROM the objects of identification in childhood to the role and collectivity structure of the adult society in order to bring out what is to me the central point of the whole analysis. This is that Freud's theory of object-relations is essentially an analysis of the relation of the individual to the *structure of the society* in which he lives. Freud analyzed this relation from the point of view of the individual rather than from the point of view of the structure of the social systems concerned. His perspective also was primarily developmental in the psychological sense; sociologically stated, he was mainly concerned with the processes by which the

269

individual comes to acquire membership in social collectivities, to learn to play roles in them, and to internalize their values, and he was most interested in the identifications entered into in early childhood.

But throughout the course of personality development, identification, object-choice, and internalization are processes of relating the individual to and integrating him in the social system, and, through it, the culture. Since these processes are a relational matter, eventually technical analysis has to be applied to both sets of relata, as well as to the relationship itself. Had Freud lived long enough to enter more deeply into the technical analysis of the object-systems to which the individual becomes related, he would inevitably have had to become, in part, a sociologist, for the structure of these object-systems is—not merely is influenced by—the structure of the society itself. Essentially, Freud's theory of object-relations is a theory of the relation of the individual personality to the social system. It is a primary meeting ground of the two disciplines of psychology and sociology.

. . . if the individual's object-relations in the course of his life history are as important as they seem to be, then the significance of internalized social objects and culture cannot, as some psychoanalysts have tended to assume, be confined mainly to the content of the superego. On the contrary, it must permeate the whole personality system, for, with all Freud's emphasis on differentiation within the personality, he consistently treated it as an integrated whole.

In certain respects the ego should provide the test case of this hypothesis. Indeed, the increasing attention of Freud himself in his later years to problems of ego psychology, an area which has been considerably further explored by such authors as Heinz Hartmann and Ernst Kris, seems to be closely related to his increasing attention to the field of the object-relations. At the same time, I do not think that the id should be exempt from the logic of this development.

First, however, let me say something about the ego. Since the ego is the primary location of interchange between the personality and the outside world of reality, and since the most important aspect of reality itself is social, the conclusion is inescapable that the ego is "socially structured." It is a particularly welcome confirmation of this hypothesis—much of which has been worked out from a sociological point of view—to find that Freud himself explicitly recognized it. The most striking passage I have found deserves to be quoted at length:

> When it happens that a person has to give up a sexual object, there quite often ensues a modification in his ego which can only be described as a reinstatement of the object within the ego, as it occurs in melancholia; the exact nature of this substitution is as yet unknown to us. It may be that by undertaking this intro- jection, which is a kind of regression to the mechanism of the oral phase, the ego makes it easier for an object to be given up or renders that process possible. It may even be that this identification is the sole condition under which the id can give up its objects. At any rate the process, especially in the early phases of develop- ment, is a very frequent one, and *it points to the conclusion that the character of the ego is a precipitate of abandoned object- cathexes* and that it contains a record of past object-choices.[1]

I think it can, then, quite safely be said that object-cathexes and identifications do not, in Freud's own mature view, simply "influence" the development of the ego, in the sense in which temperature or moisture influences the growth of a plant, but that the structure of the object-relations a person has experienced is directly *constitutive* of the structure of the ego itself.

If it can be said of the ego that it is a precipitate of abandoned object-cathexes, there does not seem to be any serious doubt that the superego is primarily social and cultural in origin. Indeed, this has been clearly recognized by psychoanalysts ever since the introduction of the concept by Freud. Freud's formula that the superego represents the parental function is to my mind the most adequate one. He also quite explicitly refers to it as the focus of "that higher nature" repre- senting the "moral, spiritual side of human nature,"[2] which we have taken into ourselves from our parents.

The role of the id is focal to the issue with which the present discussion started—namely, the relative importance of "instinctive" as compared with cultural, social, and other "environmental" influences in the motivation of personality. The concept of the id in Freud's later work is, of course, one primary heir, although by no means the only one, of such concepts as the unconscious, the primary process, and the libido in his earlier work. Furthermore, in the enthusiasm of discovery, Freud tended to contrast the id as sharply as possible with the ego, which seemed to be the closest, of all the components of the personality, to traditionally rationalistic common sense—as, for instance, when he spoke of the id as entirely lacking in organization.[3]

Against the tendency to highlight the conflicts between the ego and id must be set the view implied in the metaphor of the horse and rider, the conception of the ego as a system of control. Furthermore, the id is treated at many points in specific relation to the pleasure principle, and I have suggested various reasons for assuming that pleasure is an organizing mechanism which integrates diverse motives at lower levels of organization.

A still further consideration which points in this direction is the progressive increase in the generality which Freud attributed to the basic instinctual urges, ending up with only a single underlying duality. This is not inconsistent with Bowlby's views of the importance, in more specialized contexts, of various more particularized instinctual responses.[4] But it does imply that, from a very early phase of development, the basic *organization* of the motivational system cannot be derived from instinctual sources, but must come from identifications and internalized objects.

It is my own view that the distinction between instinctual and learned components of the motivational system cannot legitimately be identified with that between the id, on the one hand, and the ego and superego on the other. Rather, the categories of instinctual and learned components cut across the id, the ego, and the superego. The id, like the other subsystems, is organized about its experience in object-relations. It differs, however, in two fundamental respects from the other subsystems. First, it is oriented, as the other two are not, to the person's own organism as object. This seems to me to be the essential significance of the pleasure principle as the governing principle of the id. Secondly, however, the object-cathexes which are constitutive of the structure of the id are predominantly those of the earlier phases of the process of socialization, so that in any internal conflicts involving the problem of regression, id-drives represent the regressive side of the conflict.

However true it may be that advancing beyond certain early levels of development requires transcending the fixation on these early cathexes, and however much the mature personality must control them through ego and superego mechanisms, it still remains true that these are particular cases of identification and internalization of objects—not the leading example of motivation in their absence.

Thus it seems to me that the general principles of object-relations through identification, object-cathexis, and internalization must be extended to the *whole* psychoanalytic theory of personality. Indeed, this is the position Freud eventually, in all essential respects, came to, even though he had not ironed out all of the inconsistencies in his treatment of these matters, nor reconciled many of his earlier statements with his later ones.

These are two particular virtues of this position. First, it formulates psychoanalytic theory in such terms that direct and detailed articulation with the theory of social systems is enormously facilitated. This is of the first importance to the theory of the motivation of social behavior and hence, in my opinion, is an essential prerequisite of the advance of sociology in certain connections. But at the same time there are reciprocal benefits for psychoanalysis—for example, this formulation suggests ways in which personality theory must take account of variations in the structure of the social system on which it impinges.

On a more general level, however, this view should do much to relieve psychoanalytic theory of involvement in a false dilemma in its use of the categories of heredity and environment. As general biology is showing with increasing clarity, it is not a question of whether or how much one or the other factor influences outcomes—in this instance, in the field of behavior. The trend is strongly away from a "predominant-factor" explanation of the phenomena of life, toward a more analytical one. Analytically conceived variables are, except for limiting cases, always *all* important. The salient technical problems concern their clear definition and the working out of their intricate modes of *interrelationship* with each other. This paper has, in this respect, been meant as a contribution to what I conceive to be the major trend of psychoanalytic theory in this same direction.

NOTES

[1] Sigmund Freud, *The Ego and the Id,* London, Hogarth Press, 1935, p. 36. The italics are mine. The relation of this passage to Freud's late view of the role of anxiety (*The Problem of Anxiety,* New York, Norton, 1936), as concerned primarily with the fear of object-loss is clear.

[2] *The Ego and the Id, op. cit.,* pp. 46–47.

[3] For example, Sigmund Freud, *New Introductory Lectures on Psychoanalysis,* New York, Norton, 1933, p. 103.

[4] John Bowlby, "The Nature of the Child's Tie to its Mother," *The International Journal of Psycho-Analysis,* 1958, Vol. 39, Part V.

Melford E. Spiro

Religious Systems as Culturally Constituted Defense Mechanisms

In asking how we can be certain that religious behavior is not pathological behavior, Melford Spiro attempts to come to grips with one of
the social scientist's thorniest problems: cultural relativism versus universalism. The question here stems from two opposing views of the
functions of religious institutions: Freud's assertion that religious
rituals are neurotic defense mechanisms and therefore symptoms of
pathology, and the functionalists' recognition that religious systems
promote group cohesion. Though he accepts the Freudian assertion
that ritual behavior is a defense mechanism for the preservation of the
sense of self, Dr. Spiro agrees with the functionalists that religious
systems are not symptoms of pathology, but of adaptation. They are,
in fact, culturally constituted mechanisms, which in traditional societies
promote cultural participation, resolve conflicts, and reduce psychological tensions and distortion.

Introduction

Since the range of beliefs, values, and rituals related to supernatural
beliefs and events is enormous, it is obvious, as Durkheim observed
long ago, that no belief, value, or ritual is intrinsically identifiable as
"religious." Since the "religious," on the contrary, is a quality capable
of being attached to almost any instance of these three dimensions of
religious systems, the latter, to use a modern idiom, are in large
measure projective systems. It is this characteristic of religion that
poses a problem which has long confronted its students, and which

comprises the problem of this paper: If religious systems are indeed projective in character, how can we be sure that religious behavior is not abnormal behavior, requiring psychiatric, rather than socio-cultural analysis?

Anthropology, as is well known, has adopted a fairly uniform stance with respect to the cross-cultural variability which characterizes notions of the good, the true, and the beautiful. This stance, so far as the normal-abnormal distinction is concerned, was given classic expression by Benedict (1934), who maintained that judgments concerning abnormality are necessarily relative to intracultural standards. What is judged to be abnormal in one cultural setting may be properly characterized as normal in other cultural settings. This relativistic approach continues to provoke somewhat heated controversy, not only within the anthropological fraternity, but within the social sciences in general.

In a series of seminal papers Professor Hallowell has offered us important conceptual vehicles by which we can avoid the Scylla of nihilistic relativism and the Charybdis of ethnocentric absolutism. His concept of a "culturally constituted behavioral environment" (Hallowell: 1955, Chapter 8) allows us to view behavior relative to its cultural setting and, at the same time, to assess its functional consequences in terms of pancultural scientific criteria. I should like to examine the relationships between religion, abnormality, and relativism in the light of these conceptual tools. Although only these concepts are explicitly taken from Hallowell, this entire paper is heavily indebted to his work. Indeed, it is difficult to say when his ideas end and mine begin.

The persistent controversy over cultural relativism has been confounded by implicit disagreements concerning its proper antithesis. Some scholars conceive of (what I shall term) "universalism" to be the antithesis of relativism, while others take (what may be termed) "absolutism" to be its antithesis. The logic of relativism is quite different, depending upon which of these two alternative conceptions is taken to be its antithesis; indeed consensus concerning one or the other antithesis would mitigate, if not resolve, the controversy. I should like to propose absolutism as the valid antonym for relativism, and universalism as the antonym not for relativism, but for what might be called "particularism."

Universalism vs. Particularism

The question entailed by this distinction is whether a particular belief or behavior pattern found in our society—and which a clinician would characterize as pathological—occurs in all societies, in some societies, or only in our own society. This is an empirical question, concerned exclusively with the *occurrence* and relative *incidence* of a certain type of behavior. Correspondingly, the answer to this question must also be empirical, rather than judgmental. Whatever the answer to this question may be, the research task—once the answer is provided—is to identify those causal or antecedent conditions which produce the behavior or which account for its differential occurrence. In the older arguments for relativism, in which sociocultural variables were adduced as foils for, or as antidotes to, biological variables (usually, but not always, associated with racism), relativistic theorists turned to sociocultural determinants in order to explain the differential occurrence of different types of behavior. Particularism, as I shall label this variety of relativism, interprets the differential occurrence of a certain type of behavior as relative to, because determined by, differential sociocultural conditions.

Anthropological data—and, one might add, historical and sociological data as well—are unambiguous so far as the universalistic-particularistic dichotomy is concerned. The occurrence and relative incidence of certain types of behavior which, when occurring in our society, are labeled as schizophrenic, hysterical, paranoid, etc., vary not only from society to society, but they vary as well within the same society at different periods in its history, and among different social groups (class, ethnic, religious, etc.) within the same historical period. This empirical finding is independent of any judgment by which these types of behavior may be evaluated.

Absolutism vs. Relativism

This, rather than the former, dichotomy raises the genuine relativistic question, viz., can certain types of behavior which are designated as pathological when they occur in our society be properly designated by the same label when they occur in other societies? The concern here is not with the question of the differential occurrence of beliefs and practices—this is taken for granted—but with their clinical assessment.

Absolutism holds that certain types of behavior are properly designated as pathological wherever and whenever they occur. Relativism holds that judgments concerning pathology are necessarily relative. There are different types of relativism, however, differing according to what these judgments are conceived to be relative to. One type, which we may label "social relativism," holds that judgments concerning pathology are relative to intrasocietal criteria, because there are no panhuman criteria by which cross-cultural judgments can be made. A second type, which may be termed "cultural relativism," holds that the criteria for judging pathology are panhuman, but that judgments based on these criteria are relative to the cultural context in which the action occurs. I should like to examine these two types of relativism, and their respective subtypes.

Social Relativism—Social relativism holds that judgments concerning pathology can only be based on intrasocietal—and, as we shall see, quantitative—criteria. One subtype, which might be termed "objective social relativism," insists that judgments concerning the pathology of some type of behavior must be relative to its incidence in the society (or some social group within a society) in which it occurs. Hence, behavior is properly judged to be pathological if (but only if) it is statistically rare; if, that is, it deviates from the statistical norms for that society. According to this subtype, "schizophrenic" behavior is pathological in our society because it characterizes a minority; if schizophrenics were to become a majority, schizophrenia would be normal. For this subtype, then, the abnormal represents social deviation.

"Subjective social relativism" holds that behavior may be judged to be pathological if it is deemed to be pathological by the members of the society in which it is found; it is not pathological if they deem it to be normal, or, at least, if it is positively rather than negatively evaluated by them. If, according to objective social relativism, judgments concerning pathology are relative to the incidence of some type of behavior within a society, according to subjective social relativism they are relative to its evaluation by the members of society. For the former, pathology represents deviation from statistical norms discovered by the anthropologist; for the latter it represents deviation from evaluative norms held by the society.

Although their criteria differ, both subtypes of relativism agree that there can be no panhuman criteria by which judgments concerning pathology can be established. Hence, behavior which is properly labeled "paranoid" when found in our society is "normal" if found among the Kwakiutl; hysteria is normal in the case of St. Theresa, but abnormal in a contemporary middle-class woman; the belief that most mankind is doomed to eternal hell-fire is normal for a Calvinist, but abnormal for a Buddhist, and so on.

In my opinion both subtypes of social relativism are untenable. In the first place, since man (even *homo religiosus*) is a biological organism, there are I would suggest panhuman *biological* criteria by which behavior may be judged. If the majority in a given society have cancer, are we to say that they, the majority, are biologically normal, while those who do not have cancer, the minority, are biologically abnormal? This crude analogy suggests the fallacy inherent in the first subtype of social relativism. Judgments concerning biological normality or abnormality (health and illness) are indeed relative; but they are relative to specified criteria for the functioning of healthy organisms, criteria which are—or, at least, biological science takes them to be—universally applicable. Only two of the criteria which are relevant for the problem of behavioral pathology need be mentioned here: adaptation and optimum functioning.

Any organic characteristic which, like cancer, produces death, and which, if generalized, precludes the survival of the group—i.e., any maladaptive characteristic—is biologically abnormal. Furthermore, any characteristic which reduces efficient functioning—efficient relative to the potentiality of either the organ or the organism—is biologically abnormal. Thus, impaired vision or hearing, let alone blindness or deafness, are abnormal because they reduce the optimum functioning of these organs and, ultimately, of the organism. In short, maladaptive and inefficient functioning are, for the physician and biologist, pan-human criteria by which the presence of biological abnormality may be assessed; this assessment is independent of the incidence of these characteristics in a society or of their evaluation by its members. If we are prepared to accept these criteria it would seem to follow that any condition which produces these effects—whether it be a characteristic of the organism or a characteristic of behavior—is pathological. Hence, if it is the case that a religious belief or a religious ritual is maladaptive and/or reduces optimum biological functioning, such a belief or ritual is, biologically viewed, abnormal.

But man is not only a biological, he is also a psychological and a social animal. For psychological, as for biological processes, the homeostatic principle, tension→tension-reduction, holds: tension stimulates action which is intended to reduce tension. Hence the persistence of tension is abnormal. Most psychological tension stems from conflict, either between one's moral values and/or one's self-image, or between those desires which violate the one or the other (or both). Since the tension induced by such conflict is painful, the typical actor—in accordance with the homeostatic principle enunciated above—attempts to resolve the conflict and, hence, to reduce tension. This is usually accomplished by a number of maneuvers, termed "mechanisms of defense," which defend the ego against the pain induced by the tension. Although these defense mechanisms may reduce the tension, thereby satisfying the homeostatic criterion of normality, they may have other pathological consequences. Any resolution of conflict, however successful in reducing tension, which results in the impairment of psychological, social, or cultural functioning may be taken to be a universal index of pathology.

"Impairment of psychological functioning" refers to distortions of three important modes of action. (1) Cognitive distortion: This refers to any cognitive behavior in which a demonstrably false belief is held to be true. (2) Perceptual distortion: This refers to any perceptual behavior in which stimuli are perceived to be other than what they are. (3) Affective distortion: This refers to any emotional behavior which, relative to the stimulus condition, is characterized by hyper- or hypoaffectivity. "Impairment of social functioning" refers to any condition of the actor which precludes the performance of social roles. "Impairment of cultural functioning" refers to any condition of the actor which precludes compliance with cultural norms and rules.

The three psychological criteria of pathology are panhuman because, if satisfied, the reality-testing function of the ego, the agent of man's adaptation (to nature) and adjustment (to society), is impaired, and the consequence of such impairment may be either individual or social disruption. The last two sociocultural criteria of pathology are panhuman because, in the absence of adequate social and cultural functioning, the survival of the individual—and, if generalized, the survival of the group—is jeopardized. No society could persist if the behavior of its members was characterized, for example, by genuine schizophrenia or genuine paranoia. Hence any religious belief or religious ritual which is characterized by, or which leads to, these three types of impairment is properly characterized as abnormal, regardless of its incidence and regardless of its evaluation by the members of society.

Cultural Relativism—Despite these animadversions on social relativism, its rejection does not entail the acceptance of absolutism. According to absolutism certain forms of behavior and certain kinds of beliefs are pathological wherever or whenever they may be found. Thus, for example, if a religious belief or ritual in a non-Western society is phenotypically similar to a belief or behavior pattern characteristic of a Western psychotic, the former, according to absolutism, is also abnormal. This position is as untenable as social relativism. Although the criteria by which behavior is judged may be universally applicable, it does not follow that all instances of phenotypically identical behavior or belief, when evaluated by these criteria, will lead to the same judgment. Although the criteria are panhuman, the judgments based on these criteria are necessarily relative to the sociocultural context within which behavior occurs. Distortion, for example, implies the existence of some reality relative to which a cognition is false, a perception is skewed, an affect is misplaced. But this reality, as Professor Hallowell has so cogently shown, is not a universal "given." Different cultures structure reality in different ways. For any actor reality is mediated through the world view and behavioral environment constructed by his culture. Hence, judgment concerning the existence of distortion must be based on the culturally constituted world view and the behavioral environment of the actor whose behavior is being assessed. For a Western man to believe that he is the reincarnation of some ancestor is to commit severe cognitive distortion; a Buddhist who holds the same belief commits no distortion. In short, the same criterion, applied to two identical acts, yields different judgments because the judgment—but not the criterion—is relative to the sociocultural context within which action occurs.

Social and cultural inadequacy must be assessed in the same manner. Whether a particular condition does or does not permit normal social and cultural functioning is necessarily relative to the repertory of social roles and the set of cultural norms which are found in the actor's, not the observer's, society.

If the preceding discussion is sound, it may then be concluded that beliefs and rituals which characterize the behavior of religious actors in non-Western societies, although phenotypically identical with beliefs and behavior which may characterize abnormal individuals in our society, are not necessarily (or even usually) abnormal when sanctioned or prescribed by the religious systems of the former societies and taught to the actors as part of their cultural heritage. There are a number of reasons for this conclusion. (a) The religious actor acquires his beliefs and rituals, as he acquires other aspects of his cultural heritage, through the usual techniques of instruction and imitation. Hence these beliefs and rituals are expressions, rather than distortions, of (his culturally constituted) reality. They are consistent with, rather than obstacles to, social and cultural functioning. Psychotic beliefs and behavior, on the contrary, are devised by the actor himself, as an attempt to reduce the painful tension induced by inner conflict. This attempt is necessarily based on his private distortion of (culturally constituted) reality, resulting in serious impairment of his social and/or cultural functioning. (b) Since religious beliefs and practices are derived from tradition, they are frequently compulsory; but since they are not created by the actor himself to defend against forbidden or shameful impulses, they are not compulsive. Psychotic beliefs and practices, on the contrary, are not compulsory—indeed they are usually prohibited—but as attempts to reduce tension, they are compulsive. (c) Although not devised by the actor to resolve conflict, religious beliefs and ritual may be used for that end. When so used they may not only resolve conflict, but as "culturally constituted defenses" (Spiro: 1961, pp. 472–479) they are consistent with, rather than distortions of, reality; they comprise culturally sanctioned, rather than culturally prohibited, behavior; they protect the individual and his society from the disruptive consequences both of his shameful and/or forbidden needs and of his private defensive maneuvers. Conflict may also be resolved by psychotic beliefs and practices; but these idiosyncratic resolutions produce those psychological distortions and sociocultural impairments which, as I have argued, are properly characterized as abnormal. I should like to examine these propositions in the context of one empirical situation—Burmese Buddhist monasticism.

Burmese Monasticism [1]

In Burma, one of the centers of Theravada Buddhism, the monastic vocation is the most venerated of all patterns of life. Almost every village contains at least one monastery with at least one resident monk.

The monk, in theory at least, lives an exclusively otherworldly existence. His monastery is outside the village gates, and his interaction with the layman is confined to occasional ritual situations. The monk is prohibited from engaging in any form of physical labor, including any economic activity. All of his wants are attended to by the laymen, who provide his daily meals, his robes, and other necessities. Except for teaching young children, the monk's official responsibilities to the laymen are restricted to chanting of "prayers" at funerals and to public recitation of the Buddhist precepts on the "Sabbath" and other sacred days. His primary responsibility is to himself and to his attempt to attain nirvana. The latter goal is achieved through the study of Scripture and through various techniques of Buddhist meditation. These activities are believed to be instrumental to the attainment of Release from the round of rebirths because they lead to ultimate comprehension of the true characteristics of existence, viz., impermanence, suffering, and the absence of an ego. This comprehension, in turn is believed to lead to the severance of all desire for, and cathexis of, the world. With the destruction of desire or "clinging" *(tanha)*, the basis for rebirth is destroyed. Nirvana, whatever else it may be, is the cessation of rebirth.

The true monk, then, is completely absorbed in his own "salvation." Although living in a state of absolute dependence on the laymen, he has withdrawn both physically and psychologically from the physical and social world, and even—in states of trance *(dhyānas)*—from his own self. This extreme withdrawal from reality is similar to that withdrawal behavior which, in our society, would be taken as symptomatic of severe pathology, most certainly schizoid, if not schizophrenic. Is the Burmese monk to be similarly characterized? Such a judgment, in my opinion, would be grossly in error. Phenotypically, the behavior of the monk and that of the schizoid or schizophrenic patient may be very similar. Genotypically and functionally, however, they are importantly dissimilar. All of the criteria suggested in the previous section for assessing pathology are applicable to the schizophrenic; none is applicable to the monk.

In the case of the schizophrenic the actor resolves his inner conflict by constructing private fantasy and action systems; in the case of the monk, however, the actor uses culturally constituted fantasy and action systems (Buddhism) to resolve his inner conflicts. This difference not only provides the primary basis for a differential diagnosis of monk and schizophrenic, but it also provides, parenthetically, an important insight into the nature of religion. Culturally constituted religious behavior not only is not a symptom of pathology but, on the contrary, it serves to preclude the outbreak of pathology. The schizophrenic and the Burmese monk, alike, are characterized initially by pathogenic conflict, and schizophrenia and monasticism may each be interpreted as a means for resolving conflict. But this is where the similarity ends. Although schizophrenia and monasticism are both symptomatic of pathogenic conflict, the former represents a pathological, where as the latter represents a nonpathological, resolution of the conflict. Let us examine these claims.

An analysis of monastic personality, based on the Rorschach records of a sample of Burmese Buddhist monks, and without reference to their (monastic) behavioral environment, would surely lead to a diagnosis of severe pathology. Dr. James Steele (1963), who has analyzed these records, finds the following "pathological" features, among others: (1) a very high degree of "defensiveness"; (2) "pathologically regressed" expression of aggressive and oral drives; (3) cautious avoidance of "emotionally laden" situations as a means of obviating the necessity of handling affect, for which there are no adequate resources; (4) a "hypochondriacal self-preoccupation" and "erotic self-cathexis," instead of a cathexis of others; (5) latent homosexuality; (6) above-average fear of female- or mother-figures.

One of the significant characteristics of the Rorschach protocols of these monks, according to Steele, is their similarity to the records of Burmese laymen. It is not that the monastic records do not differ from those of the laymen; but the difference is one of degree, not of kind. Monks differ from laymen, not because they have different problems, but because they have more of the same problems. The monk, in other words, is a Burman *in extremis*. Burmese laymen (like Burmese monks) are constricted, ruminative, defensive, anxious about females, distrustful of others, and, perhaps, latently homosexual. The monks differ from the laymen only in that, for all these characteristics, they are *more so*. Monks are *more* constricted, *more* ruminative, *more* . . . , etc. For other characteristics, however, monks are *less so*. Compared to laymen, monks are ". . . less phallic, less self-confident, less striving, and less impulsive." In summary, Burmese monks not only appear to have "more of the basic problems" which characterize Burmans in general, but they also seem to be characterized by a "more constricted adjustment." It is the latter feature, still quoting Steele, which makes them "less accessible to social interaction with the protection that this provides."

This picture of the Burmese monks is surely a picture of pathology. Are we to conclude then—holding in abeyance a specific psychiatric diagnosis, and assuming that the Rorschach test is a reliable instrument—that these monks are abnormal? If personality existed in a social and cultural vacuum, the answer would be an unqualified "yes." Acute psychological conflicts and attendant intrapersonal tensions are marked. That these conflicts have produced defensive distortions of various kinds—perceptual, cognitive, affective—is clearly indicated. That social impairment is a most likely consequence of these conflicts, tensions, and distortions can hardly be doubted. In brief, if personality existed *in vacuo* one would probably conclude that Burmese monks resolve their conflicts in a manner which issues in severe pathology (perhaps paranoid schizophrenia).

But the proviso, "if personality existed *in vacuo*," is crucial. Although Steele's analysis of their Rorschach records is remarkably similar to my clinical impressions of these monks, impressions derived from intensive participant-observation in a score of monasteries, and from personal interviews with more than twenty-five monks—thus providing a dramatic test of the reliability of the instrument and of Steele's skill in its use—I did not ever feel that these monks, with but one exception, were pathological or, specifically, schizophrenic. Nor is this a paradox. The psychological analysis (based on Rorschachs and clinical impressions) provides a set of statements concerning the emotional problems of the subjects; it also provides, to a somewhat lesser extent, a picture of their idiosyncratic defenses, i.e., of those defenses which the subjects have constructed for themselves, in an attempt to resolve their problems. That these defenses are hardly adequate to the task is obvious from the Rorschach analysis. Left exclusively to their own inner resources many of these subjects would have become, I believe, genuine psychotics.

But personality does not exist *in vacuo,* and Burmese males, characterized by the problems described, are not confronted with the necessity of solving these problems by means of their own resources. In addition to their private resources, they are able to utilize a powerful cultural resource for their solution, i.e., they can solve their problems by recruitment to the monastic order. By utilizing the role-set prescribed for this institution as a culturally constituted defense, Burmese monks can resolve their conflicts with a minimum of distortion. Since, moreover, the performance of the roles comprising this role-set satisfies their prohibited and/or shameful needs and reduces their painful fears and anxieties, these potentially disruptive psychological variables, rather than provoking socially disruptive behavior, provide the motivational basis for the persistence of the most highly valued institution—monasticism—in Burmese society. As a culturally constituted defense, the monastic institution resolves the inner conflicts of Burmese males, by allowing them to gratify their drives and reduce their anxieties in a disguised—and therefore socially acceptable—manner, one which precludes psychotic distortion, on the one hand, and criminal "acting-out," on the other. Hence, the monk is protected from mental illness and/or social punishment; society is protected from the disruptive consequences of antisocial behavior; and the key institution of Burmese culture—Buddhist monasticism— is provided with a most powerful motivational basis. Space permits only a brief examination of these assertions.

The monastic rules which interdict *all* labor, and those Buddhist norms which guarantee that the laity provide monks with *all* their wants, combine to satisfy the monk's "regressed oral drives." The monastic life, moreover, makes no demands, either social or psychological, which might render the monk's weak "phallic-orientation," his low degree of "striving and impulsivity," and his lack of "self-confidence" nonviable modes of adjustment. Quite the contrary, the physical isolation of the monastery, and the monastic norms proscribing social participation, preclude the stimulation of "disruptive affect." At the same time the monk's, "self-preoccupation" and "erotic self-cathexis" is wonderfully expressed and institutionalized in the prescribed techniques of Buddhist meditation. Latent "homosexual" needs can be satisfied in the exclusively male setting in which the monks live. Finally, the strong interdiction on interaction with females provides little opportunity for encounters with them and for the consequent fear attendant upon such encounters. Buddhist monasticism, then, is a highly efficient means for coping with the psychological problems of many Burmese men. The differences between a monastic and a psychotic resolution of these problems are instructive.

1. In general the genesis of the psychotic's conflict is idiosyncratic, while the genesis of the monk's problem is rooted in modal features

of his society. That is, the source of the monk's conflict—which we cannot discuss here—is to be found in culturally constituted experiences which the monk shares with many other members of his social group. The monk differs from other Burmans in one of three ways: his potentially pathogenic experiences are more intense than those of other males; other Burmans utilize alternative, non-Buddhist, institutions for the resolution of equally intense problems; still others (a minority) develop idiosyncratic methods of conflict-resolution (in extreme cases, these take the form of mental illness or criminal behavior).

2. The psychotic resolves his problems by means of idiosyncratic, private, defenses; the monk resolves his problems in an institutionalized manner, by utilizing elements of his religious heritage as a culturally constituted defense. The difference between these two types of defense accounts for the following differences between the psychotic patient, on the one hand, and the normal monk, on the other.

3. The behavior of the psychotic is incompatible with any normal social role within his society, and inconsistent with important cultural norms of the larger society. The psychotic is *psychologically incapable* of performing social roles or of complying with those cultural norms which he violates. The behavior of the monk, on the other hand, is entirely appropriate to—indeed, it is the enactment of—a most important and honorific social role. The monk may be psychologically incapable of performing nonmonastic roles, but he is ideally suited for performing the monastic role.

4. As a corollary of the above, the behavior of the psychotic is bizarre in the eyes of, and disapproved by, his fellows. The behavior of the monk is not only approved by the other members of his society, but it is most highly valued.

5. Following from the last point, the behavior of the psychotic alienates him psychologically from his fellows. The behavior of the monk, on the contrary, though isolating him physically from his group, serves to integrate him psychologically into the group; for in his behavior he expresses the most cherished values of Burmese culture.

6. The world view constructed by the psychotic represents a dramatic distortion of reality, as the latter is structured by the world view of his culture; and the cognitions and perceptions that are derived from his idiosyncratic world view are highly distorted,

relative to the behavioral environment in which expected social interaction of his society takes place. The world view of the monk, on the other hand, rather than being constructed from his private fantasies, is taught to him as an integral part of the cultural heritage of his society. The private world view of the monk corresponds to the public world view of his society; his world view, in brief, is a culturally constituted world view. The Buddhist world view, of course, may be false, a distortion of reality, relative to the world view of modern science; but it is true, relative to the knowledge available to Burmese society. True or false, however, the monk's cognitions and perceptions are consistent with, rather than distortions of, reality, as the latter is structured by the world view and behavioral environment of his society. The perceptions and cognitions, the fantasies and emotions experienced by the monk in the course of Buddhist meditation and concentration may never be experienced by other Burmans—because the latter do not meditate or concentrate—but they are experiences consistent with the conception of reality which all Burmans hold, and they are vouchsafed to any Burman who is prepared to enter into these spiritual disciplines.

7. The psychotic sustains social relationships neither with the normal members of his society, nor with other psychotics. Psychotics, in short, do not participate in the society of which they are members, nor do they comprise a social group, distinct from the larger society, but nevertheless viable for its constituent members. Burmese monks, on the other hand, although socially isolated from Burmese society, are yet psychologically part of it. Moreover, although the monk may find difficulty in participating in the larger society, and in forming social relationships within it, he does enter into social relationships with other members of the monastic order. Monks are members of increasingly larger concentric groups, beginning with other members of the local monastery and extending to the entire order of monks. In short, while psychotics comprise a typological class, the monks constitute a social group. The psychotic cannot live as a member of a social group, even if it be but a subgroup of the larger society.

8. Finally, and as a corollary of the last point, the behavior of the psychotic is anomic; it violates many of the rules of his society. The monk, on the other hand, not only exemplifies the rules of Burmese society, but he must, in addition, comply with the 227 rules

of the monastic order (as outlined in the *Vinaya*). Should he violate these rules, he is expelled from the order as a charlatan, regardless of whatever wondrous visions he is alleged to have had, or miraculous powers he is supposed to possess.

In summary, then, a psychiatrically diagnosed psychotic is not only incapable of participating in his own society, he is incapable of participating in any society. An American psychotic would function no better in a Buddhist monastery than in an American city. A Buddhist monk, to be sure, while not capable of functioning in every cultural environment, functions very well indeed within *his* cultural environment. This is hardly surprising, since the latter environment is so structured that it satisfies his needs and resolves his conflicts. That he cannot function in a radically different environment does not render him "sick," nor his adjustment precarious. Typically, differential sets of human needs are differentially satisfied in different types of cultural milieux. It is doubtful if the typical Burmese peasant could adjust to an American urban environment, or a typical American to a Buddhist monastery. For neither is the new environment capable of satisfying the needs and resolving the conflicts which were produced by the old.

Summary and Conclusions

Burmese monks, as Rorschach data and clinical observations agree, are characterized by serious emotional conflicts. Their religious heritage, however, provides them with institutionalized means for resolving conflicts, and, moreover, for resolving them in a manner which satisfies none of the five criteria suggested in the first section of this chapter as panhuman indices of abnormality (psychological distortions and sociocultural impairments). Employing the monastic system as a culturally constituted defense obviates the necessity for Burmese males to erect private defenses which, necessarily, would lead to one or more of these distortions and impairments. Monasticism, in short, has important psychological functions for individual actors. By the same token, however, the psychological problems of these actors have the important cultural function of helping to perpetuate the monastic system; that is, these conflicts are not only resolved by means of the monastic system, but they provide the motivational basis for recruitment to the monastery and, hence, for the persistence of the system.

The existence of the monastic system, moreover, not only permits the resolution of emotional conflict (the latent psychological function of the monastery), but by serving this function it reduces the probability of the occurrence of other, nonsanctioned means by which these conflicts might be expressed and resolved (latent social function of the monastery). If this culturally constituted defense were not available for the resolution of conflict, the consequent persistence of tension might lead to defenses of a psychotic nature, psychosomatic disorders of various kinds, or many types of antisocial, i.e., criminal behavior. I would suggest that a study of Burmese crime, including dacoity and insurgency—both of which are, and have been, endemic in Burma—would reveal that a large percentage of dacoits and insurgents are recruited from the ranks of those for whom the monastic life is not (for reasons still to be determined) a psychologically viable means for resolving emotional conflict.[2]

The monastic system, in short, not only serves the important personal function of precluding psychotic breakdown, but it also serves the important social function of allowing potentially disruptive, antisocial drives to be channeled into culturally approved (institutional) behavior. Since the monastery, moreover—for reasons beyond the scope of this paper—is the most integrative institution in Burmese society, the social function of psychological conflict, when resolved in this fashion, cannot be overestimated.

If the foregoing analysis is correct, then—to return to the more general problem of this paper—abnormal behavior can be expected to appear under one of three conditions: (1) when emotional conflict is idiosyncratic, so that cultural means are not available as potential bases for culturally constituted defense mechanisms; (2) when emotional conflict is modal, and cultural means are available for conflict resolution, but these means have been inadequately taught or inadequately learned; (3) when, under conditions of rapid social change, culturally constituted defense mechanisms are unavailable, either because older institutions have been discarded or because the new situation creates a new set of conflicts. These three conditions, however, are necessary, but not sufficient, conditions for abnormal behavior. Although emotional conflict is potentially pathogenic, it need not produce pathology. Emotional conflict issues in pathology only if it is not resolved, or if it is resolved in a manner which is characterized by psychological distortion and/or sociocultural impairment. The latter resolutions are characteristic of neurotic and psychotic resolutions.

But neurosis and psychosis are not the only means for resolving conflict. Other private defense mechanisms may be constructed which are perceptually, cognitively, and affectively consistent with the behavioral environment of the actors, and which, moreover, constitute no obstacle to adequate sociocultural functioning. Finally, there is a third category of defense mechanisms—culturally constituted defenses—which are not only not disruptive of, but rather serve to perpetuate, the sociocultural system. Conflict, in short, may indeed produce pathological defenses; but it may also produce normal defenses, either private or culturally constituted.

In most traditional societies, where religious beliefs and practices continue to carry conviction, religion is the cultural system *par excellence* by means of which conflict-resolution is achieved. In such societies, in which religious behavior is appropriate to, rather than disruptive of, the behavioral environment of the actors, and in which a religious world view is consistent with, rather than a distortion of, "reality," religion serves as a highly efficient culturally constituted defense mechanism.

REFERENCES

Benedict, R. (1934) *Patterns of Culture* (Boston: Houghton Mifflin).

Hallowell, A. I. (1955) *Culture and Experience* (Philadelphia: University of Pennsylvania Press).

Spiro, M. E. (1961) "An Overview and a Suggested Reorientation, in F. L. K. Hsu (ed.), *Psychological Anthropology* (Homewood, Illinois: Dorsey Press).

Steele, J. (1963) *A Preliminary Analysis of the Burmese Rorschachs.* Unpublished ms.

NOTES

[1] Materials in this section are based on field work carried out during 1961–62; I am grateful to the National Science Foundation for a research fellowship which made the research possible.

[2] This generalization excludes those—and I have met them—for whom insurgency and dacoity are romantic, adventurous activities to be given up when the adventure palls. It also excludes those whose emotional conflicts are idiosyncratic, rather than culturally patterned, and for which there are no cultural institutions by which conflict can be resolved.

Harold C. Conklin

Hanunóo Color Categories

Both Freudian psychology and behaviorism have tended to stress only those aspects or qualities of man that have their source in his animal past. Little attention has been paid to human cognition, and in psychology, study of the rational or symbolic abilities of the cerebral cortex has emerged only recently in ego-psychology, existential analysis, and self-realization hypotheses. In the social sciences, cognition studies have depended, to a great degree, upon the influence of linguists who have to some degree counteracted the effect of traditional psychology. Since man's development is characterized by the excessive development of his thought-centers, the disinterest in cognition studies evidenced by most psychologically oriented social scientists seems to reflect a singular lack of awareness of basic physiological facts. The zealous attempts of social science to ignore human purposiveness, rationality, values, and goals is welded to a world view that conceived behavior either as determined by irrational and instinctual levels of human behavior, or by superorganic structures. Harold Conklin's "Hanunóo Color Categories" suggests that our ability to conceptualize may reflect our linguistic definitions rather than external sensations. It represents yet another attempt to provide a model within which abstract knowledge and concrete realities may be holistically conceived— not in terms of Platonic categories, but in terms of holistic processes.

I<small>N THE FOLLOWING BRIEF</small> analysis of a specific Philippine color system I shall attempt to show how various ethnographic field techniques may be combined profitably in the study of lexical sets relating to perceptual categorization.[1]

Recently, I completed more than a year's field research on Hanunóo folkbotany.[2] In this type of work one soon becomes acutely aware of problems connected with understanding the local system of color categorization because plant determinations so often depend on chromatic differences in the appearance of flowers or vegetative structures—both in taxonomic botany and in popular systems of classification. It is no accident that one of the most detailed accounts of native color terminology in the Malayo-Polynesian area was written by a botanist.[3] I was, therefore, greatly concerned with Hanunóo color categories during the entire period of my ethnobotanical research. Before summarizing the specific results of my analysis of the Hanunóo material, however, I should like to draw attention to several general considerations.

1.   Color, in a western technical sense, is not a universal concept and in many languages such as Hanunóo there is no unitary terminological equivalent. In our technical literature definitions state that color is the evaluation of the visual sense of that quality of light (reflected or transmitted by some substance) which is basically determined by its spectral composition. The spectrum is the range of visible color in light measured in wave lengths (400 [deep red] to 700 [blue-violet] millimicrons).[4] The total color sphere—holding any set of external and surface conditions constant—includes two other dimensions, in addition to that of spectral position or hue. One is saturation or intensity (chroma), the other brightness or brilliance (value). These three perceptual dimensions are usually combined into a coordinate system as a cylindrical continuum known as the color solid. Saturation diminishes toward the central axis which forms the achromatic core of neutral grays from the white at the end of greatest brightness to black at the opposite extremity. Hue varies with circumferential position. Although technically speaking *black* is the absence of any "color," *white*, the presence of all visible color wave

lengths, and neutral *grays* lack spectral distinction, these achromatic positions within the color solid are often included with spectrally-defined positions in the categories distinguished in popular color systems.

2. Under laboratory conditions, color *discrimination* is probably the same for all human populations, irrespective of language; but the manner in which different languages classify the millions[5] of "colors" which every normal individual can discriminate *differ*. Many stimuli are classified as equivalent, as extensive, cognitive—or perceptual—screening takes place.[6] Requirements of specification may differ considerably from one culturally-defined situation to another. The largest collection[7] of English color names runs to over 3,000 entries, yet only eight of these occur very commonly.[8] Recent testing by Lenneberg and others[9] demonstrates a high correlation in English and in Zuñi between ready color vocabulary and *ease in recognition of colors*. Although this is only a beginning it does show how the structure of a lexical set may affect color perception. It may also be possible to determine certain nonlinguistic correlates for color terminology. Color terms are a part of the vocabulary of particular languages and only the intracultural analysis of such lexical sets and their correlates can provide the key to their understanding and range of applicability. The study of isolated and assumed translations in other languages can lead only to confusion.[10]

In the field I began to investigate Hanunóo color classification in a number of ways, including the eliciting of linguistic responses from a large number of informants to painted cards, dyed fabrics, other previously prepared materials,[11] and the recording of visual-quality attributes taken from descriptions of specific items of the natural and artificial surroundings. This resulted in the collection of a profusion of attributive words of the nonformal—and therefore in a sense "color"—type. There were at first many inconsistencies and a high degree of overlap for which the controls used did not seem to account. However, as the work with plant specimens and minute floristic differentiation progressed, I noted that in *contrastive* situations this initial confusion and incongruity of informants' responses did not usually occur. In such situations, where the "nonformal (i.e. not spatially organized) visible quality"[12] of one substance (plant part, dyed thread, or color card) was to be related to and contrasted with that of another, both of which were either at hand or well known, terminological agreement was reached with relative ease. Such a defined situation seemed to provide the frame necessary for establishing a known level of specification. Where needed, a greater degree of specification (often employing different root morphemes) could be and was made. Otherwise, such finer distinctions were ignored. This hint of terminologically significant levels led to a reexamination of all color data and the following analysis emerged.

Color distinctions in Hanunóo are made at two levels of contrast. The first, higher, more general level consists of an all-inclusive, coordinate, four-way classification which lies at the core of the color system. The four categories are mutually exclusive in contrastive contexts, but may overlap slightly in absolute (i.e., spectrally, or in other measurable) terms. The second level, including several sublevels, consists of hundreds of specific color categories, many of which overlap and interdigitate. Terminologically, there is "unanimous agreement" [13] on the designations for the four Level I categories, but considerable lack of unanimity—with a few explainable exceptions—in the use of terms at Level II.

The four Level I terms are:

1. *(ma)bīru* [14] "relative darkness (of shade of color); blackness (black)
2. *(ma)lagtiˀ* "relative lightness (or tint of color); whiteness" (white)
3. *(ma)raraˀ* "relative presence of red; redness" (red)
4. *(ma)latuy* "relative presence of the light greenness; greenness" (green).

The three-dimensional color solid is divided by this Level I categorization into four unequal parts; the largest is *mabīru,* the smallest *malatuy.* While boundaries separating these categories cannot be set in absolute terms, the focal points (differing slightly in size, themselves) within the four sections, can be limited more or less to black, white, orange-red, and leaf-green respectively. In general terms, *mabīru* includes the range usually covered in English by black, violet, indigo, blue, dark green, dark gray, and deep shades of other colors and mixtures; *malagtiˀ* white and very light tints of other colors and mixtures, *mararaˀ*, maroon, red, orange, yellow, and mixtures in which these qualities are seen to predominate; *malatuy,* light green, and mixtures of green, yellow, and light brown. All color terms can be reduced to one of these four but none of the four is reducible. This does not mean that other color terms are synonyms, but that they designate color categories of greater specification within four recognized color realms.

The basis of this Level I classification appears to have certain correlates beyond what is usually considered the range of chromatic differentiation, and which are associated with nonlinguistic phenomena in the external environment. First, there is the opposition between light and dark, obvious in the contrasted ranges of meaning of *lagti*ʔ and *bīru*. Second, there is an opposition between dryness or desiccation and wetness or freshness (succulence) in visible components of the natural environment which are reflected in the terms *rara*ʔ and *latuy* respectively. This distinction is of particular significance in terms of plant life. Almost all living plant types possess some fresh, succulent, and often "greenish" parts. To eat any kind of raw, uncooked food, particularly fresh fruits or vegetables, is known as *pag-laty-un* (<*latuy*). A shiny, wet, *brown*-colored section of newly-cut bamboo is *malatuy* (not *marara*ʔ). Dried-out or matured plant material such as certain kinds of yellowed bamboo or hardened kernels of mature or parched corn are *marara*ʔ. To become desiccated, to lose all moisture, is known as *mamara*ʔ (<*para*ʔ "desiccation"; and parenthetically, I might add that there are morphological and historical reasons—aside from Hanunóo folk etymologizing—to believe that at least the final syllables of these two forms are derived from a common root). A third opposition, dividing the two already suggested, is that of deep, unfading, indelible, and hence often more desired material as against pale, weak, faded, bleached, or "colorless" substance, a distinction contrasting *mabīru* and *marara*ʔ with *malagti*ʔ and *malatuy*. This opposition holds for manufactured items and trade goods as well as for some natural products (e.g., red and white trade beads, red being more valuable by Hanunóo standards; indigo-dyed cotton sarongs, the most prized being those dyed most often and hence of the deepest indigo color—sometimes obscuring completely the designs formed originally by *white* warp yarns; etc.). Within each of these Level I categories, increased esthetic value attaches as the focal points mentioned above are approached. There is only one exception: the color which is most tangibly visible in their jungle surroundings, the green (even the focal point near light- or yellow-green) of the natural vegetation, is *not* valued decoratively. Green beads, for example, are "unattractive," worthless. Clothing and ornament are valued in proportion to the sharpness of contrast between, and the intensity (lack of mixture, deep quality) of "black," "red," and "white."

Level II terminology is normally employed only when greater specification than is possible at Level I is required, or when the name of an object referred to happens also to be a "color" term (e.g., *bulāwan* "gold; golden [color]"). Level II terms are of two kinds: relatively specific color words like *(ma)dapug* "gray" (<*dapug* "hearth; ashes"), *(ma)ᵖarum* "violet," *(ma)dilaw* "yellow" (<*dilaw* "tumeric"); and constructions, based on such specific terms—or on Level I names—but involving further derivations, such as *mabirubiru* "somewhat *mabīru*" (more specific than *mabīru* alone only in that a color which is *not* a solid, deep, black is implied, i.e., a color classed within the *mabīru* category at Level I, but not at or near the focal point), *mabīru (gid)* "very *mabīru*" (here something close to the focal center of jet black is designated), and *madīlawdīlaw* "weak yellow." Much attention is paid to the texture of the surface referred to, the resulting degree and type of reflection (iridescent, sparkling, dull), and to admixture of other nonformal qualities. Frequently these non-colorimetric aspects are considered of primary importance, the more spectrally-definable qualities serving only as secondary attributes. In either case polymorphemic descriptions are common.

At Level II there is a noticeable difference in the ready color vocabulary of men as compared to women. The former excel (in the degree of specification to which they carry such classification terminologically) in the ranges of "reds" and "grays" (animals, hair, feather, etc.); the latter, in "blues" (shades of indigo-dyed fabrics). No discernible similar difference holds for the "greens" or "whites."

In short, we have seen that the apparent complexity of the Hanunóo color system can be reduced at the most generalized level to four basic terms which are associated with lightness, darkness, wetness, and dryness. This intracultural analysis demonstrates that what appears to be color "confusion" at first may result from an inadequate knowledge of the internal structure of a color system and from a failure to distinguish sharply between sensory reception on the one hand and perceptual categorization on the other.

BIBLIOGRAPHY

BARTLETT, HARLEY HARRIS (1929) *Color Nomenclature in Batak and Malay* (Papers, Michigan Academy of Science, Arts and Letters, vol. 10, pp. 1–52, Ann Arbor).

BROWN, ROGER W., AND ERIC H. LENNEBERG (1954) *A Study in Language and Cognition* (Journal of Abnormal and Social Psychology, vol. 49, pp. 454–462).

CONKLIN, HAROLD C. (1954a) *The Relation of Hanunóo Culture to the Plant World* (Doctoral dissertation, Yale University, New Haven).

——— (1954b) *An Ethnoecological Approach to Shifting Agriculture* (Transactions, New York Academy of Sciences, ser. II, vol. 17, pp. 133–142, New York).

EVANS, RALPH M. (1948) *An Introduction to Color* (New York: Wiley).

HJELMSLEV, LOUIS (1953) *Prolegomena to a Theory of Language* (Indiana University Publications in Anthropology and Linguistics. Memoir 7 of the International Journal of American Linguistics [translated by Francis J. Whitfield], Bloomington).

LENNEBERG, ERIC H. (1953) *Cognition in Ethnolinguistics* (Language, vol. 29, pp. 463–471, Baltimore).

LENNEBERG, ERIC H., AND JOHN M. ROBERTS (1954) *The Language of Experience, a Case Study* (Communications Program, Center of International Studies, Massachusetts Institute of Technology, Cambridge: hectographed, 45 pp. and 9 figs.).

LOUNSBURY, FLOYD G. (1953) "Introduction" [section on Linguistics and Psychology] (in *Results of the Conference of Anthropologists and Linguists*, pp. 47–49, Memoir 8, International Journal of American Linguistics, Baltimore).

MAERZ, A., AND M. R. PAUL (1930) *A Dictionary of Color* (New York: McGraw-Hill).

OPTICAL SOCIETY OF AMERICA, COMMITTEE ON COLORIMETRY (1953) *The Science of Color* (New York: Crowell).

OSGOOD, CHARLES E. (1953) *Method and Theory in Experimental Psychology* (New York: Oxford University Press).

RAY, VERNE F. (1952) *Techniques and Problems in the Study of Human Color Perception* (Southwestern Journal of Anthropology, vol. 8, pp. 251–259).

——— (1953) *Human Color Perception and Behavioral Response* (Transactions, New York Academy of Sciences, ser. II, vol. 16, pp. 98–104, New York).

THORNDIKE, E. L. AND I. LORGE (1944) *The Teacher's Word Book of 30,000 Words* (Teacher's College, Columbia University, New York).

NOTES

[1] Field work among the Hanunóo on Mindoro Island (1952–1954) was supported by grants from the Social Science Research Council, the Ford Foundation, and the Guggenheim Foundation.

[2] Conklin, 1954a, 1954b.

[3] Bartlett, 1929.

[4] Osgood, 1953, p. 137.

[5] Estimates range from 7,500,000 to more than 10,000,000. (Optical Society of America, 1953; Evans, 1948, p. 230).

[6] Lounsbury, 1953.

[7] Maerz and Paul, 1930.

[8] Thorndike and Lorge, 1944.

[9] Lenneberg, 1953, pp. 468–471; Lenneberg and Roberts, 1954; Brown and Lenneberg, 1954.

[10] Lenneberg, 1953, pp. 464–466; Hjelmslev, 1953, p. 33.

[11] Cf. Ray, 1952, 1953.

[12] The lack of a term similar in semantic range to our word "color" makes abstract interrogation in Hanunóo about such matters somewhat complicated. Except for leading questions (naming some visual-quality attribute as a possibility), only circumlocutions such as *kabitay tīda nu pagbantāyun?* "How is it to look at?" are possible. If this results in description of spatial organization or form, the inquiry may be narrowed by the specification *bukun kay ?anyu?* "not its shape (or form)."

[13] Lenneberg, 1953, p. 469.

[14] These forms occur as attributes with the prefix *ma-* "exhibiting, having" as indicated above in parentheses, or as free words (abstracts).

William A. Gamson

Community Issues and Their Outcome:
How to Lose a Fluoridation Referendum

One of the arguments usually launched against social science is its inability to conduct controlled experiments—that is, to hold all variables constant except the one that is being tested. To be sure, this limitation of scientific method is most pronounced in the social sciences where the variables are numerous and questions of morality usually interfere with attempts to create experimental situations. Social science has attempted to conduct controlled experiments in small group situations, but by and large, the method most characteristically used is that of comparison based upon empirical study of situations as they have come up. Such an empirical situation is the one presented by William Gamson in the following paper. By studying this particular situation—in this case, the failure of a fluoridation referendum to gain popular approval—he attempts to expose the dynamics of social inter-action that lie beneath the rejection of a reform that, in rational terms, seemed inevitable. Numerous studies of this kind provide the comparative data which can be used to discover general laws.

A NUMBER OF SOCIOLOGISTS HAVE suggested that students of community decision-making compare several communities on similar issues. This paper represents an informal assessment at the midpoint of such a study in 18 New England communities. Two issues from among such stalwarts as school bond proposals, zoning, parking, and sewerage are studied in each town, with a fluoridation controversy common to all. Fluoridation lends itself to this purpose because of its frequent occurrence and essentially "internal" character, i.e., most of the important determinants come from within the community.

In studying a community, we make use of documents and interviews. The documents include informal accounts in community newspapers, formal statistical data from the state and federal census, city planning reports, annual town reports, and various state manuals. The interviews are with active participants on both sides of each issue and with people named by these "issue leaders" as influential in the community. We call this latter group "reputational leaders" to avoid prejudging their actual influence on specific issues.

Systematic analysis of these interviews and other data has hardly begun, but several impressions have emerged. I am wary about stating these impressions, for they may not be our conclusions when the analysis is complete. However, with this caveat, I shall undertake the risk.

What I wish to say centers around fluoridation but applies, I believe, to other community issues as well. A major focus of this study is the set of conditions which determine whether political and other community leaders will become involved in an issue or will remain neutral. Originally, we reasoned that most community issues involved competing economic interests. Certain traditional alignments will arise around these issues and political leaders will draw their major support from among these segments. But if an issue upsets these alignments and offers no stable basis for new ones, we thought that political leaders would be under pressure to avoid involvement in the controversy. We reasoned that fluoridation was just such an issue, and that the failure of politically skilled individuals to exercise their influence on it paved the way for its defeat.

If this explanation is adequate then, as a minimum, we should find in studying the course of the controversy, first, that fluoridation divides the community in unusual ways, compared to other issues, and second, that it is not possible to identify most community leaders with either side on this issue.

We are discovering that these premises are true only in certain cases, and perhaps not even in a majority. Fluoridation often divides a community along cleavage lines similar to those of other issues—particularly school issues. This does not always bring strange bedfellows together. Instead, in some communities the controversy deepens and intensifies the cleavages partially formed by other issues.

Our evidence suggests that it is fruitless to ask if, in general, fluoridation follows conventional or unusual cleavage lines. Seen as a variable, the question becomes, "What conditions determine whether fluoridation divides the community along normal or unusual lines?" After answering this, we would also need to know how given strategies affect the outcome under each of these alternatives. Similarly, the second part of the original explanation—that community leaders will remain neutral—is also variable, and dependent on the distribution and functioning of power in a given community.

In short, neither fluoridation nor any other issue studied seems to follow some invariant pattern independent of the social structure and leadership patterns in the communities involved. Our hope is to be able to characterize certain modal patterns and to determine the conditions under which each occurs. I would like to describe my impressions of what now seems to me the most significant of these patterns.

Pro and Anti Voters

There has been a good deal of research on why people vote for or against fluoridation which suggests that both groups are heterogeneous. Among the active opponents are the disingenuous professionals, the sincere but rather emotional individuals, and the calm, rational citizens who object on grounds of individual rights or public policy. Among those who simply vote against fluoridation, are all of the above plus those who are confused and unconvinced by either side. The proponents of fluoridation are also varied; many confuse fluoridation with some water purification process such as chlorination. In short, it is difficult to predict that any given strategy will be effective without specifying the audience and the characteristics of the community involved.

But in spite of the variable character of both sides, a dominant theme runs through many of the findings. There seem to be substantial differences between the advocates and the opponents of fluoridation on the degree to which people feel able to control the important forces in their lives. This has been variously characterized as alienation, feelings of deprivation, and low sense of political efficacy. Essentially, those who vote against fluoridation have greater feelings

of helplessness than those who favor it. Studies of voters in a predominantly lower-middle-class and working-class precinct in Cambridge, Massachusetts, and of a cross-section of voters in a medium-
sized and a small city in the northeastern United States have yielded
the same result. Those who voted against fluoridation were more
likely to agree with such statements as "Public officials don't really
care what people like me think," and "Sometimes politics and government seem so complicated that a person like me can't really understand what's going on." Additional data are needed to establish these
differences conclusively for various populations. But I will assume at
this time that these differences are valid and I will try to relate them
to community decision-making on fluoridation.

One further contrast between the two groups of voters is worth
mentioning here. Some proponents have incorrectly argued that opponents are anti-scientific. This assumes that opponents perceive
scientific unanimity on this issue and refuse to respect it. There is
evidence that many who vote against fluoridation see the "experts"
as divided on the merits of the proposal. How, one might ask, can
they continue despite endorsement by the United States Public Health
Service, the American Medical Association, and the American Dental
Association?

To answer this, it is necessary to make a distinction between "experts" and "authorities." Many active opponents point out that the
doctors and dentists in their community have done no special research
on fluoridation. They perceive such organizations as the American
Medical Association and the American Dental Association, not as
technical experts, but as medical *authorities* with the power to punish
individual doctors and dentists who do not follow their policies.
Furthermore, they frequently do not believe that these organizations
use their power in a disinterested fashion. They may easily interpret
the self-interested attitude of the American Medical Association on
medical care for the aged as evidence for such a belief. On the
other hand, when an occasional doctor or dentist opposes fluoridation, they may see him as a technically qualified "expert" with the
courage to oppose the "authorities." These partisan opponents, then,
will see the authorities as united, but the experts as divided. In a
less explicit fashion, many ordinary voters may be unconsciously
making this kind of distinction.

A Hypothetical Campaign

To explain why a fluoridation referendum passes or fails, it is not sufficient to simply point out differences between opponents and proponents. In some way, the fluoridation campaign in a community must make these differences salient. The description which follows of a campaign in the hypothetical town of "Fluoradale" suggests how the actions in a campaign can make feelings of political helplessness relevant. While my hypothetical community is "purer" than any actual community through the omission of extraneous complicating factors, it is not simply a straw town designed for easy criticism. The actions I will describe have all been done in one or more actual communities studied.

The health officer in Fluoradale is a conscientious, intelligent, but somewhat rigid person. He is aware that fluoridation has been a controversial issue in many places, but he sees no reason why it can not be adopted in Fluoradale if it is handled correctly. In his view, opposition in these other communities has come from a handful of "crackpots" who have managed to scare or hoodwink a gullible populace.

The health officer goes to other health officials and finds that they also favor fluoridation. He contacts various physicians and dentists in town. One of the dentists points out that fluoridation does poorly on referenda and that it would be wise to try to have fluoridation adopted directly by the town council. Up to this point, no opposition has developed and everyone concerned is optimistic.

The council is sympathetic, although one member has some doubts, and they decide to hold a public hearing on the proposal. In response to a notice in the paper, an unexpectedly large number of people attend the hearing and most of them are hostile to fluoridation. Proponents are heckled and asked hostile questions from the floor. One opponent, a retired chiropractor, asks to be allowed to testify. The health officer argues that he is unqualified. "There is no sense in letting a lot of scientifically untrained people shoot their mouth off about this," he tells the council. Several people in the audience loudly object and the meeting threatens to get out of hand. One of the councilmen most sympathetic to fluoridation makes a short speech about democracy. "This is a public hearing and anyone here who wishes to speak may do so," he announces.

The retired chiropractor makes a moderate plea: "There is a lot of controversy about this question of fluoridation and I think we should study it thoroughly before we adopt it. In a lot of places, they've tried to rush it through and suppress the opposition. I hope the people of Fluoradale will be given a chance to hear both sides and decide for themselves on this question."

The health officer is annoyed at the response of the partisan audience. He reacts by reasserting the technical nature of the question and the lack of qualifications of the average citizen to pass judgment on a scientific matter. *He* is willing to take the word of reputable scientific organizations on faith. Why should those so much less qualified than he insist on exercising their own judgment?

After lengthy discussion the council decides to place the question on the ballot at the next town election and to set up a study committee to publish an impartial report. The health officer, another physician, and a dentist are appointed along with the chiropractor and another opponent, a housewife.

The active proponents begin mobilizing quickly. They contact all the dentists and physicians execpt one, who is retired and rather senile. They publish advertisements over the names of most of the leading business and civic leaders, three of the five council members, the Chamber of Commerce, and a service club.

By misreading the operation of community power (a misreading which many sociologists have helped to perpetuate), they believe that they have followed the politically realistic strategy of enlisting the "community powers" on their side. In the community where there is no "ruling elite" who can implement decisions at their collective will (and there are many such localities) this strategy backfires. Anti-fluoridation leaders, who have already begun to broadcast the message that something is being "put over" on the community, see this list of endorsements as additional evidence of the "power play" that is being conducted. "They" are beginning to turn on the heat.

The proponents see their campaign as "educational" rather than "political." They decide to hold a large public meeting to present their point of view. The active opponents bring in an anti-fluoridation "expert" from outside the community. The proponents charge that he is a "quack," that this is an educational forum, not a debate. Opponents claim that this is a deliberate effort to keep the people from being told both sides. Finally, the proponents consent to questions from the floor, and a free-wheeling, highly emotional debate ensues. Anti-fluoridation speakers repeatedly challenges the motives of the proponents.

As the controversy in Fluoradale grows more heated, several of the civic leaders among the original endorsers ask that their names be removed from the advertisements. They begin to let it be known that they are neutral on the issue, but intend to see that both sides are heard.

The opposition campaign begins to gather momentum. They point to the array of community leaders and medical people who endorse the proposal as evidence of powerful forces—not of scientific judgment. The defectors to neutrality are seen as men of conscience who are really opposed but do not have sufficient courage to buck the "powers." The elderly physician who was not contacted by the pro-fluoridation committee published a letter attacking fluoridation and the endorsing physicians. This is used as evidence of how an "expert" who is beyond the reach of sanctions will act. Any doubt privately expressed by a doctor or dentist is viewed as his "honest," unpressured opinion.

In the atmosphere of mistrust generated by the campaign, people whose normal skepticism would lead them to dismiss the usual flamboyant stories of pipe corrosion, deaths from cancer, dying goldfish, stillbirths and what-have-you, are left in doubt. Furthermore, the pro-fluoridation partisans follow the policy of not responding to opponents' charges—"to avoid dignifying such hogwash."

On election day, fluoridation is beaten decisively. The nature of the campaign leaves most community leaders—active proponents—feeling that it would be a bad thing for the community to have the issue brought up again.

Conclusion

It is an important characteristic of political debate in a democracy that proponents and opponents recognize the legitimacy of disagreement. When a person responds to an opponent by attempting to refute the logic of what he has said, we are implicitly accepting his "right" to express an opinion. When we respond with an *ad hominem* attack, we are asking people to ignore his opinions, not because they are wrong, but because he is not qualified to make them.

Fluoridation involves issues that go beyond the technical questions of effectiveness and safety. In many communities studied, proponents —irked by irresponsible and unqualified opinions on technical matters —have tended to challenge the legitimacy of opposition. They have done this by calling opponents "crackpots" (perhaps some are, but by no means all), refusing to debate the issue or answer charges, and doing other things which imply that this is not a fit subject for democratic political debate.

I am not interested in arguing here whether fluoridation is or is not an appropriate question for the citizenry to decide. I *am* interested in what, I believe, are the consequences of such a position. If I feel that some mysterious "they" make all the important decisions, if I distrust power as such, and find it difficult to distinguish between its use for selfish or for disinterested ends, I may easily misinterpret certain actions of the proponents.

I do not intend this unsuccessful fluoridation campaign to illustrate any specific tactical errors. I am not commenting on the general wisdom of getting endorsements from civic leaders, avoiding referenda, answering opponent charges, or any of the other specific acts which were performed. Such considerations are largely dependent on the conditions existing at a given time.

If I were to attempt listing "don'ts" they would center on certain characteristic attitudes among many active proponents in the fluoridation controversy:

Don't assume that all opponents are the same; that they are stupid, emotional crackpots. For every person this description fits, you'll convince several it doesn't fit to vote against it.

Don't assume that the mere multiplication of medical and political authorities will convince doubters that the experts agree. Attitudes of trust or distrust toward the influence held by such authorities may be decisive. Their endorsements of fluoridation may be given a different meaning by potential opponents.

Don't assume that those who are influential on some types of issues will necessarily be influential on fluoridation. An individual who wields a great deal of power on a sewerage or new school proposal may or may not be able to influence the outcome of a fluoridation vote.

Don't be annoyed that your role as expert is challenged. Some active proponents, by allowing themselves to be "baited" by hostile questions, seem to confirm opposition charges of high-handedness or concealment.

I wish to illustrate a more general criticism which grows out of the earlier discussion on the sources of opposition. Many people have feelings of political helplessness. This in itself does not turn them against fluoridation. That differences exist on this issue between voting proponents and opponents seems to indicate that there is something about fluoridation which arouses these feelings. This "something" may be inherent in the nature of the issue (its technical quality or some other feature) and beyond the control of anything proponents do in a campaign. On the other hand, it may be the partisans' attitude which stimulates these reactions. I have tried to illustrate in my hypothetical example how well-intended actions in a fluoridation campaign can have such unintended consequences.

Most of us are annoyed and self-righteous when an unqualified person challenges our opinion on a subject on which we feel we are to some degree an expert. This kind of legitimate "arrogance" is more refreshing than false humility. But legitimate or not, it is a poor posture to take on fluoridation or any other issue which will be decided by the voters of a community.

Claude Lévi-Strauss

The Particular Task of Anthropology

One of the most controversial and most interesting figures in anthropology today is Claude Lévi-Strauss. Much of his thinking about structural anthropology has its roots in the Durkheimian conception of the *conscience collective*. He has also been called a Zen Marxist—by anthropologist Robert Murphy—as a result of his attempts to synthesize the concepts of the superstructure with those of the unconscious. Lévi-Strauss's structuralism is, in part, an artistic method—a search for wholeness outside of strict empiricism. His insistence that anthropology can use both the intuitive methods of art and the empirical methods of science has been sharply criticized. Nevertheless, his formulations have revived anthropology's waning interest in myths and in history, and his approach represents another vantage point from which man can view human behavior.

WE MUST . . . examine how we can define what anthropology, as such, has to say—the message which the proper organization of its teaching should enable it to transmit under the best possible conditions.

Objectivity. The first aim of anthropology is to be objective, to inculcate objective habits and to teach objective methods. Not simply an objectivity enabling the observer to place himself above his own personal beliefs, preferences, and prejudices; that kind of objectivity characterizes every social science, or they could not be regarded as sciences at all. The objectivity aimed at by anthropology is on a higher level: The observer must not only place himself above the values accepted by his own society or group, but must adopt certain definite *methods of thought;* he must reason on the basis of concepts which are valid not merely for an honest and objective observer, but for all possible observers. Thus the anthropologist does not simply set aside his own feelings; he creates new mental categories and helps to introduce notions of space and time, opposition and contradiction, which are as foreign to traditional thought as the concepts met with today in certain branches of the natural sciences. This connection between the ways in which the same problems are stated in apparently very different disciplines was admirably perceived by the great physicist Niels Bohr when he wrote: "The traditional differences of [human cultures] . . . in many ways resemble the different equivalent modes in which physical experience can be described." [1]

Yet these unrelenting efforts to achieve complete objectivity can go forward only on a level where phenomena retain a meaning for humanity and can be apprehended, in mind and feeling, by an individual. This is a very important point, for it enables us to distinguish between the type of objectivity to which anthropology aspires and that aimed at by the other social sciences, of which it can be said that it is no less rigorous, although it is on another level. The realities in which economic science and demography are interested are no less objective, but they are not expected to have a meaning so far as the subject's own personal experience is concerned, for in the course of his historical evolution he never encounters such things as value, profitableness, marginal productivity, or maximum population. These are all abstract notions; their use by the social sciences brings the social sciences closer to the natural sciences, but in a quite different way, for in the case of anthropology the connection is more with humanistic studies. Anthropology aims to be a *semeiological* science, and takes as a guiding principle that of "meaning." This is yet another reason (in addition to many others) why anthropology should maintain close contact with linguistics, where, with regard to this social fact of speech, there is the same concern to avoid separating the objective basis of language *(sound)* from its signifying function *(meaning)* . [2]

Totality. The second aim of anthropology is *totality.* It regards social life as a system of which all the aspects are organically connected. It readily admits that, in order to acquire a more thorough knowledge of certain types of phenomena, it is essential to subdivide— after the manner of the social psychologist, the jurist, the economist, and the political scientist—and it is too much concerned with the method of models (which it employs itself in certain fields, such as that of kinship) to question the validity of these particular models. But when the anthropologist endeavors to create models, it is always with the underlying motive of discovering a *form that is common* to the various manifestations of social life. This tendency underlies both the notion (introduced by Marcel Mauss) of the *total social phenomenon,* and that of *pattern* (an idea which has loomed large in Anglo-Saxon anthropology during recent years).

Meaningfulness. The third original feature of anthropological research—unquestionably more important than the other two—is not so easy to define. We are so accustomed to attaching negative terms to the types of society that interest the ethnologist that it is difficult for us to realize he is interested in them for positive reasons. Anthropology, we are apt to say—and this is evidenced by the title of the chairs themselves—is concerned with societies that are *non*-civilized, *without* a system of writing, and *pre-* or *non*-industrial in type. Yet behind all these qualifying negative expressions there is a positive reality: These societies are, to a far greater degree than the others, based on personal relationships, on concrete relations between individuals. It would take some time to prove this point, but, without entering into details, it will suffice here to emphasize that the small size of the societies known as "primitive" generally permits of such relationships and that, even where this is impossible because the societies of this type are too extensive or scattered, relations between individuals who are extremely remote from one another are based on the most direct kind of relationship, of which kinship is usually the prototype. Radcliffe-Brown has given us examples in Australia, which have become classic, of this process of projection.

The Criterion of Authenticity

In this respect it is, rather, modern societies that should be defined in negative terms. Our relations with one another are now only occasionally and fragmentarily based upon global experience, the concrete "apprehension" of one person by another. They are largely the result of a process of indirect reconstruction, through written documents. We are no longer linked to our past by an oral tradition which implies direct contact with others (storytellers, priests, wise men, or elders), but by books amassed in libraries, books from which we endeavor—with extreme difficulty—to form a picture of their authors. And we communicate with the immense majority of our contemporaries by all kinds of intermediaries—written documents or administrative machinery—which undoubtedly vastly extend our contacts but at the same time make those contacts somewhat "unauthentic." This has become typical of the relationship between the citizen and the public authorities.

We should like to avoid describing negatively the tremendous revolution brought about by the invention of writing. But it is essential to realize that writing, while it conferred vast benefits on humanity, did in fact deprive it of something fundamental.[3] The international organizations, and particularly UNESCO, have so far entirely failed to appreciate the loss of personal autonomy that has resulted from the expansion of the indirect forms of communication (books, photographs, press, radio, etc.). But the theorists of the most modern of the social sciences (that of communication) treat this as a major question, as is shown by the following passage from Wiener's *Cybernetics:* "It is no wonder that the larger communities . . . contain far less available information than the smaller communities, to say nothing of the human elements of which all communities are built up."[4] Taking an illustration from a field which is more familiar to the social sciences, there is the dispute—well known to French political scientists—between supporters of the individual constituency poll *(scrutin d'arrondissement)* and supporters of voting for several unknown or little-known members out of a list drawn up by the political parties *(scrutin de liste).* Under the latter system, there is a great loss of information suffered by the community, owing to the substitution of abstract values for personal contacts between the electors and their representatives.

NOTES

[1] Niels Bohr, "Natural Philosophy and Human Culture," *Nature,* CXLIII (1939).

[2] Just after writing these lines, we came across very similar views expressed by Jean-Paul Sartre. After criticizing an out-of-date sociology, he adds: "The sociology of primitive peoples is *never* open to this criticism. There we study *meaningful wholes* [*ensembles signifiants*]." *Les Temps Modernes* (October–November, 1952), p. 729, n. 1.

[3] Regarding this point, see C. Lévi-Strauss, *Tristes Tropiques* (Paris: 1955), Chapter XXVIII.

[4] Pages 188–9. Speaking generally, I should say that all of pages 181–9 of that book would deserve inclusion *in extenso* in UNESCO's Constitution.

F. S. C. Northrop

Philosophical Anthropology and World Law

Our inability to construct a world legal system that can function without the use of force, has, in the opinion of F. S. C. Northrop, been unsuccessful largely because it has been erected upon Western legal models which often contradict the living law of other major peoples and cultures. He suggests that the construction of a comparative legal science is a major prerequisite for the achievement of peace. More significantly, he insists that the legal systems of others are comprehensible only in terms of the meaning which each group gives to the system itself. In calling for a reintroduction of philosophy into social science, Northrop rests his case upon the nature of the human nervous system, which, he contends, does not order its neurons linearly and therefore cannot be understood in terms of stimulus-response models favored by mechanical psychology. Instead, the nervous system orders its neurons circularly, so that an impulse representing a stimulus that is long since gone may be passed continuously around the circuit. Behavior—even on a neurological level—is not merely a response to stimuli from below, but to symbols and ideals, systems of belief that are intrinsic to human neurological makeup.

THE NEED IN AN atomic age for settling disputes between nations by peaceful rather than violent means is obvious. History gives no evidence, as Dean Roscoe Pound [1] has recently reminded us, that a peaceful settling of disputes in any sphere has ever been achieved without recourse to legal procedures or rules. Legal procedures and rules applied to international disputes mean a world law.

Notwithstanding this need for a world law, previous attempts to achieve it have been most disheartening. One need only recall the disillusionment following the founding of the League of Nations at Versailles, or the present cold war and vituperation supplanting the high hopes for the United Nations which were voiced and officially affirmed at San Francisco.

These discouragements suggest that perhaps we have been going about the achievement of an effective international law in the wrong way. Apparently the conditions for an effective law have not yet been met in the international sphere. It behooves us, therefore, to turn aside momentarily from the world at large to examine what legal science has to teach us about the criterion for an effective law.

This criterion, the Criterion of Effective Law, is well known to all contemporary legal thinkers. It has been laid down by the great Austro-Hungarian sociologist of law, Ehrlich, as is expressed in Ehrlich's formula that the positive law must be grounded in and correspond to the living law. By "positive law" Ehrlich means the legal constitutions, statutes, institutions, and officials which are introduced. By the "living law" he means the *de facto* behavior, mores, and norms of the people, or at least a majority of the people, quite apart from the positive law. When the positive law is not rooted in the living law, it is Ehrlich's thesis that legal institutions and processes for handling disputes break down. The failure of the prohibition amendment in the United States, even though it was legally passed, is an instance.

Ehrlich's criterion of effective law has implications in the international sphere—implications moreover which have not received the attention they merit. What his principle means, internationally, is that no positive legal rules or institutions for bringing the settlement of disputes between nations under the rule of law, rather than of force, can be successful unless these positive rules and institutions are rooted in, and are the expression of, the living law of all the major peoples and cultures of the world.

The first task, therefore, in the attempt to obtain an effective world legal order is to determine the underlying living law of the world's major different peoples and cultures. Clearly this is an undertaking for which the lawyer and the statesman are quite incompetent. The living law of the diverse cultures and peoples of the world can be determined only by a direct scientific study of those cultures, and the science whose business it is to pursue this study in anthropology. Hence the importance of anthropology, and in particular cultural anthropology, for world law.

But not everything with which cultural anthropology concerns itself is relevant to or necessary for the statesman's or international lawyer's purpose. Only certain factors supplied by the science of cultural anthropology are required. These relevant factors become evident when one notes that positive law is concerned always with norms. Positive law always prescribes certain normative rules, statutes, or procedures which serve as a normative measuring rod to distinguish the behavior in society which is permissible from that which is not. In short, law is concerned with the normative factor in cultural and social organization. What the international lawyer needs, therefore, from the anthropologist is the normative factor in the living law of the different peoples and cultures of the world. What is wanted from the cultural anthropologist is the living, vital, indigenous ethos of each culture in the world; the living ethos which will sustain the international lawyer's positive world law providing he constructs this positive world law out of, and in accord with, this living ethos.

At least we are now able to see why the traditional attempts at a world legal order have been so disheartening. The positive law which defined these traditional attempts corresponded at most only to the living law ethos of but one culture in the world, the modern French and Anglo-American Western culture. It was little more than a positive law brought into correspondence with the living law of this solitary, relatively small Western culture and then generalized for the rest of the world. By the very nature of the case, such an international law fails to correspond to the plurality of living laws of the other European, Latin American, African, Islamic, and Asian cultures of the world and hence, of necessity, must be ineffective.

Having noted that the first step toward an effective world law is the determination through cultural anthropology—and it may be added, through sociology—of the living ethos of each of the major cultures and nations of the world, the second task becomes evident. It is that of determining the key independent variable or variables in the science of cultural anthropology which, when its values are determined empirically for any specific culture, give us the ethos of that culture. What is this independent variable?

Fortunately the sciences of sociology, anthropology, and psychology converge upon the specification of the answer to this question. The work of many different sociologists, anthropologists, and psychologists could be brought to the support of the conclusion upon which these three sciences converge. For purposes of brevity, we shall restrict ourselves to one or two scientists for each of these three sciences. Those which we chose are Sorokin for cultural sociology, Kluckhohn for cultural anthropology, and McCulloch and Pitts for neurological psychology. More specifically we shall restrict ourselves to Sorokin's concept of logico-meaningful causality,[2] Kluckhohn's study of the legal norms of the Navaho Indians,[3] and McCulloch and Pitts'[4] concept of cortically trapped universals in their relation to any person's response to a stimulus.

Sorokin's Concept of Logico-Meaningful Causality. Sorokin noted that there is a difference between causality in any system of natural science and causality in any system of cultural science. Whereas the former is mechanical, causality in cultural science is logico-meaningful.

The mechanical causality characterizing the systems of nature is illustrated in Newtonian mechanics, Einstein's theory of relativity, and Schroedinger's quantum mechanics. These examples show that a natural system is governed by mechanical causation when an experimentally verified, deductively formulated, theory of the subject matter to which the system refers specifies independent variables defining any state of the system; and specifies such postulates that when the values of these independent variables for a specific state of the system at a given time t_1 are determined empirically, the postulates of the theory enable us to mathematically calculate, or in other words, logically deduce, the values of these independent variables for any other state of the system at any earlier or later time t_2. In the case of Newtonian mechanics, these two independent variables are but two in number: the position and the momenta of the entities of the system.

The nature of logico-meaningful causality begins to become evident when one pursues the analogy of Newtonian mechanics in the cultural sciences as far as it will go. Any natural system designated by Newtonian mechanics has its entities. They are the physical or scientific objects. The cultural systems also have their entities. They are the human persons and their physical environment. When, in Newtonian mechanics, the postulates and values of the variables defining the state of any system are specified, the ordering relations of the system are made determinate. The mere specification, however, in any cultural system of the positions and momenta of the persons in that society is not sufficient to specify the ordering relations which define the culture of those persons.

An example will suffice to make this clear. In many village communities of India, Moslems and Hindus have lived together for centuries. Most of the Moslems are converts from Hinduism; thus ethnologically the peoples are for the most part identical. Hence, the cultural differences between Moslems and Hindus which are so great as to necessitate the present division of nineteenth century India into Pakistan and New Delhi's India are not to be explained by physical, ethnological differences. The momenta and positions of the bodies of the Hindus and Moslems in any single village hardly account for the differences in their two cultures. The position of Moslems and Hindus is identical since both are located in the same village. If one watched both groups walking down the street there might be slight differences in their momenta, but hardly differences sufficient to account for the differences in culture. In fact we would suspect that where differences in momenta between Moslems and Hindus in the same village appeared, these differences would be the effect rather than the cause of the cultural differences. Clearly the cultural ordering relations are not given after the manner in which the ordering relations of natural systems exhibiting their mechanical causation are given.

What is the unique factor, in addition to the aforementioned physical factors, which must be determined in order to make the ordering relations, which incidentally define the ethos of a culture, determinate? Sorokin's answer is that this additional key variable, unique to cultural systems, is to be found in the meanings that the persons making up any single culture hold in common and use to conceptualize, order, and integrate the raw data of their experience. It is because meanings are the key factor that Sorokin calls this unique causality of cultural science "logico-meaningful causality."

What this entails is that wherever there are two different cultures, the persons in those cultures are using different basic meanings or concepts to describe, systematize and integrate the data of their experience. The Hindus in the Indian villages are using those of Hinduism; the Moslems, those of Islam; and so we could go on beyond the Hindu villages to the rest of the world. Then we would say Soviet Russians are using those of Marx as interpreted by Lenin and Stalin. The traditional Chinese, those of Confucius; the Siamese, those of Buddhism, with a slight top layer of Hinduism; the Roman Catholics those of St. Thomas; the Americans those of Locke and Jefferson and Adam Smith and Mill and Jevons, and more recently Keynes.

Our example of the Indian village suggests also another point noted by Sorokin. The meanings used by a given people to describe, organize, and interpret the data of their experience determine the ethos of their culture. I would even go further and say that they *are* its ethos. The word "good" is literally nothing more than the name for the basic meaning of the hierarchy of all meanings used by a people to conceptualize themselves and their universe. This follows from what has been said. For if the basic meanings define the ordering relations of a culture, they automatically define its living law, and the living law of a culture is its ethos. To these basic conceptual meanings the word "good" adds but one thing in addition to its designation of them, *i.e.,* their application to, and use as a measure of, conduct. In short, ethics is the conceptualization of the data of experience applied.

But what are the basic meanings of a people or culture? The traditional term used everywhere for the basic concepts of anything is philosophy. This is the reason why the international lawyer, if he is to be effective in meeting the world's present need, must go to not merely anthropology but to philosophical anthropology. This brings us to the second of our three contemporary scientists.

Kluckhohn's Philosophy of the Navaho Indians. What makes this study especially relevant is the fact that the Navaho have no written literature. Nonetheless, Kluckhohn found after years of firsthand study of them that he did not understand what he saw until he teased out of them their philosophy. Before this he had been doing what so many other cultural scientists have done, namely, he had been conceptualizing what he saw in his terms rather than theirs. This is but Sorokin's point, proved over again quite independently in the science of anthropology. Even a so-called primitive people devoid of a written literature order their relations in terms of their conceptual meanings. Moreover Kluckhohn was able to formulate their legal norms and found them to derive from their philosophy.

But how can philosophy have this basic significance? Is not the response to stimuli of sex and hunger basic, with philosophy a mere afterthought? To answer these questions we must turn to the psychologists.

McCulloch and Pitts' Neurologically Trapped Universals. McCulloch and Pitts have noted that ideas would be irrelevant in behavior were the neurons of the human nervous system ordered linearly. Then the firing of the sensory neuron by the stimulus would fire the cortical neurons and in turn the motor neuron. Thus the stimulus alone would determine behavior.

Lorente de Nó has shown, however, that cortical neurons are ordered in a circle to which a sensory neuron comes and from which a motor neuron goes. Suppose the firing of the sensory neuron fires one of the cortical neurons in the circle and that this cortical neuron in turn fires the next neuron in the circle and so on. Then the impulse produced initially by the stimulus firing the sensory neuron will be passed continuously around the circle. But this impulse represents the stimulus that is gone. When something represents something else, it is a symbol. Thus McCulloch and Pitts noted that in the trapped impulses of Lorente de Nó's reverberating cortical circuits one has the neurological correlate of what introspective psychology calls a meaning or a universal.

Suppose there are several such neurally connected circuits with their different trapped representatives of diverse stimuli or environmental facts. Connected meanings give propositions and connected propositions give theories. Suppose also that some trapped impulses representing certain facts in experience (*i.e.,* stimuli) are used to define others. The trapped universals will then be ordered hierarchically in the cortex. Thus the distinction between basic or philosophical concepts and derived, more inductively given, concepts will arise.

Suppose also that this hierarchy of meanings can both effect the firing of one motor neuron and inhibit the firing of another, as McCulloch shows to be the case. Then we see how philosophy not only can, but must, serve as the normative judge and censor of any stimulus striking a sensory neuron, determining what passes over into overt behavior and what does not. Thus, both law and ethics as grounded in the trapped universals placed at the top of the cortical hierarchy because of their capacity to prepare the human organism for any stimuli hitting it, become intelligible. Neurological as well as introspective psychology hereby combine to affirm that behavior is a response not to stimuli alone, but to ideas found to be basic in remembering, describing, and integrating the stimuli, and in enabling one to anticipate tomorrow's stimuli. When many people agree on these basic meanings, one has a single culture.

Cultural sociology and anthropology and neurological behavioristic, as well as introspective, psychology converge upon the following conclusion: The way to an effective world law is through philosophical anthropology.

This way involves several steps. First, the basic meanings or philosophy which define the ordering relation or living law ethos of each major people and culture of the world must be determined. This entails a study of their basic philosophical and religious classics. Second, the corresponding positive law for each philosophy defined living law must be made explicit. Only thus will the operational consequences in practice of a given living law cultural ethos become evident; and this necessitates a study of the legal classics and practices. Third, with this knowledge from philosophical anthropology of the living law and the corresponding positive law of each culture of the world, the international lawyer is then for the first time able to construct an effective world law. He does this following Ehrlich's criterion of effectiveness by formulating it so that as far as possible it draws upon, is rooted in, and corresponds to the vital living law norms, or in other words the philosophy, of all; rather than, as has been the case in the past, merely one of the peoples and cultures of the world.

Clearly the basic principle underlying this more effective world law must be ideological and cultural pluralism. Its ideal must be a symphony of the world's diverse cultures.[5]

NOTES

[1] R. Pound, "Toward a New *Jus Gentium*," in *Ideological Differences and World Order* (New Haven, 1949).

[2] See P. Sorokin, *Social and Cultural Dynamics* (New York, 1937).

[3] See C. Kluckhohn, "The Philosophy of the Navaho Indians," in *Ideological Differences and World Order*.

[4] See W. S. McCulloch and W. Pitts, "How We Know Universals," *Bull. Math. Biophysics*, 1943, 5:115. See also McCulloch, "A Hierarchy of Values Determined by the Topology of Nervous Nets," *Bull. Math. Biophysics*, 1945, 7:89.

[5] See also F. S. C. Northrop, "Ideological Man in His Relation to Scientifically Known Natural Man," Chap. 19 in *Ideological Differences and World Order*; "Naturalistic and Cultural Foundations for a More Effective International Law," *Yale Law Journal*, 1950, pp. 1430–1450; "The Importance of Deductively Formulated Theory in Ethics and Social and Legal Science," in *Structure, Method and Meaning* (New York, 1951), pp. 99–116.

Erwin W. Straus

The Upright Posture

The emergence of Existentialist philosophy at the end of World War II brought yet another conceptual framework into the study of human behavior. The sources of Existentialism extend back into the nineteenth century, but its influence is largely a postwar phenomenon. Although fully aware of the unconscious and the irrational, the Existentialists insist that man must be dealt with as a rational animal, whose ability to make a choice is what gives meaning and purpose to life. Existentialists object to the view that sees the world as either a purely irrational, mental phenomenon or a purely physical one. Instead, they insist—as does Erwin Straus—that man's development takes place in a physical world and proceeds through interaction of mind, body, and culture. Straus's view is one that has been fruitfully explored by psychologists, and by physical anthropologists whose concern with the changing shape of the human body has led them to hypothesize about the nature of man's physical relationship to the world and the effect of this relationship upon mind and culture. Investigations of physical anthropologists indicate that evolution of the brain may not have preceded the development of culture and language, but, in fact, cannot be understood at all except in terms of a continual process that involved man's mind, body, and environment in an intricate, inseparable, interactive dynamic.

Introduction

A breakdown of physical well-being is alarming; it turns our attention to functions that, on good days, we take for granted. A healthy person does not ponder about breathing, seeing, or walking. Infirmities of breath, sight, or gait startle us. Among the patients consulting a psychiatrist, there are some who can no longer master the seemingly banal arts of standing and walking. They are not paralyzed, but, under certain conditions, they cannot, or feel as if they cannot, keep themselves upright. They tremble and quiver. Incomprehensible terror takes away their strength. Sometimes, a minute change in the physiognomy of the frightful situation may restore their strength. Obviously, upright posture is not confined to the technical problems of locomotion. It contains a psychological element. It is pregnant with a meaning not exhausted by the physiological tasks of meeting the forces of gravity and maintaining equilibrium.

Language has long since taken cognizance of this fact. The expression "to be upright" has two connotations: first, to rise, to get up, and to stand on one's own feet and, second, the moral implication, not to stoop to anything, to be honest and just, to be true to friends in danger, to stand by one's convictions, and to act accordingly, even at the risk of one's life. We praise an upright man; we admire someone who stands up for his ideas of rectitude. These are good reasons to assume that the term "upright" in its moral connotation is more than a mere allegory.

The upright posture distinguishes the human genus from other living creatures. To Milton, Adam and Eve appeared as ". . . Two of far nobler shape, erect and tall, God-like erect, with native honor clad. . . ." Some biologists, however, would like to take exception to this praise, and, in slightly more prosaic statements, they indict the upright posture is an excellence or not, in any case it is a distinction. be, whether the poet is right or his misanthropic opponents, whether upright posture is an excellence or not, in any case it is a distinction. It does not occur in any species other than man.[1]

Upright posture, while unique, is also essential. This is no necessary consequence. The exceptional might be nothing but a peculiarity, an accidental caprice of nature. However, there is no doubt that the shape and function of the human body are determined in almost every detail by, and for, the upright posture. The skeleton of the foot; the structure of the ankle, knee, and hip; the curvature of the vertebral column; the proportions of the limbs—all serve the same purpose. This purpose could not be accomplished if the muscles and the nervous system were not built accordingly. While all parts contribute to the upright posture, upright posture in turn permits the development of the forelimbs into the human shoulders, arms, and hands and of the skull into the human skull and face.

With upright posture, the vertebral column takes on, for the first time, the architectural function of a column. The skull rests on the articular surfaces of the atlas (which here, indeed, deserves its name) like an architrave on the capitals of columns. This arrangement makes it possible and necessary for the atlanto-occipital joint to be moved forward toward the center of the base of the skull, resulting in the typical configuration of the human skull, the extension of the base, and the closing vault, which in turn provides wider space for the orbitae. The skulls of the other primates still show the shape characteristic of other quadrupeds, in which the head does not rest on the vertebral column but hangs down from it. The foramen magnum accordingly is in a more caudal position; the clivus cuts the vertical at a more obtuse angle. The other primates—as has been said—are built to stand upright but not for upright posture. . . .[2]

Upright posture characterizes the human species. Nevertheless, each individual has to struggle in order to make it really his own. Man has to become what he is. The acquisition does not make him an "absentee landlord." While the heart continues to beat from its fetal beginning to death without our active intervention and while breathing neither demands nor tolerates our voluntary interference beyond narrow limits, upright posture remains a task throughout our lives. Before reflection or self-reflection start, but as if they were a prelude to it, work makes its appearance within the realm of the elemental biological functions of man. In getting up, in reaching the upright posture, man must oppose the forces of gravity. It seems to be his nature to oppose nature in its impersonal, fundamental aspects with natural means. However, gravity is never fully overcome; upright posture always maintains its character of counteraction. It calls for our activity and attention.

Automatic regulation alone does not suffice. An old horse may go to sleep standing on its four legs; man has to be awake to keep himself upright. Much as we are part of nature with every breath, with every bite, with every step, we first become our true selves in waking opposition to nature. In sleep, we do not withdraw our interest from the world so much as we surrender ourselves completely to it. We abandon ourselves to the world, relinquishing our individuality. We no longer hold our own in the world, opposed to it. Awakeness and the force of gravity are mutually interdependent. While awakeness is necessary for upright posture, that is, for counteracting gravity, gravity determines waking experience. The dreams of one night are not related to the dreams of another night, but days are related to one another. They form a continuum where every hour, every moment, anticipates the next and prepares for it. Held back by gravity to a precise point, we can overcome distance only in an orderly sequence. During our waking hours, sequence means consequence. Gravity, which holds us in line, imposes on waking experience a methodical processing. In sleep, when we no longer oppose gravity, in our weightless dreams, or in our lofty fantasies, experience becomes kaleidoscopic and finally amorphous. Sequence, then, no longer means consequence. Awakeness is no mere addendum, still less an impediment, to an otherwise happily functioning id. The waking man alone can preserve himself, and he alone can help drives to reach their goal.

In the Hobbesian philosophy, man, haunted by fear of violent death, creates the commonwealth to keep disruptive natural tendencies in check. A permanent, never resolved discord ensues between man in the state of nature and man as a member of society. Locke, Rousseau, Freud, and many others took up the theme and added to it variations of their own. If only these many descriptions of man's state of nature were more than historical fantasies! Yet, one need not invent prehistory; we can make use of a very concrete experience. We can read man's natural endowment from his physique. Considering man in his upright posture, we do well to envisage the possibility not that society has first brought man into conflict with nature, but that man's natural opposition to nature enables him to produce society, history, and conventions.

The direction upward, against gravity, inscribes into space worldregions to which we attach values, such as those expressed by high and low, rise and decline, climbing and falling, superior and inferior, elevated and downcast, looking up to and despising. On Olympus, high, remote, inaccessible, and exalted, dwell the Homeric gods. On Mount Sinai, Moses receives the Ten Commandments. Below, in the depths, is Hades and the world of shadows. There, also, is the Inferno. However, such evaluations are not unequivocal. "Base" (adjective) and "base" (noun) have, in spite of their phonetic resemblance, different etymological roots and opposite meanings. "Base," the adjective, is derived from the Latin root *bassus* with the connotation "short" and, later, "low"; "base," the noun, originated in the Greek root *baino*—"walking" or "stepping." The earth that pulls us downward is also the ground that carries and gives support. The weighty man signifies, by his dignified gait, that he carries a heavy burden but sustains it well. Upright posture as counteraction cannot lack the forces against which it strives.

Standing

In getting up, man gains his standing in the world. The parents are not the only ones who greet the child's progress with joy. The child enjoys no less the triumph of his achievement. There is a forceful urge toward the goal of getting up and of resisting, in a state of dangerous balance, the downward-pulling forces. There need not be any other premium, like satisfaction of hunger, attention, or applause. The child certainly does not strive for security. Failure does not discourage him. He enjoys the freedom gained by upright posture— the freedom to stand on his own feet and the freedom to walk. Upright posture, which we learn in and through falling, remains threatened by falls throughout our lives. The natural stance of man is, therefore, "resistance." A rock reposes in its own weight. The things that surround us appear solid and safe in their quiet resting on the ground, but man's status demands endeavor. It is essentially restless. We are committed to an ever renewed exertion. Our task is not finished with getting up and standing. We have to "withstand." He who is able to accomplish this is called constant, stable.

Language expresses well the psychological meaning of standing, with all its facets. The coupling of the transitive and the intransitive meaning "to stand" and "to stand something" characterizes them as resisting and, therefore, enduring against threat, danger, and attack. The etymological root of standing—*sta*—is one of the most prolific elements not only in English but also in Greek, Latin, French, and German. It may suffice to mention only a few derivatives of an almost exhaustible store. Besides such combinations as "standing for," "standing by," and "making a stand," there are many words where the root has undergone slight changes but is still recognizable: e.g., "state," "status," "estate," "statement," "standard," "statute," "institution," "constitution," "substance," "establish," "understand," "assist," "distant." This entire family of words is kept together by one and the same principal meaning. They refer to something that is instituted, erected, constructed, and, in its dangerous equilibrium, threatened by fall and collapse. Falling is not always tragic. Clowns, modern and old, primitive and sublime, all have made use of falling as a reliable trick to stir up laughter.

With upright posture, an inescapable ambivalence penetrates and pervades all human behavior. Upright posture removes us from the ground, keeps us away from things, and holds us aloof from our fellowmen. All of these three distances can be experienced either as gain or as loss.

1. *Distance from the ground.* In getting up, we gain the freedom of motion and enjoy it, but, at the same time, we lose secure contact with the supporting ground, with Mother Earth, and we miss it. We stand alone and have to rely on our own strength and capacities. With the acquisition of upright posture, a characteristic change in language occurs. In the early years, when speaking of himself, a child uses his given name. However, when he has reached the age when he can stand firmly on his own feet, he begins to use the pronoun "I" for himself. This change marks a first gaining of independence. Among all words, "I" has a peculiar character. Everyone uses "I" to refer to himself alone. "I" is a most general word. At the same time, it has a unique meaning for every speaker. In using the word "I," I oppose myself to everyone else, who, nevertheless, is my fellow-man.

Because getting up and standing are so demanding, we enjoy resting, relaxing, yielding, lying down, and sinking back. There is the voluptuous gratification of succumbing. Sex remains a form of lying down or, as language says, of lying or sleeping with. Addicts, in their experience, behavior, and intention, reveal the double aspect of sinking back and its contrast to being upright. A *symposium* found the ancient Greeks, a *convivium* the Romans, stretched on their couches until, after many libations to Dionysus and Bacchus, they finally sank to the ground. *Symposium* means "drinking together," or "a drinking party." It could be well translated by the characteristic German word *Gelage*. Plato's dialogue first helped the word *symposium* to reach its modern connotation. The old and new are not so far apart as one might assume. Their relation can also be expressed— Plato clearly indicates this—as the difference between being upright and sinking.

2. *Distance from things.* In upright posture, the immediate contact

with things is loosened. A child creeping on his hands and knees not only keeps contact with the ground but is, in his all-fours locomotion, like the quadrupeds, directed toward immediate contact with things. The length-axis of his body coincides with the direction of his motion. With getting up, all this changes. In walking, man moves his body in a parallel transposition, the length-axis of his body at a right angle to the direction of his motion. He finds himself always "confronted" with things. Such remoteness enables him to see things, detached from the immediate contact of grasping and incorporating, in their relation to one another. Seeing is transformed into "looking at." The horizon widened, removed; the distant becomes momentous, of great import. In the same measure contact with near things is lost.

Thales, the philosopher and astronomer, fell into a ditch while watching the stars. A young child is close to the ground; to him the stars are far off. He does not mind picking things up from the ground; but, growing older, he will learn to accept our table manners, which remove even food to a distance. We set the table; we serve the meal; we use spoon and fork. Our feeding is regulated by a ritual, which we like to discard at a picnic. Artificiality and tools interfere with the direct satisfaction of hunger. The mouth is kept away from the plate. The hand lifts the food to the mouth. Spoon and fork do not create distance; tools can only be invented and used where distance already exists. In the early months of life, hands hold on to things in a grasping reflex. Not until the immediate contact of grasping is abandoned is the use of tools possible. This development is not simply the result of motor maturation. An imbecile may never learn and a paretic may unlearn manners, not so much because of failure of the motorium as because of the loss and lack of distance. Pointing likewise presupposes distance. It appears to be a human activity. Animals do not easily, if at all, understand pointing to distant things.[3] Pathology reveals an antagonistic relatonship between grasping and pointing. There are cases where pointing is distorted while grasping either remains undamaged or is later intensified and becomes forced grasping (Goldstein, 1931).[4]

3. *Distance from fellow-men.* In upright posture, we find ourselves "face to face" with others, distant, aloof—verticals that never meet. On the horizontal plane, parallel lines converge toward a vanishing point. Theoretically, the vanishing point of parallel verticals—to which we are comparable, standing vis-à-vis—is in infinite distance. In the

finiteness of seeing, however, parallel verticals do not meet. Therefore, the strict upright posture expresses austerity, inaccessibility, decisiveness, domination, majesty, mercilessness, or unapproachable remoteness, as in catatonic symmetry. Inclination first brings us closer to another. Inclination,[5] just like leaning, means literally "bending out" from the austere vertical.

Dictators, reviewing their parading troops, try to show by their rigid poses their imperturbable and unshakable wills. Formalized attitudes and pantomimic, signifying gestures follow the pattern set by spontaneous expressions. When we lower our heads or kneel in prayer, when we bow or bend our knees in greeting, the deviation from the vertical reveals the relation to it.

So it is with expressions of reverence, of asking and granting a request, and many others. The formalization and shortening of social gestures sometimes make it hard to recognize their origin; but even the stiff forms of military greeting may, with a slight courteous bending of the head, be revitalized by spontaneous expression.

There is only one vertical but many deviations from it, each one carrying a specific, expressive meaning. The sailor puts his cap askew, and his girl understands well the cocky expression and his "leanings." King Comus at the Mardi Gras may lean backward and his crown may slip off-center. However, even the disciples of informality would be seriously concerned if, on his way to his inauguration, the President should wear his silk hat (the elongation and accentuation of the vertical) aslant. There are no teachers, no textbooks, that instruct in this field. There are no pupils, either, who need instruction. Without ever being taught, we understand the rules governing this and other areas of expression. We understand them not conceptually but, it seems, by intuition. This is true for the actor as well as the onlooker.

One may argue that these are cultural patterns with which we grow up and that our final attitudes are the result of many infinitesimal steps. To support this view, one may point to the fact that gestures of greeting were different in the old days from ours and are different in the Occident and the Orient. Yet, in spite of their divergences, they all are variations of one theme. They are all related to the vertical; they are all modifications of the upright posture. Exceptions only confirm the rule. We give our assent by nodding the head, which is obviously also a motion that carries the head downward following gravity, away from the vertical. It has been observed that this gesture is not universal, that there are peoples to whom the same vertical motion of nodding means negation or denial. However, these two forms of expression, which indeed resemble each other, are not identical. Our mode of assertion, as well as their negation, consists of a two-phased motion—the motion downward and the movement up and backward. While in assertion the accent is on the downward motion, negation chooses the opposite direction. The head is moved from the position of inclination back to the vertical, expressing inaccessibility and denial.

Cultural patterns do not arbitrarily create forms but, within the given framework, formalize a socially accepted scheme valid only for its group and period. With upright posture counteracting gravity, the vertical, pointing upward and away from the center of gavity, becomes a natual determinant. The vertical is a constancy phenomenon. Its apparent position does not change, even if the head is tilted, and, therefore, its projection on the retina varies. At an early age, children are able to draw a vertical or a hoizontal line, to copy a cross or a square, but they fall when asked to copy the same square presented as a diamond.[6]

Upright Posture and the Formation of the Human Head

Upright posture has lifted eye and ear from the ground. In the family of senses, smell has lost the right of the first-born. Seeing and hearing have assumed dominion. Now, these really function as senses of distance. In every species, eye and ear respond to stimuli from remote objects, but the interest of animals is limited to the proximate. Their attention is caught by that which is within the confines of reaching or approaching. The relation of sight and bite distinguishes the human face from those of lower animals. Animal jaws, snout, trunk, and beak—all of them organs acting in the direct contact of grasping and gripping—are placed in the "visor line" of the eyes. With upright posture, with the development of the arm, the mouth is no longer needed for catching and carrying or for attacking and defending. It sinks down from the "visor line" of the eyes, which now can be turned directly in a piercing, open look toward distant things and rest fully upon them, viewing them with the detached interest of wondering. Bite has become subordinated to sight.

Language expresses this relation in signifying the whole, the face, through its dominating part—the eyes, as in the English and French word "visage," in the German *Gesicht,* and in the Greek *prosopon.* While the origin of the Latin word *facies*—and therefore, also, of the English noun "face"—is uncertain, the verb "to face" reassumes, in a remarkable twist, the original phenomenological meaning: to look at things straight ahead and to withstand their thrust. Eyes that lead jaws and fangs to the prey are always charmed and spellbound by nearness. To eyes looking straight forward—to the gaze of upright posture—things reveal themselves in their own nature. Sight penetrates depth; sight becomes insight.

Animals move in the direction of their digestive axis. Their bodies are expanded between mouth and anus as between an entrance and an exit, a beginning and an ending. The spatial orientation of the human body is different throughout. The mouth is still an inlet but not longer a beginning, the anus, an outlet but no longer the tail end. Man in upright posture, his feet on the ground and his head uplifted, does not move in the line of his digestive axis; he moves in the direction of his vision. He is surrounded by a world panorama, by a space divided into world regions joined together in the totality of the universe. Around him, the horizons retreat in an ever growing radius. Galaxy and diluvium, the infinite and the eternal, enter into the orbit of human interests.

The transformation of the animal jaws into the human mouth is an extensive remodeling: mandible, maxilla, and teeth are not the only parts recast. The mark of the jaws is brute force. The muscles that close the jaws, especially the masseter, are built for simple, powerful motions. Huge ridges and crests, which provide the chewing muscles with an origin appropriate to the development of power, encompass the skull of the gorilla. They disapear when the jaws are transformed into the mouth. The removal of these pinnacles permits the increase of the brain case while, at the same time, the reduction of the mighty chewing muscles permits the development of the subtle mimic and phonetic muscles.

The transformation of jaws into the mouth is a prerequisite for the development of language but only one of them. There are many other factors involved. In upright posture, the ear is no longer limited to the perception of noises—rustling, crackling, hissing, bellowing, roaring—as indicators of actual events, like warnings, threats, or lures. The external ear loses its mobility. While the ear muscles are preserved, their function of adapting the ear to actuality ceases. Detached from actuality, the ear can comprehend sounds in the sounds' own shape—in their musical or phonetic pattern.This capacity to separate the acoustical Gestalt from the acoustical material makes it possible to produce purposefully and to "re-produce" intentionally sounds articulated according to a preconceived scheme.

Just as the speaker produces his words—articulated sounds which function as symbols or carriers of meanings—these should be received and understood by the listener in exactly the same way. The articulated sound, the phoneme, has an obligatory shape. The phoneme itself is a universal. The relation which connects speech and speaker can be held in abeyance so that speech as such can be abstracted, written down, preserved, and repeated. Speech, while connecting speaker and listener, keeps them at the same time at a distance. The most intimate conversation is bound to common, strict rules of phonetics, grammar, and intended meanings. A spontaneous cry can never be wrong. The pronunciation of a word or the production of the phoneme is either right or wrong. The virtuosity acquired by the average person in expressing himself personally and individually in the general medium of language hides the true character of linguistic communication. It is rediscovered by reflection when disturbances of any kind interfere with the easy and prompt use of language or when the immediateness of contact does not tolerate linguistic distance, and the word dies in an angry cry, in tender babble, or in gloomy silence.

In conversation, we talk with one another about something. Conversation, therefore, demands distance in three directions: from the acoustical signs, so that the phoneme can be perceived in its pure form; from things, so that they can be the object of common discourse; from the other person, so that speech can mediate between the speaker and listener. Upright posture produces such distances. It lifts us from the ground, puts us opposite to things, and confronts us with one another.

The sensory organs cannot change without a corresponding change in the central nervous system. No part could be altered alone. With upright posture, there is a transformation of sensorium and motorium, of periphery and center, of form and function. While upright posture permits the formation of the human skull and, thereby, of the human brain, the maintenance of upright posture demands the development of the human nervous system. Who can say what comes first and what comes last—what is cause and what is effect? All these alterations are related to upright posture as their basic theme. "In man, everything converges into the form which he has now. In his history, everything is understandable through it, nothing without it" (Herder, 1784, p. 129).

The phenomenon of upright posture should not be neglected in favor of the lying man, or the man on the couch. To do this is to ignore facts that are obvious and undebatable, accessible without labyrinthine detours of interpretation, facts which exact consideration and permit proof and demonstration. It is true that sleep and rest, lying down and lying with someone, are essential functions; it is no less true that man is built for upright posture and gait and that upright posture, which is as original as any drive, determines his mode of being-in-the-world.

"The upright gait of man is the only natural one to him, nay, it is the organization for every performance of his species and his distinguishing character" (Herder, 1784, p. 128). Human physique reveals human nature.

Summary

The wound cut by the Cartesian dichotomy of mind and body is covered over, but not yet healed, by mere reference to the mind-body unity. This term is useful only if it is filled with definite meaning and classified in its presuppositions as well as in its consequences. The idea of a mind-body unit demands, first of all, a revision of those traditional concepts of psychology which are shaped in accordance with a theory of a mind-body dichotomy. Experience can no longer be interpreted as a train—an accumulation or integration of sensations, percepts, thoughts, ideas, and volitions occurring in the soul, the mind, the consciousness, or the unconscious for that matter. In experiencing, man finds himself always within the world, directed toward it, acting and suffering.

This study discusses the mind-body relation from one well-defined point of view. In analyzing upright posture, it points out in detail the correspondence between human physique and the basic traits of human experience and behavior. It also sets forth how some expressive attitudes of man are related to his basic orientation in the world as an upright creature.

Upright posture, which dominates human existence in its unity, makes us see that no basis exists for claiming any kind of priority for the drives. The "rational" is as genuine a part of human nature as the "animal."

REFERENCES

Aristotle. *De anima.*

Asch, S. & H. Witkin. Studies in space perception. *J. exper. Psychol.*, *1948.* **38,** 325–337, 435–477.

Browning, R. Andrea del Sarto.

Darwin, C. *The expression of the emotions* (1872). New York: Appleton, 1910.

Foerster, O. Die motorischen Bahnen und Felder. In O. Bumke & O. Foerster, *Handbuch der Neurologie.* Vol. VI. Berlin: Springer-Verlag, 1936.

Gesell, A., *et al. The first five years of life.* New York & London: Harper, 1940.

Gibson, E., & Mowrer, O. Determinants of the perceived vertical and horizontal. *Psychol. Rev.*, 1938, **45.**

Goldstein, K. *Über Zeigen und Greifen.* Vol. 4. Berlin: Dèr Nervenarzt, 1931.

Gregory, W. K. *The humerus from fish to man.* American Museum Novitates, January 31, 1949.

Herder, G. W. *Ideen zur Philosophie der Geschichte der Menschheit.* Riga: 1784.

Jackson, H. *Selected Writings. . . .* Vol. 2. London: J. Taylor, 1932.

Katz, D. *Der Aufbau der Tastwelt.* Leipzig: Engelman, 1925.

Kleist, K. *Gehirnpathologie,* Leipzig: 1934.

Minkowski, E. Les notions de distance vécue. *J. de Psychol.*, 1930, **27,** 727–745.

Moskati. *Vom Koerperlichen Wesentlichen Unterschiede der Thiere und Menschen.* Goettingen: 1771.

Nielsen, N. J. *Agnosia, apraxia, aphasia.* (2nd ed.) New York & London: Hoeber, 1946.

Portmann, A. *Biologische Fragmente zu einer Lebre vom Menschen.* Basel: 1944.

Ramon y Cajal, S. *Histologie du système nerveux de l'homme et des vertébrés.* 1909.

Revesz, G. *Die menschliche Hand.* New York & Basel: Karger, 1944.

Schilder, P. The image and appearance of the human body. *Psychol. Monogr.*, 1935, No. 4.

Sherrington, Ch. *The integrative action of the nervous system.* (9th ed.) Cambridge: Cambridge Univ. Press. 1947.

Sittig, O. *Über Apraxie.* Berlin: S. Karger, 1931.

von Uexkuell, J. *Theoretical biology.* New York: Harcourt, Brace, 1926.

Weidenreich, F. *Apes, giants and man.* Chicago: Univer. of Chicago Press, 1946.

NOTES

[1] F. Weidenreich (1946) discusses the relationship between man and his simian ancestors. He enumerates the main peculiarities that, compared to the condition of the apes, characterize man in his upright posture. The human leg, which he mentions among other things, "is stretched in hip and knee points to its maximum extent and adduced toward the midline, so that the knees touch each other, while in anthropoids, even if the latter succeed in standing and walking upright, the legs remain bent in hip and knee joints and are held in abduction, so that anthropoids always stand stooped, with their knees crooked and turned outward" (p. 6). In the so-called normal attitude of man, therefore, the lines connecting the centers of hip, knee, and ankle joints are all located in the same frontal plane. The plumb line passes through this plane. Furthermore, the center of the hip joint is, for each leg, vertically above the center of the knee and ankle joints.

[2] The comparison of man and other primates is a time-honored topic, widely discussed among pre-Darwinian zoologists. Most of the characteristic differences enumerated by Weidenreich (1946) were known to the anatomists of the eighteenth century, who also considered the possibility of a common origin. Daubenton published, in 1764, a paper about the different positions of the foramen magnum, in man and animals (Herder, 1778). Even the sentence passed on upright posture because of its inherent evils is old enough. Moskati (1771), comparing the essential differences of man and animals, came to the conclusion that upright posture disposed heart, circulation, and intestines to many defects and diseases.

[3] It is the hunter who understands and interprets the dog's aiming as pointing. The "point" is the natural outgrowth of the dog's pausing previous to springing the game.

[4] Experimental ablations of cortical areas indicate that grasping is under the control of Brodman's area 6.

[5] The root is Latin, *clino*, to bend. It is interesting to see how greatly language is shaped in accordance with expressive phenomena. Not only does the English language have two words of the same structure from different roots; but there is the German word *Zuneigung*, with still another etymological derivation, which, however, expresses the same meaning with the corresponding space experience. All this points to the fact that metaphors do not simply carry over a meaning from one medium to another. There is a much more intimate relation—that between expressive motion and emotional attitude.

[6] Gibson and Mowrer (1938) assumed that our orientation in space is determined by postural factors, while visual stimulation is of secondary importance. Asch and Witkin (1948), however, in their more recent experiments, came to the opposite conclusion.

Index

337